GHOSTHUNTER

GHOSTHUNTER

Investigating the World of Ghosts and Spirits

Eddie Burks and Gillian Cribbs

LONDON NEW YORK SYDNEY TORONTO

This edition published 1995
by BCA
by arrangement with
HEADLINE BOOK PUBLISHING

CN 9386

First published in 1995
by HEADLINE BOOK PUBLISHING

Typeset by
Letterpart Limited, Reigate, Surrey

Printed and bound in Great Britain by
Mackays of Chatham PLC, Chatham, Kent

Gillian Cribbs

To my parents,
Allan and Elsie Corkindale

Eddie Burks

To my good friends,
Mary Beattie and Martin Shaw

Contents

Acknowledgements

This book would not have been possible without help and advice from the following people: Barbara Peters; Father Francis Edwards; Lady Mary Mumford and Lady Winefride Freeman; the Earl and Countess of Arundel; Lord Charles and Lady March; No. 10 Downing Street Security Guards; Lieutenant John Stevens, R.N.; Captain John Cuninghame; Michael Brooks, Brenda Jenkinson and Flt. Lieutenant David Taylor; Liz and Bill Rich; Joanne Silverwood, Stephanie and Neil Barton; Dr Faustina Raciti; David Roper, Damien Considine, Andrew Wagstaff and Peter Martin; Sarah Woodcock of the Theatre Museum, Covent Garden; Nina Smirnoff, Tommy Baxter, Callum Cunningham, Mark Stradling and Robert Ross; Fred and Harold Panton; Paul Crowther; Joseph Wright and Christine Kerr; Major-General Christopher Tyler and Sue Tyler; Anne Broadbent; John Wellens and Clare Cleary; and Donald Macer-Wright.

Alan Brooke and Sarah Hughes of Headline never wavered in their encouragement and support, and Gillian Bromley edited the manuscript sensitively and intelligently.

Extracts from *Rosencrantz and Guildenstern are Dead*; *The Gentlemen's Clubs of London*; and *No. 10 Downing Street: The Story of a House* by kind permission of Faber and Faber; Little, Brown and Company; and BBC Books.

Gillian Cribbs

I would like to thank Elsie Midgley for her astute observations on the first draft and Max Rhodes for his encouragement throughout 1994. Last, but never least, my special thanks to Simon Freeman, who supported and advised me during my long hours at the keyboard. An outstanding journalist, his enthusiasm, humour – and scepticism – were an inspiration. Without him, *Ghosthunter* would not exist.

Introduction

We cannot all be friars, and many are the ways by which
God bears his chosen to heaven.

Miguel Cervantes, *Don Quixote*

It was a freezing cold Saturday morning in January 1993 and the
rain was driving against my window. Reluctantly, I got up and
shuddered through the icy hall, where a fresh batch of unwanted
mail was waiting for me. Over a cup of tea I picked through the pile
of envelopes: bills, circulars, bank statements – and a large white
envelope postmarked South Kensington.

Inside was *Light*, the College of Psychic Studies' quarterly
newsletter, which always made me smile because it was so precious.
I had joined the college in 1992 intending to try out one of its
classes in psychic development, but my membership had long since
lapsed, and I could never understand why they continued to send
me the newsletter. There, sandwiched between a tedious account of
the life and times of the outgoing president and a collection of
turgid book reviews, a curious story stood out, entitled 'Psychic
disturbance in a bank'. In August, I read, the college had received a
letter from a bank in the Strand asking for help with a rather
delicate problem. Switchboard staff had been alarmed by 'a vague
human shape lacking a head' which had appeared near the computer terminals at the entrance to the building. Could the college

1

help? Brenda Marshall, editor of *Light*, had passed the letter to Eddie Burks, a retired civil engineer who had become a ghosthunter. The account of his visit to the mysterious bank followed.

Accompanied by the terrified receptionists, Mr Burks had apparently made contact with an entity who berated him for not getting on with the job; the ghost wanted to escape as soon as possible and urged Mr Burks to help him. Then he complained that he had been executed on a trumped-up charge of treason and that his bitterness had left him trapped on earth. Mr Burks had a brief conversation with the entity before sending him on his way – and, according to the article, the ghost had not made an appearance at the bank since.

I was intrigued. Who was the mysterious Eddie Burks? How did he do it? What was the name of the bank, and who was the ghost? The bank had insisted that it should not be identified, although I thought that it would be easy to work this out from some of the details in the article. But that would have taken time and effort – and I could not risk it. This was a potentially excellent story for the national press and *Light* might well be read by a psychically aware reporter. So I decided to go straight to the man who had the answers: Eddie Burks, ghosthunter.

'Mr Burks cannot be contacted directly, but we can pass a letter on to him,' said a nervous receptionist at the college the following Monday morning. 'He is very helpful, and I'm sure he'll reply.' I was not so sure, but I wrote a friendly letter expressing my interest in the case and setting out my own psychic credentials: three generations of interest in the paranormal on both sides of the family and fifteen years of personal research.

Four days later Mr Burks telephoned, thanked me for my letter and asked how he could help. Just tell me the name of the bank, I thought to myself, though I did not put it quite like that. 'I was fascinated to read about your work in *Light*. Could you tell me some more about it? Perhaps we could meet,' I said. For a moment I feared that I had been a little too forward, but Mr Burks said that he would be pleased to see me at his home in Lincoln.

Drawing into Lincoln station at 10.30 a.m. on 12 January 1993, I wondered what kind of day was in store. Would Mr Burks, ghosthunter, turn out to be as otherworldly as he sounded over the telephone? I scanned the platform for a figure that matched the unsettling description he had given of himself: a tall man with a beard who would be wearing a hat and black raincoat. I stepped off the train and – as if from nowhere – he was at my side. He shook my hand and escorted me out of the station. 'I thought we'd walk to my house,' he said. 'It's such a fine day.'

No-one who lives in a city is ever prepared for the cruel and sudden exposure of the open countryside. As we walked beside the old Roman canal towards Mr Burks' house, an icy wind cut through me and ruined my attempts at polite conversation. Mr Burks (at this early stage I thought it polite to address him formally) lumbered along: he did seem a bit odd, but then he was in a very peculiar line of business, I thought. We stopped at a neat, modern housing estate flanking the canal which reminded me of Brookside Close, the Liverpool estate of the eponymous television soap opera: small, brick houses, neat gardens and gleaming new hatch-backs. I was taken aback; I had expected the Gothic splendour of a crumbling vicarage, at least. 'Just moved in here,' he said. 'It's very easy to run.'

Without his hat, coat and scarf, Mr Burks seemed less intimidating: tall, straight-backed and dressed in blue jumper and beige slacks, he looked more like a woodwork teacher than a ghosthunter. Over tea I gathered my thoughts and prepared my line of attack. I wanted to leave with what would be a classic story: a major bank, a ghost, a scandal, a ghostbuster . . . 'The incident at the bank was intriguing,' I began. 'Can you tell me a little more about it?' Ponderously Mr Burks recited – verbatim – what I had already read in *Light*. Then I changed tactics. I explained that I only wrote for quality newspapers – the *Independent*, the *Sunday Telegraph*. The story would be safe in my hands . . .

But Mr Burks was unmoved; he showed no sign of wanting to tell me the name of the bank, and without that I could not write a story. So, in desperation, I plunged in. 'This is all very interesting, Mr Burks, but exactly *where* did it all happen?' He looked at me, and in a tone that reminded me of my bank manager on a bad day, said: 'That is a confidential matter; I never divulge the names of my clients.' 'Never?' I asked. 'Only if they give me permission,' he replied. 'My work is to release trapped souls. I seek neither money nor recognition.'

3

I decided that it would be prudent to change the subject. We were discussing hauntings in general when he told me that there was 'someone' in the room. 'Get a pen and paper,' he said. He moved from an armchair on to a hard-back chair and was swaying to and fro; his breathing had become heavy and his face was contorted. My first thought was that he was having palpitations and I wondered whether I should call an ambulance.

'I heard you tell of me and take this opportunity to return to give you my thanks,' he said slowly. 'I cannot do justice to the joy which has come to me . . . the beauty of this place is beyond my describing. Thank you again. One day we shall meet face to face and it will give me great joy to embrace you. Farewell.'

Mr Burks opened his eyes and rubbed his hands together. 'It's the ghost from the bank – he's come back to say thank you. They do that sometimes.' I stared at him and, with what I later realized was a stroke of inspiration, took my chance: 'Well, he's obviously happy with me, or else he wouldn't have come through while I was here,' I said. 'So why don't you fill me in on the details?' He looked at me and nodded. 'You're right. The bank was Coutts – but don't say I told you so,' he said with a surprisingly conspiratorial chuckle.

In the following weeks I contacted Coutts, which confirmed that Mr Burks had indeed paid a visit, but declined to comment further, and the College of Psychic Studies, which for some reason was even more publicity-shy. Inexplicably, its president, Dudley Poplak, insisted that the college should not be mentioned in relation to the incident at Coutts, even though its own magazine, *Light*, had been the source for my story. Mr Poplak said that the college did not want to be associated with the haunting, which was baffling since it was, after all, dedicated to the study of psychic phenomena.

I was right about the impact of the story. The *Sunday Telegraph* ran my article, headlined 'Haunted Coutts calls in the ghostbuster', on the front page on 21 February. The following morning, *Today*, the most prestigious current affairs programme on radio, carried the story. Then Mr Burks' phone in Lincoln was ringing constantly: would he take part in a live CBS phone-in in New York? . . . The BBC World Service would like to interview him . . . The *News of the World* was sending a reporter to his house . . . LWT would like to make a documentary . . . At Coutts the main switchboard was jammed that morning; the College of Psychic Studies was also inundated with calls, but remained aloof and refused to take messages for Mr Burks. Meanwhile, the serious and the not-so-serious press raced against each other to identify the ghost. Mr Burks was now a celebrity. Although he had previously featured in a handful of magazine articles and had appeared a few times on television, he had never attracted such widespread and serious interest.

The following week Father Francis Edwards, a Jesuit priest and historian based at Farm Street Church in central London, identified the Coutts ghost as Thomas Howard, fourth Duke of Norfolk, who was beheaded in 1572 by Elizabeth I for his alleged role in a plot to overthrow the Crown. Father Edwards had spent his life trying to clear the poor man's name, and was certain that Howard was the ghost. At a family memorial service for Thomas Howard in Corpus Christi Church, Covent Garden, the following November, Father Edwards spoke of his delight in helping to restore the fourth Duke's reputation. Listening to his address were the present Duke of Norfolk and his family, gathered together to pay their last respects. An astonished pack of reporters and photographers looked on as Britain's leading Catholic family led the prayers with a ghosthunter, a Jesuit priest and staff from Coutts Bank. All this, I realized, would make a wonderful opening chapter for a book: and so the quest began.

Eddie Burks was born in Bow, east London, in 1922, the eldest son of a man who worked for a hay merchant in the City. He had two brothers and a sister. Money was tight, but he had a stable and happy childhood. It was uneventful, but one incident, when Eddie was five years old, marked the beginning of his involvement with the psychic world. Eddie recalled: 'I went into hospital for a minor operation and as I was coming round I found myself hurtling along a tunnel at great speed, finally emerging into the hospital ward. As this was happening I was filled with intense frustration because I had been forced to leave the wonderful garden. The memory stayed with me all my life. I used to go to Sunday school and I remember saying to myself: "They are not telling the truth," although I could not for the life of me recall what the truth was.'

A few years later the family moved to Edmonton, north London, and Eddie would often call into the local library on his way home from school. He discovered Nandor Fodor's *Encyclopaedia of Psychic Science*, and shortly afterwards a neighbour invited him to a spiritualist church where he watched clairvoyants relaying messages from deceased loved ones to enthralled audiences. But although he visited the church regularly he had no psychic experiences himself during this period.

During the war Eddie served in the Royal Electrical and Mechanical Engineers in Britain and the Far East. After the war he took a degree in Civil Engineering at South-west Essex Technical College and in 1951 he joined the Air Ministry Works Directorate, where he worked on airfield construction. He was eventually made a Principal Scientific Officer at the Road Research Laboratory, but left the Civil Service in 1966 to set up his own practice in Lambley, Nottingham. He retired in June 1989.

In 1970, Eddie's wife of twenty-eight years died of a heart attack. He said: 'The day after she died our son came to visit me. I was preparing lunch and I suddenly sensed her beside me. She told me that I had taken the best pieces of chicken for myself the previous day, when they were meant for her. It made me smile; from that moment on I knew that she was happy.' It also prepared him for the death of his son, who died in exactly the same way ten years later.

In 1975 Eddie discovered a gift for healing when he visited a friend who was recovering from a serious operation. She asked him if he had brought a spirit presence with him; he surprised himself when he said that he may well have done. 'When I acknowledged this fact I felt a strong urge to take her hands in mine,' he said. 'As I did so, I felt a surge of energy pass through me and into her. It was healing power.' A few weeks later Eddie stopped by again and found that the woman could walk without pain. After this, Eddie performed many more healings, and although he was still working full-time as a civil engineer, he devoted his spare time to healing.

On 15 June 1983 Eddie was talking to Brenda Marshall, president of the College of Psychic Studies, in her office in South Kensington when a pneumatic drill started up outside. Suddenly Eddie became aware of an entity approaching. It was a man, who told him:

'London always was a noisy place – it doesn't seem to improve. I'm a little lost. There's change been going on and I'm a bit confused. I've been told I have to make an effort if I'm to be helped, but I'm not sure what to do.

'I was bullied; I can't let go of the memories, and I know they are holding me back. My life was drudgery. I don't know where my master has gone, but I don't want to go there too – I'm still afraid of him. But I want to leave. Oh God . . . can you help me?'

Eddie then received an explanation for this message from a group of spirit helpers who had also approached. 'He had a deformity,' they said, 'an affliction of the right hand, which caused him to shake. His master used him as a run-about. But he has seen the light and unburdened himself . . . we can help him now. It is important that we now clear the earth of as many such lost souls as possible. The spiritual power that is coming to the earth in the New Age will be of such brightness that those who are trapped could suffer more than they need, unless we can free them now.'

That day was a turning point in Mr Burks' life; it was the first time he had released a trapped soul, and it set the pattern for his subsequent psychic work.

On 21 February 1994, exactly a year after the Coutts story appeared in the *Sunday Telegraph*, work began on this book. There is no shortage of books on ghosts and haunted houses, but usually they do little more than recount stories that have been passed down through generations. The Ghost Club of London has tried to take a more analytical approach in documenting hauntings, but reducing ghost stories to a list of flying objects and bumps in the night is, frankly, ridiculous as well as dull. This book would have to appeal to a wide audience – sceptics included. I thought it would be unique because Eddie could engage the ghosts in conversation: it was their story that had to be told.

Eddie's main concern had always been to guide people through troublesome hauntings rather than to seek out and release Britain's most famous ghosts. His stories concerned ordinary people in ordinary places. Of course, it is important to remember that ghosts do not belong exclusively to aristocrats and their stately piles; they are just as common in council flats and modern houses as they are in ancestral castles. But I wanted Eddie to extend his range and look at some of Britain's best-known ghosts. This country is widely acknowledged as the most haunted in the world, so there was no shortage of material. At first Eddie could not understand why we needed to include 'celebrity cases'; in the spirit world, he argued, ghosts were not graded according to how famous they once were. But he relented as I escorted him around the country and he made contact with some of the most fascinating and influential figures in English history.

I had to adopt a sceptic's persona – strange territory for me because I have been involved in paranormal research for much of the last fifteen years. I had joined psychic development groups and had trained as a healer, but I realized that for this book I had to put myself in the shoes of a sceptical reader. So I constantly had to ask myself whether a sceptic would believe what Eddie said, or whether I could push him to give further, irrefutable details.

My whole approach was, therefore, designed to test Eddie. Scouring libraries and reading countless newspaper cuttings on haunted Britain, I drew up an eclectic list of ghosts and haunted houses. It was not possible to cover every place and person – that would have been a lifetime's work – but my list included classic cases such as Hampton Court, said to be haunted by Cardinal Wolsey, and the site of the Battle of Naseby, where annual ghostly re-enactments of the Civil War battle had been reported. I also found some more earthy locations which had their own special ghosts, including the Duke of Wellington's local pub in Hyde Park Corner and the Theatre Royal, Drury Lane.

Next, I set the ground rules for our quest: Eddie and I would visit all the locations together, but he was not to know any background history to the hauntings in advance. I set up the appointments, interviewed the people involved and kept all reference material well out of Eddie's sight. Living in Lincoln, Eddie had no access to my research material in London, and anyway he seemed to prefer working 'blind'; he said that too much detail in advance interfered with his psychic communications. For me the crucial thing was to see how accurately Eddie's account matched the received history.

Each visit followed a set pattern. We met at the location,

introduced ourselves and then went to the rooms or places where disturbances had been recorded. Sometimes Eddie paced around like a bloodhound, sniffing out the exact spot where an incident had taken place; at other times he calmly waited for the entity to approach. Sometimes it worked, sometimes it did not. On our visits we worked a full day, with obligatory breaks for lunch and afternoon tea. This, I soon discovered, was vital for Eddie; on several occasions I became exasperated when he decided it was time to break for lunch just as we were nearing an important breakthrough, but in the end I had to accept the fact that his psychic work was often draining and he needed regular sustenance.

There are always difficulties, of course, when two people collaborate on a project, whether they are scientists trying to find a cure for AIDS, astronomers searching for black holes or historians examining Hitler's final days. Eddie and I had much less in common than the average team: he was in his seventies, knew nothing about the media and, though he tried to be modern, naturally exhibited the attitudes of a generation where women played a limited and modest role; I was in my early thirties and a journalist on national newspapers. We were very different and were united really only by our interest – and belief – in the paranormal.

I knew that it was unfair – considering his age – but I often became frustrated that Eddie's pace was much slower than my own. He also did not appreciate, since he was not a journalist, that it was not enough just to turn up at a place and communicate with a ghost; interviews and background research had to be done, otherwise the book would have consisted simply of unfocused psychic anecdotage. So, after Eddie had done his work I had to try to make sense of what the ghost had told him: sometimes I succeeded and discovered supporting evidence; occasionally I was unable to corroborate his story, which was both dispiriting and frustrating.

As I listened to Eddie communicating with the ghosts, in castles, theatres, gentlemen's clubs and great country houses, I was puzzled by the language used by the ghosts who talked through him; sometimes they spoke in contemporary English, sometimes in language not heard since the last war, sometimes in an odd concoction of Shakespeare and Chaucer. I asked Eddie whether ghosts actually spoke to him in their native tongue or idiom; if they did, I asked, how could he understand someone who had lived five hundred years ago and who would have spoken what was, to Eddie, a foreign language? It was vital to press him on this as cynics would inevitably use inconsistencies in language – whether Eddie was communicating with the ghost of Charles I or a Second World War bomber pilot – as proof that he was a charlatan. To his credit, Eddie did not pretend that there was an easy explanation; depending on the strength of the psychic contact, he said, his communications would come through in clear phrases and sentences or as thought forms which he would verbalize. He was aware that this would not satisfy sceptics; but, he argued, what the ghost said was more important than how it was said.

Our journey around England developed into a great psychic odyssey, peopled with an extraordinary cast of characters, both spectral and living. As well as being a test of Eddie's psychic skills, this quest was also a good gauge of the British public's attitude to the paranormal. Remarkably, there was usually little opposition when I asked if Eddie could have a word with the resident ghost. The managers of London's greatest theatres – the Adelphi, the Haymarket and the Theatre Royal, Drury Lane – were the most enthusiastic and flung open their doors to us; I could not bring myself to tell them later that Eddie had sent their beloved ghosts on their way.

The only places where we were refused entry were Number 10 Downing Street (on security grounds) and Glamis Castle, Scotland's oldest inhabited castle and supposedly the scene of Duncan's murder in *Macbeth*. It was also the childhood home of the Queen Mother and birthplace of Princess Margaret. Its occupants in 1994, the Strathmore family, wanted to shake off Glamis's reputation as a haunted castle. Legend has it that the hideously deformed eleventh Earl of Strathmore, who was disinherited and locked away in the castle in the nineteenth century, haunts Glamis, so their reluctance is perhaps not surprising.

As the weeks went by, several cases came to us quite by chance. In May 1994 Eddie was invited to the Tower of London for a private viewing of the Crown Jewels by the (then) Governor, Major-General Christopher Tyler. He had heard about Eddie through a friend and wanted him to look into some disturbances he had witnessed in the Governor's House. On 19 May Eddie visited the Tower where he contacted, among others, the spirit of Anne Boleyn. Again, in June I was invited to a private reception at 10 Downing Street, where I uncovered a fascinating history of hauntings from the security guards and staff. I drew a plan of the building for Eddie and, working with this and some pictures of the rooms, he managed to contact several ghosts. Later that month we were invited to Goodwood, East Sussex, by Lord and Lady March, who were convinced that a ghost was causing the depressing atmosphere in the house.

After a while I began to encourage Eddie to ask for more information about the ghosts so I could build up a stronger picture of them; then, as I became more confident, I interviewed them myself through Eddie. At times I doubted his ability, especially when he failed to contact well-known ghosts that had appeared on many occasions. But, as Eddie said, ghosts come when they are ready, not on demand for a book. On the other hand, there were times when he exceeded my expectations by adding startling new details to a case which I had researched.

The book contains the five most interesting cases that Eddie had worked on before we met; these are inevitably presented from a different perspective and have a different tone as I researched them retrospectively. (These cases are described in Chapters 5, 8, 9 and the second half of Chapter 15.) Each chapter includes Eddie's communications with the ghosts, which I have set in an historical context and interpreted where necessary, and also testimony from the individuals who had been affected by the haunting. These people span the social spectrum, from royalty and aristocracy to professionals such as doctors, architects and services personnel and, last but not least, ordinary people – secretaries, farmers, housewives and pensioners. The sections of text describing Eddie's psychic communications are indented to help distinguish them from the surrounding narrative.

I hope that these stories will entertain and – above all – inform. I did not set out to ascertain whether or not ghosts exist (that, surely, is an impossible task), but to examine the phenomenon in a new way – from the viewpoint of the unfortunate people who found one in their midst and, most importantly, from that of the ghosts themselves.

Ghostly Questions

Our birth is but a sleep and a forgetting:
The soul that rises with us, our life's star,
Hath had elsewhere its setting,
And cometh from afar.

William Wordsworth, 'Ode: Intimations of
Immortality, from Reflections of Early
Childhood'

Ghost stories are as old as time itself. The theme of spirits of the dead returning to haunt the living occurs in most literatures and religions around the world. Ghost stories may be entertaining, but at their heart lies a universal concern: whether there is life after death. This book is not a religious or philosophical tract; everyone must make up their own minds about the nature of God, the soul and the afterlife. But I hope to shed fresh light here on some of these great questions – by giving the ghosts themselves, who know so much more than we do, their own, unique public platform.

Every religion has a mystical element. At the heart of most cultures lies the concept of good and evil: the Egyptians, Romans, Celts and American Indians used complex spells and strange talismans to ward off evil spirits, while many contemporary African tribes still rely on the judgements of witch doctors to preserve social order. The world religions of Judaism, Christianity, Islam, Hinduism and Buddhism rely on the central belief that there is a world beyond the physical earth which only the good may enter.

In the Old Testament Book of Job, a terrifying spectre rose which caused the prophet's bones to shake and his hair to stand on end, while Jesus himself is said to have travelled into the under-world to help the tormented spirits of the dead; the ancient Jewish Kabbalah records the great magical traditions of Judaism; while the Tibetan Book of the Dead (Bardo Thodol) gives the reader precise instructions on how to pass through the portals of death – the most important being to ensure that emotional ties are not able to draw the spirit back to the earth.

Western culture has taken an ambivalent view of the supernatu-ral since the witch hunts of the Middle Ages, when even those with a passing interest in the psychic world were persecuted. Ostracized by society, mystics and clairvoyants were regarded as little better than devil-worshippers. But people have always clung to the fundamental belief – or at least hope – that part of us survives our physical death, and interest in the paranormal has never waned, even when it was forced underground. As its adherents adopted a code of silence, the paranormal acquired a new name: the occult – the 'hidden' world. In the popular imagination the occult eventually became confused with the more sinister aspects of black magic, Satanism and the cult of death.

Scientific rationalism assumed anyone with a belief in ghosts to be illogical, eccentric or simply mad. However, although modern society still ridicules the psychic world, there has been a resurgence of interest during the last twenty years; the arrival from the US of spiritualism – a divertissement for late nineteenth-century aristo-crats – sowed the seeds for this revival by making clairvoyants celebrities. Today – for the first time in over 600 years – writers, intellectuals, businessmen and even some scientists have begun to acknowledge the value of ancient wisdom. Philosophers are grap-pling with the teachings of ancient and modern mystics; British and European doctors are studying the phenomenon of near-death experience; psychiatrists are treating some cases of schizophrenia with exorcism; American businessmen are using psychics to advise them in multi-million-dollar business deals; and governments are researching ESP as a potential military weapon.

13

Although Western scientists have long maintained that it is necessary to prove the existence of ghosts in order to believe in them, that view is now changing. This is, in part, due to the foundation of the London Society for Psychical Research (SPR) in 1882. Drawing its members from among the élite of Oxbridge graduates and the educated upper middle classes, the society attracted such eminent Victorians as Lord Tennyson, William Gladstone, John Ruskin and Lewis Carroll. They set about collecting first-hand accounts of apparitions and other psychic phenomena which they subjected to careful and painstaking analysis. One study, the Census of Hallucinations, carried out in London between 1889 and 1892, drew 17,000 replies: around 10 per cent reported having seen or heard a ghost. The results of the census were recorded in the seven-volume work *Human Personality and the Survival of Bodily Death* in 1892. If the census was an accurate reflection of society as a whole, more than one million adults in Victorian Britain would have seen or heard a ghost.

More recently, a survey in Britain showed that over half the population believed in psychic phenomena and that 44 per cent of people believed in ghosts; of these, one in seven claimed to have seen a ghost or been haunted by one. The figures in the US are even higher; similar studies revealed that 57 per cent of the adult population believed in the phenomenon. The sheer volume of accounts of ghosts and hauntings is probably the strongest argument for their existence. To deny ghosts exist is to ignore the millions of ordinary witnesses to them.

Physicists are now investigating what mystics have been talking about for years. They have observed that quarks – sub-atomic particles vibrating at tremendous speed – can pass through solid matter in the same way that apparitions seem to move effortlessly through solid walls. Physicists proved many years ago that the solidity of our world is illusory, as everything we see, touch, taste and feel consists of minuscule particles composed of millions of protons and electrons. Everything and everyone can be reduced to patterns of energy; only our minds – or consciousness – separate us from the inanimate objects around us.

One of the questions that is taxing twentieth-century scientists is this notion of consciousness. Galileo was the first scientist to ask whether the mind is contained within the brain or distributed throughout the body in the form of a soul. Until recently scientists dismissed the idea of a soul because they believed the brain was the seat of consciousness; when the brain dies, they said, consciousness died with it. But the growing number of people who recall a near-death experience – the remembrance of an event that occurred when they were clinically dead – is undermining this theory. Researchers are now close to proving scientifically that consciousness survives when a person biologically dies.

We live in a technologically advanced society, but we are still a long way from answers to the fundamental questions of life. It is no wonder, then, that psychics like Eddie Burks pose such a threat. He is neither a mystic nor an intellectual; nor is he trained in the natural sciences. He is an ordinary man who matches the image of a civil engineer perfectly – quiet, unimaginative, methodical and practical. He should not even understand the questions; yet he does, and he offers some thought-provoking answers.

I questioned Eddie on these issues; I tried to forget my own beliefs in the paranormal and, instead, to put myself in the position of a sceptic. Having listened to Eddie, and watched him working during the research of this book, I am sure that he is sincere – and, more important, that what he does defies glib explanation.

What happens to a person when they die?
In the dying moments consciousness begins to drift to a higher level of existence; often relatives and loved ones will appear, sometimes accompanied by a spirit presence. Then the person passes out of the physical body and into the etheric body. This process is sometimes witnessed as a silver thread rising out of the abdomen or top of the head. The spirit will then linger by the body for a short while – usually a few days at most – before casting off the etheric body and moving through a tunnel into the spirit world.

What is the etheric body?
The etheric body is a halfway house between the physical and spiritual bodies. The etheric body is very closely knit with the physical body; when you are alive it conveys the energies of the

spirit world and, when intact, prevents damaging entities intruding. Protection through the etheric body is our birthright, but it can be breached in many ways – by repeated use of hallucinogenic drugs, by injuries to the body (especially the head) and by consulting ouija boards. When breached, the etheric body is less able to protect the consciousness from invasion by entities from the lower realms of the spirit world; some cases of schizophrenia are thought to be caused by this invasion.

When you die your consciousness moves out of the physical body and operates through the etheric body. But if you remain in the etheric body for too long your consciousness begins to cloud; this is why ghosts have no idea how long they have been trapped – in the etheric body there is no difference between a day and a hundred years. When you are released into the soul or spirit body – the next stage of development – there is a great sense of freedom and expansion of the consciousness.

Are evil people always trapped when they die?
No, they don't necessarily remain earthbound, but their nature tends to determine where they are going. A murderer would probably find himself in a dark region, whereas a person who has led a good and kind life will find himself in a beautiful place. Our spirituality – or lack of it – determines our next destination.

How many people get trapped?
Up to one in five hundred, but this is only a guess.

Does a ghost become trapped unwittingly or is it a matter of choice?
In most cases unwittingly. It's usually because some part of them still clings to the life they had on earth; the memory of death or the sorrow of leaving a loved one behind could hold them back. Most ghosts want to go, but can't.

Is a ghost simply a soul that is not very developed spiritually?
Definitely not. I recently released a woman who was alcoholic but spiritually evolved. She was earthbound because her husband had taken her children from her and she was still grieving over her loss.

16

Do ghosts seal their fate when they hold on to earthly emotions?
Yes, but most people let these feelings go; ghosts are trapped by very powerful thoughts or feelings.

Why do they come to you? Do they instinctively know you can help?
They come to me because I throw out a psychic light – a sort of beacon that only they can see. I don't know what it's like, but it obviously means something to them.

Is that why ghosts are attracted to certain people and places?
Yes; if they are not trapped in a particular place, ghosts will take temporary refuge where they see a light; this can emanate from anyone who is spiritual.

How do they make themselves known?
A very sensitive person might feel as if an invisible presence is following them. If nothing is done to help the entity at this stage, it can quickly become a nuisance; as it grows more frustrated it will start to draw attention to itself by banging doors, switching off lights or giving off strange smells. Sometimes there will be a sudden drop in temperature and people in the house might feel unnaturally tired; this is because the entity is drawing on their energy to create the disturbances. It is very rare for a ghost to appear physically as it would require a lot of energy to manifest.

Have any ghosts refused your help?
One or two have avoided me, and I can't do anything about that as it is their choice whether or not to come forward.

How do you make contact with the ghost?
This happens in two ways. Often a trapped spirit will come to me unbidden; in that case, I sense a change in my mood – I feel uneasy, frustrated or depressed. I know that this feeling does not belong to me because it often happens when I'm feeling quite cheerful. I try to adjust my consciousness to allow it to get closer to me; I suppose I bring it into a conscious focus. This is not a rational process, except that I recognize what is happening mentally. It's more a matter of the heart – I develop an empathy with the spirit. As I

17

focus on it, I begin to find out about its situation; first, I get some idea of whether it's a man or a woman and then I begin to get an understanding of the problem.

Do you then switch off your rational side and let the intuitive side take over?
Yes, it's as though my intuition – or psychic faculty – reaches out and engages with the entity, but my rational side continues to work so I am able to describe what is happening. It's as though I'm keeping one foot in the real world and one in the psychic world. The two sides are working together, as the psychic side pulls in information which is filtered through the rational mind.

What sort of information do you receive?
First of all, the emotional state of the person. For example, if a person died a violent death and left things undone, they may be held back by the guilt over that and I feel their remorse. I share their emotions in a way that is very cathartic for them; I am reading from their memories of the event and I have to encourage them to go back to their death, because sometimes they have wiped it from their consciousness. It's very important for me to share these feelings because these are usually at the root of the problem. By helping them to express emotional energy they can be released.

How do you communicate with a ghost?
I usually pick up words and phrases before I see the ghost. It's as though they share their emotions first and then their thoughts. I respond to them telepathically too, either encouraging them to talk or asking direct questions. I often say: 'Look, I have to share your death experience with you before we can go any further.' And: 'I'm not driving you out into the dark, I'm helping you; there's a far better place for you to be than here.'

What sort of information do you pick up then?
I usually pick up the physical pain of their death, although occasionally this comes through very strongly at the outset. A hanged man once came through to me and I immediately felt the noose around his neck. It's far more traumatic for them than it is

18

for me; although I do pick up terrible pain sometimes, I have trained myself to let it go. I share enough of their burden to encourage them to shed it; if you are not prepared to go through this process you risk leaving them in a worse position than before. This is the mistake most exorcists make.

Is there also a visual stage?
When the person has gone through the emotional and physical catharsis of their death, they suddenly emerge into their soul body. If a person has had disabilities which have caused them unhappiness on earth, these disappear with the etheric body. My psychic vision becomes much clearer once they are in their soul body. It's as though my consciousness suddenly comes into focus again; sometimes I see the clothes they are wearing or their face.

Would you describe yourself as a psychotherapist for ghosts?
Yes, the process is very similar to a psychiatrist taking a patient back to the deep cause of a neurosis. The difference is that a release happens more quickly and it's usually accompanied by a great burst of energy. I have to remain calm to hold the ghost steady and steer it through this important stage. Many of the entities I deal with have gone through a terrible experience and I must ensure that they are not traumatized. I gently urge them to let go of the experience. They are then ready to move into the light.

What you mean by moving into the light?
Jesus himself said: 'I am the light of the world'; in the spiritual world a highly developed soul has a very strong light, while an undeveloped soul shows no light and may show darkness. Anyone who is spiritually developed will recognize an entity's progress by the strength of the light around them. When I release a soul it has to come into the light; if I succeed, it's as if a background light comes into the foreground, signifying that the spirit world is ready to accept them. The release is complete when the person steps into the light.

Does everyone move into the light?
No. If someone is not prepared, either morally or spiritually, the light will not appear; a path will appear instead, often with a gate. If

the person opens the gate, it indicates that they are willing to begin their spiritual journey towards the light. On that journey, which is a sort of Pilgrim's Progress, they will encounter all sorts of obstacles which symbolize the things about that person's personality that need to be corrected – a quick temper, stubbornness, selfishness or greed, for example. It's allegorical, of course, but nonetheless very real to the person on the journey. They may have to climb rocks and squeeze through narrow openings, or they may be presented with such insurmountable obstacles that they have to pause and work out what to do.

What are the differences between hauntings, psychic imprints, revenants and poltergeists?
A *haunting* is characterized by the fact that phenomena associated with it vary and often attract attention. The ghost exists in its own right with a consciousness: if I make contact with a ghost it is aware of me; and in some cases the person who is being haunted can also communicate with the ghost.

A *psychic imprint* is like a psychic video; it will replay the event to whoever is sensitive enough to pick it up. Psychic imprints are often experienced when people are in a relaxed state of mind, and they are characterized by repetitiveness – the same event will recur time after time. A psychic imprint does not interact or communicate because it belongs to a specific moment and has no consciousness associated with it.

The term *revenant* is used to describe someone who is not trapped at the earth level, but has moved to the spirit world, and whose memories or desires take them back to the place where they first felt them. Occasionally the person will manifest and is mistaken for a ghost; it's only through contact that I can determine that they are a revenant. Fear, sorrow and bitterness usually indicate a ghost, whereas a revenant is more likely to bring feelings of happiness.

I've never dealt with a *poltergeist* case, but I agree with the theory that a poltergeist is not necessarily a discarnate spirit, but a manifestation of the unconscious mind of a person – usually a teenager. It's as though the psychic energies of the teenager are externalized and this causes disturbances such as flying objects and rushing winds. It usually stops when the teenager grows up.

Why does the spirit world need you *to release ghosts?*
For two reasons. The first is that I have the advantage of being on
the earth; I can therefore hold the ghost steady as it is released. If I
didn't do this, the emotional backlash could send them into a
psychic wilderness. But I do get help from the spirit world; a team
of helpers usually comes to assist. This team always includes
someone who knew the ghost and has some love for them; this is
the person that takes the ghost to the spirit world.

*Why are some ghosts more aware of what's going on in the twentieth
century than others?*
This has something to do with how alert the person was when they
were alive; someone who died from a drugs overdose, for example,
would have little awareness of what's going on around them.
Sometimes it seems as if they are looking at the earth through a
smokescreen; they cannot get back to earth or see the light to the
spirit world.

*Are ghosts aware of their predicament? Do they know that you are
there to help?*
There's a lot of variation. Some are anxious to get away; others
have no idea of their situation. Their consciousness is dimmed once
they enter the etheric body, but some begin to have an understanding – maybe after a year or two, or maybe after a hundred years –
and they begin to look around for some way out. At this stage they
will begin to grow frustrated and can develop into a nuisance.

What does it take for a ghost to become aware?
Although the consciousness has dimmed, it slowly dawns on them
that they are in the wrong place and they have to move; this feeling
becomes more and more urgent. Sometimes other spirits come to
them and prompt them to leave. When I draw close to a ghost I
empathize with him and at the same time he becomes aware of
anything that is affecting me. One ghost insisted I closed the
window because he was disturbed by the noise of passing traffic on
a busy road.

Can ghosts ever spontaneously release themselves once they are trapped?
No, I haven't come across that, but I imagine it could happen.

Have you ever failed to release a ghost?
Yes, where someone has been reluctant to let go of some aspect of their past life it can prove impossible to help them. One should never try to force them to change their minds or interfere with their free will. This has happened to me on a couple of occasions; I made contact with the ghost but then it withdrew from me because it was not ready to let go of whatever had happened in its earthly life.

How do groups of ghosts manage to coexist?
I've occasionally encountered several ghosts haunting one house at the same time, but generally they are not aware of each other because they are from different periods of time. Sometimes a group of souls can be trapped at an intermediate level between the etheric and spirit plane, held together by a common interest. Two good examples of this are the group of Battle of Britain pilots and the courtiers of King Charles I, who were held back by a strong desire to reconstruct the glamour and position of their earthly life. I usually tell them to look away from the earth, towards the spirit world.

Is it true that you can work over the telephone and from pictures?
Yes. I was talking to someone in Australia who was describing a haunting in their house, and as they talked I became aware of the ghost involved. I went through the usual process and the person on the phone wrote down what I said. It's possible because I'm dealing with time and space in the spiritual, not physical sense.

Are there other people doing the same work as you?
There are a few who work in the same way as I do. But there are others who do more harm than good. If they charge for their services, it may be a bad sign.

Why should people believe you?
The best judges of my skills are the people who call on me to deal with a haunting; they don't need to be persuaded of the reality of

22

the entity that has invaded their lives. I make contact with the ghost and free it; the proof lies in the fact that the same ghost never reappears – you have their testimony for that.

Why do you specialize in hauntings?
Because the demand is there; but I'm still interested in healing and psychic counselling.

Do you feel you are doing some good at a haunting?
Releasing someone is like turning a key to their cell. I sense their feeling of liberation and I feel great joy from the spirit world.

Do you believe in God?
Yes. I have been sure about God's existence since I experienced an intense white light which brought a feeling of unconditional love. That happened in a church over twenty years ago.

Could you be described as an exorcist?
I would not like to be thought of as an exorcist as this conjures up images of rituals involving holy water. Nor do I like the term 'ghostbuster', because it implies aggression; the last thing I do is to behave aggressively towards these poor souls. I have been called in after exorcism has failed, but my work is different because I help the trapped spirit move on to a better place. Anglican exorcists are usually more interested in ridding the house of the ghost than what happens to it afterwards; very few exorcists can guide the spirit into the next world.

There's also a tendency to think that ghosts are evil spirits. The ghost is not necessarily evil. Entities often tell me they don't want to be pushed out into the dark again. In the Roman Catholic church they seem to have a better understanding of the problem – they talk about people being trapped in purgatory, the halfway house between this world and the next.

Why do there seem to be more ghosts in Britain and the US than the rest of the world?
It may just be that we have a higher state of awareness in this

country, but I find it hard to believe that there are any more here than in Germany or France. Also there's more openness about ghosts here and in the US than in Europe, for example.

How do you know when to stop?
If I do too much in the course of the day I feel a strain in the head.

Do you need to regenerate yourself after you have worked with ghosts?
Yes, through sleep – too much psychic exertion leaves you feeling mentally and physically drained.

How do you protect yourself against evil or dark forces? Are there any places you have refused to visit?
I have never refused to go anywhere, and I never feel fear in a spiritual sense. I protect myself with prayer before I visit a place and ask for help from the angelic realms. My experience has also built up a degree of protection.

What do you think about the Society for Psychical Research and their methods? How do your methods differ?
There are many people involved in psychic work who make contact with spirits at various levels. The SPR tries to set the subject in a scientific framework; but their methods – trying to record ghosts on tape or film – are pointless. The only way you will capture a ghost on film is if it is able or willing to materialize through ectoplasm, a semi-physical matter that some mediums can produce. If a ghost remains at the etheric level – the next stage on from the earth – it will not be possible to capture its image with electronic devices. The only things you could record are the sounds of disturbances, such as doors banging, floors creaking and windows opening.

Those of us with psychic awareness know it is an experiential thing; we don't need evidence, we have to go along with what we experience. I am not worried about whether people believe or disbelieve. As long as my work is useful I will keep doing it; if people are interested I will explain.

What about the future? Some psychics believe that as we enter the Aquarian Age the earth is attracting powerful new energies from the spirit world that will clear these trapped souls in a single wave.

It is said that Jesus journeyed into Hell to preach to trapped souls; you could say that He entered this realm in order to release them. There were many more trapped souls then than today because the times were so cruel and understanding of the psychic world was limited. Although there are trapped souls today, there are not so many; they are coming to light rapidly, because the energy of the spirit world is exposing them. As the New Age dawns, those who are trapped will become uncomfortable; they will realize that they are in the wrong place and, as their frustration grows, it will become crucial to deal with them.

Part I

People and Places of Influence

Chapter 1

The Queen's Bank

Say to the Court, it glows
And shines like rotten wood;
Say to the Church, it shows
What's good, and doth no good;
If Church and Court reply,
Then give them both the lie.

Sir Walter Raleigh, 'The Lie'

On 17 January 1572 Thomas Howard, fourth Duke of Norfolk, was beheaded at Tower Hill for plotting the overthrow of Queen Elizabeth I. Howard was thirty-seven years old and had been a widower since the death in 1557 of his wife, Mary Fitzalan, daughter of the twelfth Earl of Arundel. He was also innocent.

Howard was a victim of the complex power struggles in Elizabethan England and Europe which are so difficult for modern readers to understand. Historians describe the events which led to Howard's conviction using the tidy language of contemporary politics, but this is misleading. Howard's England was governed by a tiny landed élite and by the church; the feuds and schemes flowed from nationalism spiced with religious dogma, personal hatreds and brutal self-interest. Thomas Howard was not a great historical personage; he became a footnote in the history of the Elizabethan era. Then, more than 400 years later, forgotten by all but a handful of scholars, Thomas Howard once again became a public figure.

★

Coutts & Co., the Queen's bank, is justifiably proud of its head office at 440 Strand in London. In the huge, airy marble atrium cultivated trees and trailing plants flank a steep escalator which leads up to the bank's secluded offices on the first floor. Male staff, wearing traditional nineteenth-century frock coats, circle the ornamental pool that shimmers with iridescent koi carp, and discreetly welcome customers to the bank. Like most places frequented by people of wealth and privilege, there is a decorous hush in the air.

The casual visitor is left in no doubt that Coutts is an exceptional institution. From its giant cheque-books to the absence of advertisements to attract new customers, Coutts prides itself on good taste and discretion. Although it is not the oldest bank in London – Hoare & Co. lays claim to this title – it is certainly the most prestigious. Founded in 1692, its customers have included the explorer David Livingstone, the eighteenth-century prime minister William Pitt and King George III. Today, it maintains the same high standards; in 1994, personal customers had to show that they enjoyed an annual income of at least £75,000 and had to keep at least £3,000 in their current account in order to avoid bank charges.

Coutts' personnel director was understandably alarmed in August 1992 when a receptionist complained that she had been disturbed one afternoon by a shadowy black figure crossing the atrium towards the door. The lighting and computers had malfunctioned and minutes before the ghost appeared the temperature had plummeted, leaving the receptionist and her colleagues shivering with cold. Worse, she was not the first person to see an apparition; three of her colleagues had also seen it on separate occasions. By that stage the four women were too terrified to work.

The director passed the note on to Barbara Peters, the archivist. She had heard of ghosts appearing in Coutts' other London branches, such as Angela Burdett-Coutts, granddaughter of the founder, Thomas Coutts, who was supposed to haunt the Strand. But none had been sighted as regularly as the ghost seen by the receptionists. Determined to find out who it was, Barbara wrote to the College of Psychic Studies in South Kensington, hoping it would point her in the right direction. Her letter, dated 10 August, told how the Archivist's Department had recently received reports from the bank switchboard staff about 'a vague human shape lacking a head' at the entrance to their new offices at 440 Strand. It had been seen by several of the staff at different times through the day and early evening, and the details of the phenomenon tallied when compared. There was also a distinctly chilly temperature in the area of the sightings. The archivist asked whether the college had any details of the area from the point of view of known ghosts or other psychic phenomena, and whether it could help uncover any background to the apparitions.

The bank had moved into its Strand offices in the late 1970s. The building, which was refurbished by Coutts, formed part of the West Strand Development, constructed in the 1820s and 1830s. Before that, the site had been a maze of alleys and courtyards and the position of the switchboard (now at the corner of Adelaide Street and William IV Street) would have been close to the former Seymour Court; Church Court, Church Lane and Hewers Court would also have been demolished to make way for the building.

Brenda Marshall, the president of the College of Psychic Studies at this time, read the letter with interest. She was flattered that such a prestigious institution should be asking for help. For ten years she had worked tirelessly to promote the college, but it had not been easy; psychics were an easy target for ridicule by the media and she knew she still had a long way to go to convince a sceptical public of the value of their work. She called Eddie, whom she had known for many years and who had relayed several messages from her deceased husband. Mrs Marshall was confident that if anyone could get to the bottom of the Coutts mystery, Eddie could. The date and time were arranged; Eddie was to travel up from Lincoln on 14 August and meet Barbara Peters at 1.30 p.m.

Three days later Eddie arrived at King's Cross station on the Newark train and took a taxi to Charing Cross. He paused for a moment outside Coutts' marble and glass edifice, admiring the bright exterior, and then walked through the lower atrium towards the escalator. Barbara Peters, a neat woman in her late forties, was waiting on the first floor for him. After a brief introduction, he asked the three receptionists what they had seen; at least one thought that the apparition had been headless. They then went to a small office close to the switchboard and continued their discussion. Eddie became aware of an entity approaching and asked one of the women to record what he was about to say.

He is a man of considerable pride and he is somewhat haughty; I feel his impatience. He says: 'I have been waiting a long time, yet you continue to keep me waiting needlessly. I practised the law. I would not bend to the Queen's command conveyed to me through her servant, the one who held the great seal. By this time I knew too much. Did I become indiscreet I could threaten Her Majesty, so when it was discovered that I would not be amenable, a case of treason was trumped up and I was beheaded not far from here on a summer's day, which made me loath to depart.

'I have held much bitterness and I am told that if I am to be helped I must let this go. In the name of God I ask your help. I cannot do this alone. The memory is still strong. Thank you, my hope is growing. If you can get me from this place I shall be much obliged.'

He is much calmer now. I shall try to hold him steady. He is wearing a dark red or black doublet and hose. The doublet has puffed upper sleeves and lace around the cuffs; it is taken in around the waist slightly and flared below. He is wearing a ruff at his neck and dark shoes with silver buckles. I think he is Elizabethan. He is tall and slim, with a thin face and an aquiline nose.

He says: 'That is a fair description, but you have not mentioned my ornaments.' He is drawing my attention to the jewelled rings on his left hand and the gold or silver chain around his neck; at the end of the chain is a disc with delicate tracery worked in gold or silver. He says: 'At my execution I took off my doublet and ruff, for I did not wish them to be spoiled. They were to be given to my son. I put around my shoulders the black mantle which was part of my accoutrement in law. I did not mind if this were stained, for it was stained already through this injustice . . . I wait upon you now.'

I sense his daughter approaching; I know he had a great love for her. He immediately responds: 'You lift my heart, for she was dear to me.' I see her clearly as she approaches him; she is dressed in Elizabethan costume, entirely in white, and she radiates a bright light. She takes both his hands in hers. He is awe-struck by her beauty. They turn now and walk towards the light, she holding his left hand in her right hand. He looks back for a moment to thank us. I am getting the impression now that there was some dispensation after his death, for he was buried in consecrated ground.

Eddie left it to the Coutts' archivist to find out the identity of the man; he had done his work by freeing the ghost.

A few days later he called Brenda Marshall to tell her what had happened. At the time she was editing *Light*, the college's newsletter, and she asked for an account of the haunting so she could feature it in the next issue. Eddie agreed, on condition that the name of Coutts would not be used. Had Mrs Marshall decided not to use the story, the matter would have rested there. As it was, I came across it as I was leafing through the winter issue of *Light*, and one month later, on 21 February, my front-page story in the *Sunday Telegraph* heralded Eddie as 'Britain's most celebrated ghostbuster'. After years of treating the paranormal with disdain, the media treated the case in an intelligent way.

Unlike Eddie, who was only too happy to discuss his work with the media, the College of Psychic Studies shied away from the press. Although Brenda Marshall, who had by this time stepped down from the presidency, was initially thrilled at the prospect of publicity she was quickly brought into line by the new president, Dudley Poplak, a flamboyant South African. As interior designer to the Prince and Princess of Wales – he had supervised the redecoration of Highgrove, the Prince's Gloucestershire home, after the royal wedding in 1981 – he had a high profile in London society and his reputation to consider. Curiously for a president of a society dedicated to the study of psychic phenomena, Mr Poplak seemed embarrassed that the Queen's bank was haunted.

But Mr Poplak's disapproval did not matter to the newspapers, who were determined to identify the Coutts' ghost. The *Daily Mail* consulted historian Paul Slack, fellow of Exeter College, Oxford, who thought the most probable candidate was Robert Devereux, Earl of Essex, who was beheaded in 1601. Commander of the British fleet and a favourite of Queen Elizabeth after his spectacular defeat of the Spanish navy in 1596, five years later he was arrested and tried for treason after riding up and down the West End trying to drum up a rebellion against Elizabeth.

It was Father Francis Edwards, a Jesuit priest and a member of the Royal Historical Society, who identified the ghost as Thomas Howard, fourth Duke of Norfolk. Father Edwards knew that Thomas Howard's path to the executioner's block could be traced to the return in 1561 to her native Scotland of Mary Stuart, the young widow of the French king Francis II. As daughter of King James V and Mary of Guise, Queen of France, Mary had inherited the Scottish crown and now believed she was the rightful successor to the childless Elizabeth I. The English court immediately recognized the potential importance of Mary's next marriage and watched nervously for any signs of an impending union.

In an attempt to heal the rift between Protestant England and Catholic Scotland, Elizabeth's courtiers put forward the names of several leading Protestant noblemen, hoping Mary would choose one for a husband. But Mary was more concerned with appeasing her European allies and considered a long list of Catholic suitors. In an effort to limit the damage, Elizabeth proposed one of her trusted courtiers, Thomas Howard, fourth Duke of Norfolk, who was a Protestant although his family later became the country's most notable Catholics.

Mary eventually chose Henry, Lord Darnley, who was good-looking but feeble. Their marriage was short-lived: Darnley was murdered in 1567 by the Earl of Bothwell, a Protestant soldier with whom Mary had fallen in love. Elizabeth appointed Thomas Howard to oversee an inquiry into the murder; finding that several of Mary's letters incriminated her in the murder, he consulted Elizabeth, who ordered a full-scale investigation at Westminster. Sir William Maitland, a Scottish diplomat and Mary's adviser, quickly approached Norfolk in an attempt to prevent this. Cleverly, he appealed to Norfolk by suggesting that Mary was interested in marriage. Thomas Howard had never met Mary Stuart, but their courtship developed through regular correspondence and Mary soon began to address him as 'My Norfolk'.

A group of highly placed Scottish and English noblemen, including John Leslie, Bishop of Ross and Mary's ambassador at Elizabeth's court, also thought that the marriage would be useful, though for their own selfish reasons. They wanted to curb Sir William Cecil, who had assumed dominance of Elizabeth's Privy Council, and whose foreign policy – particularly his hostility towards Spain – they regarded as damaging to England's commercial interests.

Since Elizabeth had originally suggested him as a possible husband for Mary, Thomas Howard naturally assumed that she would not now disapprove of the marriage. However, he was mistaken; Elizabeth now calculated, for complex political and religious reasons, that the marriage would threaten her, and in 1569 imprisoned Mary at Chatsworth and sent Howard to the Tower. He was released the following August in return for persuading Mary not to take part in yet another plot dreamt up by ambitious nobles, to snatch her from England and return her to Scotland.

Unfortunately for Howard, a further plot was being hatched. This centred on a man called Roberto Ridolfi, a Florentine banker and adventurer who was trying to mastermind an invasion of England, supported by the Spanish and Pope Pius IV. The plan was preposterous: having stirred up Catholic feeling in England, they would seize Elizabeth and install Mary on the throne with Thomas Howard as consort. Nevertheless Mary, tired after long years of uncertainty, wrote to Ridolfi endorsing his scheme; she named Howard as head of the enterprise and guardian of Catholic rights in England, and said that all practical details were to be left to him.

In the spring of 1571 Elizabeth received a private warning about Ridolfi's plot and discovered letters which revealed that Norfolk was sending money to Mary's supporters in Scotland. On 7 September Howard was arrested and sent to the Tower. Under interrogation John Leslie claimed that recent Catholic uprisings in the north were the direct result of correspondence between Mary and Norfolk. William Cecil pounced and from that moment Howard had no hope.

Father Francis Edwards knew every twist and turn of the Thomas Howard story. A kind, intensely donnish man, Father Edwards had spent many years researching the Duke's life for his book *The Marvellous Chance*, which examines in detail Howard's alleged part in the Ridolfi plot. He had been convinced that the ghost at Coutts was Thomas Howard by a few clues that were, at least to an expert like him, crucial: the ghost at Coutts had practised law, had been condemned on a trumped-up charge and had been executed on a summer's day.

Father Edward's letter to the *Sunday Telegraph*, which appeared the week after my story, said:

> I do not know what the archivist at Coutts' bank will come up with, but the apparition that appeared in the Strand seems to correspond remarkably well with what we know of Thomas Howard, fourth Duke of Norfolk. Born in 1536, he was executed on a trumped-up charge of treason on Tower Hill on June 2, 1572. He was tall and slim, with aquiline features that were beautifully drawn by Lukas de Heere around 1569. He is yet another character waiting in the wings of history for a fairer deal at the hands of historians. Although he technically disobeyed Queen Elizabeth I by persisting in a project to marry Mary Queen of Scots, then in captivity in England, he had no evil design on Elizabeth. He was a devout Anglican to the last. He really owed his death to Sir William Cecil, who feared him as a rival for power. The Duke, I may say, has not seen fit to call on me, although I regard myself as a supporter of his, if not exactly a friend.

Father Edwards invited Eddie to Farm Street Church, London, in March 1994 to discuss the Coutts incident. It is unusual for a Catholic priest – especially one from such a prestigious order – to work with psychics. But Father Edwards felt a strong link with Eddie, perhaps because of their shared interest in Thomas Howard. Although he believed that the experience left some questions unanswered for him, Father Edwards accepted that the broad facts of the Coutts case fully corroborated the Catholic doctrine of purgatory – an intermediate state between heaven and hell, where souls are prepared for their entry into heaven. It was also good Catholic doctrine that souls in this intermediate state cannot help themselves, but need prayers and intervention from those still living on earth.

When they met, Eddie told Father Edwards about his latest communications from Thomas Howard. On 12 January 1993 the spirit had approach Eddie while I was interviewing him for the *Sunday Telegraph*. We were talking about the Coutts case when Eddie told me to start writing:

'I heard you tell of me and take this opportunity to return to give you my thanks, for I had not time when you did free me from my imprisonment. I cannot do justice to the joy which has come to me. I give praise to God for all his goodness. My daughter has stayed with me to bring me familiarity with this new abode, but soon she will return to her heavenly place which is as yet beyond me. But I have made friends and feel secure, for the beauty of this place is beyond my describing. Thank you again. One day we shall meet face to face and it will give me great joy to embrace you. Farewell in the love of God.'

Again, on 2 June, while Eddie was sitting with some friends in his home in Lincoln, the entity made contact. Eddie realized that the ghost had returned to him on the anniversary of his execution.

'This is the anniversary of my execution and I must confess that it still saddens me, but this will pass. In all the time I was in the dark I never noted the day. So I feel today, your day, something of the weight of the many past anniversaries which went unnoticed. 'Tis a strange feeling, a hole in time, it seems. And somehow I know I have to fill it, if only to satisfy my curiosity about events from that sad day to this, and I know that when I have done this I shall be able to let go finally of the sorrow and sadness. Forgive my sombre note, but I did not wish this day to pass once more unnoticed. God's blessing upon you.'

The Duke of Norfolk and his family had been intrigued by the return of the fourth Duke. Relieved that he had finally been helped to move on to a more restful place, they agreed to hold a memorial service for Thomas Howard in London the following November. As head of Britain's most eminent Catholic family and lay head of the Catholic community, the seventeenth Duke understood the importance of his family finally laying Thomas Howard's soul to rest.

On a cold, rainy afternoon on 15 November newspaper and television journalists were huddled in the entrance to the tiny Corpus Christi Church in Maiden Lane, Covent Garden. They had been waiting since lunchtime for the arrival of the Duke and Duchess of Norfolk and their family, who were to pay their last respects to Thomas Howard that afternoon. Inside the freshly painted church, the Duke chatted to Father McDonald, the parish priest of Covent Garden, who was to lead the service. His son and heir, the Earl of Arundel, with his wife Georgina, Countess of Arundel, stood nearby with Lady Mary Mumford, daughter of the sixteenth Duke, and her aunt Lady Winefride Freeman. The Duke's other children, Lady Carina, wife of the television presenter Sir David Frost, Marsha Fitzalan, the actress, Lord Gerald and Lady Tessa could not attend. But the congregation was nonetheless strong, swollen by friends, associates, representatives from Coutts Bank – which had donated the spectacular plants adorning the church – and the College of Psychic Studies.

At four o'clock the service opened with an address by Father Edwards, who gave thanks for the extraordinary life of Thomas Howard. After the first hymn, 'Praise to the Holiest in the height', Father McDonald led the family in prayers for the fourth Duke; his father Henry Howard, also beheaded, in 1547; and Thomas's son, St Philip Howard, who was imprisoned for eleven years and later died in the Tower for refusing to renounce his faith, and was canonized by the Roman Catholic church in 1970. The Earl of Arundel then gave a moving reading from Ecclesiastes, the eulogy of the ancestors.

As the words of Vivaldi's 'Laudate Pueri' echoed the earlier rendition of Mozart's 'Laudate Dominum', the congregation bowed and said a private prayer for the fourth Duke. As the last strains of the music died away, Eddie took his place in the pulpit and gave his address. The journalists, who had somehow managed to creep into the back of the church and were now looking around rather nervously, listened open-mouthed as Eddie explained the unusual circumstances of his meeting with Thomas Howard.

The service closed with a rousing hymn written by St Philip Howard while he was imprisoned in the Tower: 'Oh Christ the glorious crown/of virgins that are pure'. The day had gone extremely well; the service had not embarrassed the Norfolks, and the media had had their story. As they filtered out of the church one reporter stopped to ask the Duke, a bluff and normally taciturn retired major-general, what he thought of the service. Pausing for a moment, he said: 'I don't believe in ghosts, it's all a load of rubbish.' With this he stomped off.

Other members of the family kept a more open mind on psychic matters. Lady Mary was delighted with the service: 'It was the least we could do for poor Thomas,' she said. 'I hope he's happy now.' After the service she invited us to Arundel Castle, the Norfolks' family seat. She wanted us to check whether any more distressed spirits were wandering through Arundel's stately halls. A devout Catholic herself, she was acutely aware that it was up to the living to help lost souls by prayer and kind thoughts, and she wanted to do everything to ensure that no-one else was suffering as Thomas Howard had done.

We travelled to Arundel the following day. That evening, after dinner at Lady Mary's comfortable cottage in North Stoke, a village a few miles away from the castle, Eddie told us that Thomas Howard was with us again:

> 'You pleased me greatly with the honour you did me yesterday. I saw more of this than would have met your eyes. I sensed the love and concern for my well-being and it pleased me greatly. Please put aside any doubts concerning the true value of the ceremony, for it has relieved me of the last vestiges of my sadness and I now feel free to view the scene in which I find myself and step forward into the greater light which beckons me.

'I owe you all a debt which I can only repay in the coinage of a love whose quality has been raised by my greater awareness of the presence of our God. Therefore accept my love and, when you can and when you will, reflect upon me and send me a token of your love. You may think, as I did, that a gulf of time does separate us, but it is a moment only and to me you are my brothers and sisters forever united and bound in the love of God. Remember me in your prayers as I will remember you until the blessed day when we meet in joy.'

Arundel Castle nestles in the rolling South Downs, above the River Arun in West Sussex. For over a thousand years it has been the family home of the Fitzalan and Howard families; in 1994 it was inhabited by the Earl of Arundel, his wife Georgina and their four small children. An army of staff manages the castle, caring for its priceless furniture, glass and silverware, which are as great a national treasure as the building itself.

Arundel's history dates from 1067 when William the Conqueror made Roger de Montgomery Earl of Arundel in return for governing Normandy while William was conquering England. De Montgomery was also given a third of the county of Sussex, and he proceeded to build a motte and bailey castle at Arundel. Roger's son, Hugh, died without an heir in 1094; his brother Robert de Belesme was imprisoned after rebelling against Henry I, who took control of the castle and its grounds and withdrew the title of Earl of Arundel from the family. This he bestowed on the d'Albini (d'Aubigny) family, one of whom, William d'Albini, married Henry's widow, Adela of Louvain, in 1138.

In 1243, on the death of William's great-grandson Hugh d'Aubigny, the estates were divided and John Fitzalan, Lord of Clun and Oswaldestre, inherited the castle and Honour of Arundel through his mother Isabel d'Albini. The Fitzalans held the castle with a few short interruptions until 1556 when Mary Fitzalan married Thomas Howard, fourth Duke of Norfolk, thereby uniting the Fitzalans with the Howards and bringing Arundel to the Dukes of Norfolk, who have held it to this day.

Thomas, the third Duke, was the most notorious: an unscrupulous Tudor courtier who was determined to survive the treacherous politics of Henry VIII's court, he was prepared to sacrifice both his religion and his family to retain Henry's favour. He introduced the King to two of his nieces: the first, Anne Boleyn, became Henry's second wife and mother of Elizabeth I; the second, Catherine Howard, married Henry as his fifth wife and, like Anne Boleyn, was beheaded at the Tower while her uncle stood back and refused to intervene.

Thomas left a son, Henry, the 'Poet Earl of Surrey', a highly cultured man and a competent soldier, who was executed in 1547 on a trumped-up charge of quartering the arms of Edward the Confessor. The fourth and fifth Dukes, Thomas Howard and St Philip Howard, each suffered a tragic fate, as I have already described, and thereafter the family's fortunes declined for a while, reviving in the seventeenth century.

★

As Lady Mary and the Countess of Arundel escorted us around the castle, Lady Winefride reminisced about life as a child at Arundel. A sprightly and sharp-witted old lady, Lady Winefride was born in the castle in 1914. She remembered the long, cold winters when the only warmth was provided by log fires kept going by woodmen. The castle had its own electricity supply for lighting, but it was not powerful enough for heating or cooking; food had to be cooked on a gas stove and then warmed in an oven in the pantry next to the dining room. They had only one telephone and got their first radio in 1922. 'But as a family we had a very happy life, always remembering what a privilege it was to be living here – always ready to show others our home,' she told me. 'Of course, it was a wonderful place for children's games, treasure hunts and the amateur theatricals which my brother and two sisters would perform at Christmas for our relations. On Christmas Eve all those on the Arundel estate would come to the Barons' Hall, which was decorated with enormous coloured baubles and lights, and after tea the children would be given presents. As they left we handed each one a bag of sweets and an orange.'

As we walked through the breathtaking Barons' Hall, with its polished wooden floor and hammerbeam oak roof, I stole a sidelong glance at Lady Winefride, moist-eyed and wistful after recalling her idyllic childhood. We turned into the picture gallery and paused for a while. Portraits of all the Dukes and Duchesses of Norfolk lined both walls, arranged mainly in chronological order beginning at the west end. This priceless collection is one of the few comprehensive sets of family portraits in Europe. Eddie was drawn to a posthumous painting of the Poet Earl of Surrey, dressed in a fur cape and hat and standing languidly beneath an arch flanked by a man and woman bearing the Norfolk coats of arms. He said:

There is a strong imprint in front of this painting. I think the Poet Earl wants to communicate. He says:
'I beg you to complete the task which you have begun. Strike the chain from my legs, I beseech you. My soul reaches forth but part of me remains anchored, fastened to the cruelty of mine end. You have helped me already to see a light beyond. Help me free myself, I pray you.
'I look at the richness and pomp that was my lot at times in life and which I have clung to for so long, but now I am coming to understand how little these things signify in the sight of God. I must let go now of these baubles, of the importance I took upon myself, and reach the humility of soul which I see I must acquire. Help me in this. My sufferings are so little set beside those of our Lord. I must fasten my mind upon this and find forgiveness for those who did me wrong.'
I feel him resting now, although his soul is still struggling. He says: 'Praise be to God, the chains have fallen away and my beloved Thomas doth approach.'
Thomas is coming to Henry as the boy he remembered, not the adult. There is an overwhelming feeling of joy coming through as they greet each other warmly.

After Eddie had finished, Lady Arundel said that she wanted us to see a final portrait, of St Philip Howard, Thomas's son, in her private apartments. Tall and elegant, with short dark hair and cornflower-blue eyes, Lady Arundel was a thoroughly down-to-earth chatelaine. As we entered the apartments, our eyes were immediately drawn to the saint's poignant gaze. Philip's life was even more tragic than that of his father or grandfather; his wilful refusal to denounce Catholicism at a time when the Anglican church was gaining power led to his arrest and detention in the Tower. He was accused of having said a Mass for the success of the Spanish Armada and died in the Tower in 1595, probably poisoned. Eddie received the following communication from him:

> 'I see such distinctions as I made and suffered for as of little or no account from where I now stand. But mark this: I did right at the time as I then saw the truth. It is how a man behaves in relation to the truth as he perceives it that matters, and the growth of the soul doth depend on this. So I am happy that I made the stand I did. I am warmed by your interest and enquiry, so I am emboldened to say these few words to help you understand that what is right at the time may look different from a loftier viewpoint, but still remains right in its context. God bless you and farewell.'

The sun had set by the time we were ready to leave Arundel. The prospect of afternoon tea was appealing, but Lady Arundel was too busy with her children to entertain us any longer. Before Eddie could accept her gracious invitation I declined on his behalf, to her obvious relief. As we drove out of the courtyard across the moat and through the barbican I looked back at Arundel's massive walls and towers, wondering if Thomas Howard was watching us leave. Then, driving out through St Mary's gate, we left the past behind and returned instead to the twentieth century.

★

Eddie received one further communication from Thomas Howard, on 23 December 1993. He had been reading Neville Williams's book, *Thomas Howard, IV Duke of Norfolk: A Tudor Tragedy*, when he felt the Duke approaching. He said:

> ' 'Tis concerning my story. I have followed the writings in the book at one remove as it were and find the story somewhat

bland, though the intention was honest enough. The priest was nearer the mark as for the sake of my earthly reputation, though it matters little to me now. I feel I owe the father a debt of gratitude. It required much patience to unravel the events as he described. Please convey to him my gratitude. I take this opportunity to wish you the joy of this Holy Season. God be with you.'

Chapter 2

Glorious Goodwood

You . . . are the great oaks that shade a country and perpetuate your benefits from generation to generation.

Edmund Burke to Charles Lennox, Third Duke of Richmond

And both were young, and one was beautiful.

Lord Byron, 'The Dream', II

On 30 November 1991 Charles March, only son of the Earl of March and Kinrara, married the Honourable Janet Astor, daughter of the late Viscount Astor, in one of the society weddings of the year. It was his second marriage, so the couple had a simple registry office ceremony, in front of just two witnesses. Later, 450 guests gathered for a marriage blessing in the chapel of the bride's family home, Cliveden in Buckinghamshire. After a glittering reception, the young couple zoomed off, under a cascade of fireworks, in the black Ferrari which the bride had given to her new husband as a wedding present.

Lord March, thirty-six, tall, dark with the smouldering good looks of a top fashion model, had already enjoyed a successful career as a fashion photographer in the early 1980s. Approaching his forties, he had decided to devote himself full-time to Goodwood, the family home in Sussex. The new Lady March, six years his junior, was a strikingly attractive Oxford graduate who had pursued an equally successful career as a fashion designer.

Charles March and Janet Astor were the couple with everything: they were good-looking and wealthy and commuted from breathtaking country estates to smart London town houses. They came from that colour supplement world of beauty and power that ordinary people could only dream of. Lord March's father entertained the Queen, when she visited for Goodwood's famous July race week. In 1970 Charles's elder sister, Lady Ellinor Gordon Lennox, held an eighteenth birthday ball attended by the Queen, the Duke of Edinburgh, Prince Charles and Princess Anne. Janet's grandmother, Nancy Astor, had been England's first woman MP.

Charles March had been expelled from Eton at sixteen for organizing a classroom revolt; he spent the following nine months travelling in Africa, where he developed a passion for photography. Back in England he became a top fashion photographer, using the family name Settrington. His new wife, Janet, more reserved than her husband, took an MA in philosophy at Oxford and trained in Paris as a designer with Chanel. She later returned to London as a senior designer for Victor Edelstein, the English couturier.

By 1994 the Marches regularly stared out of newspapers and magazines; they were the perfect, enviable couple. But Lord March's private life had not always been so happy. In 1989 his twelve-year marriage to Sally Clayton, a dancer with Hot Gossip, a well-known dance group, had broken down and they had separated, selling their £2.5 million London home, Hurlingham Lodge. Their daughter, Lady Alexandra, ten, remained with Sally. When he fell in love with Janet Astor, a Catholic, Charles was a non-Catholic divorcé, which posed significant problems. But he was determined to marry her and converted to Catholicism.

They kept their house in London but decided to base themselves on the 12,000-acre Goodwood estate, a few miles from the great house. In 1988 Lord March's father, the Earl of March and Kinrara, had inherited Goodwood and the title of tenth Duke of Richmond at the age of fifty-nine. Although he was an active man, who had had a distinguished career in business and academia, he also suffered from clinical depression, so it was no surprise to his family when he announced that he intended to hand over the family estates to his son. 'It's very important for the next generation to get into the saddle reasonably early on,' he said. 'There have been a number of places in this country where the old man has gone on too long, sitting in the house trying to run things. Places like Goodwood mustn't be allowed to stand still.' True to his word, in April 1994 the Duke swapped Goodwood for Lord and Lady March's small house on the estate.

His son, Charles, told me that the Goodwood house had not been properly lived in since the war. 'My grandparents only came here for the horse and motor racing and it was kept going with a housekeeper and skeleton staff,' he said. 'My great-grandfather would much rather have been Scottish – he'd open up for the motor racing and then go straight back to Scotland. When my father took it over it was in a sorry state. They did it up, redid the electrics, made it watertight – all the boring bits. You don't think about the decor being drab when you're worried about the roof.'

Unlike his father and grandfather, Lord March had strong views about the house. He said that it was important that a house like this worked for him, rather than his being controlled by it. Although both his father and grandfather had a horror of selling works of art from Goodwood, he regarded this as a straight business proposition and used the money to finance much-needed restoration.

Lord and Lady March set themselves the task of restoring the 300-year-old house to its former glory in time for the traditional ball which accompanies Glorious Goodwood – the Festival Meeting on the racecourse which is held every July. The restorations were intended to emphasize the history of the house, without compromising the comfort. Fine art experts from London advised the Marches on how to rearrange the countless priceless paintings, pieces of furniture and works of art, closely following the original plan for the house by the third Duke, who had commissioned Goodwood in the eighteenth century. Supervising the restoration work was a respected interior designer, Robert Kime, who oversaw the redecoration of Highgrove for the Prince of Wales after his separation from Princess Diana.

On schedule, Lord and Lady March opened their doors on 28 July to 450 society guests who danced away the small hours at the Goodwood Ball. He decided that the theme of the night should be

'Dress to Dazzle' – which meant that everyone should wear as many jewels as possible. Assisted by Rosa Monkton, a friend who was managing director of the society jeweller, Tiffany, the Marches raised thousands of pounds for charity. Lord March may have looked like just another well-groomed and privileged member of the aristocracy but he also showed that he had a fine business brain in his management of the Goodwood estate. As well as the motor circuit and racecourse, Goodwood has a golf club, aerodrome, hotel and country club and 12,000 acres of parkland. He consolidated and expanded. There were corporate seminars for blue chip companies, antiques fairs, orienteering championships, dressage competitions and golf tournaments. But he was determined not to be tacky; Goodwood had to be tasteful or it would lose its unique appeal. So he ruled out pop concerts and theme parks.

★

The news that Lady March was expecting her first child coincided with their move to Goodwood in spring 1994. Soon Lady March noticed that after a few days in the house she felt lethargic and depressed; but friends told her that this was normal in the early stages of pregnancy. Then, after a couple of months, and after her doctor assured her she was perfectly healthy, she began to wonder whether, somehow, the house was responsible; she always felt so much better if she spent time away from it.

It was Lady March's neighbour, Georgina, Lady Arundel, who suggested that Eddie might be able to improve the atmosphere at Goodwood. She said that she was inviting Eddie to perform a psychic inventory at Arundel and urged Lady March to ask him to do the same at Goodwood. By that time Lady March was spending most of her time at the house and was feeling more and more unwell. The Marches had already invited a number of psychics there, but without any improvement in Lady March's health.

Lord and Lady March invited us to stay overnight at Goodwood on 6 June 1994. We arrived there from Arundel just as the sun was beginning to set; as we turned into the long drive rabbits skipped away into the woods and then Goodwood came into view: an imposing, ivy-clad façade with four round towers, fronted by a perfect circular lawn. As we drove into the car park we saw a tall figure striding towards us. Immaculately dressed in a dark business suit, Lord March looked more like a city banker than a country gentleman.

After showing us to our rooms, Lord March asked us to meet him in the small library for a drink. As I entered the library, I saw that Eddie and his son, Christopher, who had come to photograph the house, were already sitting in deep armchairs nestling drinks in their hands. Lord March, who was putting an extra log of wood on the fire, asked me what I would like. A generous gin and tonic in an enormous crystal glass soon arrived and I sat down to survey the room. Well-worn armchairs surrounded a heavy oak coffee table loaded with magazines and newspapers – *Tatler*, *Country Life*, the *Economist*, the *Independent*; a large desk with an antique leather chair (which we later discovered was Napoleon's campaign chair at Waterloo) stood squarely behind me and antique books lined the walls, from floor to ceiling, the topmost of which could be reached by a spiral staircase leading to a reading gallery.

Lord March began to tell us about the house. 'There's nothing specific, just a feeling of unease – it has a very debilitating, negative effect on whoever lives here. It all began with my sister Ellinor. She kept seeing Aunt Ellinor – my mother's aunt – who had committed suicide in India years ago after her bankrupt lover killed himself. She was perfectly normal until we moved into the house in 1968, but then she began to have strange mood swings and was finally diagnosed as schizophrenic in 1972 when she was twenty. I've often wondered if her illness is due to the fact that she is extremely sensitive to influences in the house,' said Lord March. 'I sense presences here, but they don't affect me in the same way as my wife, who feels tired whenever she's here. My mother is quite sensitive to these feelings too, and has been much happier since she left the house.'

He said that there had been a brief improvement after one psychic had visited the house. But it had not lasted. 'My wife says that the oppressiveness has returned – it's as if a cloud has descended on the house. We have tried to do something about this by moving all the furniture and pictures around, and although I feel the house has responded in a very positive way, she still feels something has to be done. The land around the house has some ancient Druid sites and we wonder if this has something to do with the negative atmosphere.'

At this point there was a loud crash from above. We went upstairs to check for intruders but the house was secure. Then I noticed that a picture had fallen down outside the door of my room. It was the third Duke, whose staring eyes, said Lord March, always unsettled guests. Back in the library Lady March joined us. A petite, vivacious blonde dressed in black leggings and a grey jumper, she had just driven down from London where she was training as a psychotherapist. 'Obviously there's something wrong with the house,' she said. 'I think it's something to do with ten generations of strong men controlling it – there's been very little feminine influence here.

'It's quite a challenge to live with all this history and lead a healthy, normal life. If you are completely oppressed by the house – as the last few generations have been, struggling to make ends meet – your life can be absolutely miserable. I don't want that sort of pressure for Charles and myself.'

★

Goodwood House, the historic seat of the Dukes of Richmond and Gordon, was built by James Wyatt between 1780 and 1800. Commissioned by the third Duke of Richmond, it was built on the site of the original Jacobean house, erected in the early 1600s by the ninth Earl of Northumberland and bought by the first Duke of Richmond for £4,100 as a hunting lodge. The second Duke, born at Goodwood in 1694, led an extraordinary life. When he was eighteen years old he was married off to the Earl of Cadogan's daughter, Sarah, to settle a gambling debt between the two men. Then he set off on a three-year tour of Europe. On his way home he visited the opera in Brussels, saw a beautiful woman and immediately fell in love; it was his wife, Sarah, whom he had fled. They lived together for the next twenty-eight years and had twelve children.

Modern Goodwood is the result of the dedication of the third Duke, the seventh child of the second Duke, who was born on 22 February 1735. A major-general at the age of twenty-six, he became Master of Ordnance, supervising the famous Martello

Towers which warded off Napoleon's invasion in the next century. As ambassador extraordinary to Louis XV's court at Versailles, he immersed himself in French culture and brought back a fine collection of Sèvres china and Louis XV furniture to Goodwood, as well as the priceless Gobelin tapestries depicting the adventures of Don Quixote. In 1760 he employed Sir William Chambers to rebuild the house around the Jacobean original; later, James Wyatt began extending the house on an ambitious octagonal plan, but the Duke ran out of money before it could be completed. He died in 1806, childless, leaving debts of £180,000.

The third Duke was succeeded by his nephew, son of his brother Lord George Lennox. As Lord Lieutenant of Ireland, and later Governor-General of Upper and Lower Canada, the fourth Duke did not spend much time at Goodwood. In 1818 he was bitten by a rabid fox in Canada and died an excruciating death. He was buried at Quebec's Anglican cathedral. The fifth Duke followed his father into the army, which was the usual career in the nineteenth century for aristocrats hungry for the glory and status of military service. But there was to be no heroic battlefield death for the fifth Duke; he died of gout in 1860.

Duke number six was a home-builder, like the third Duke, and spent large sums of money on the estate, building 400 cottages for employees, planting trees, building a reservoir and installing his own gas-works in the house. In 1876 Queen Victoria created him first Duke of Gordon in return for his services to the Crown. The two world wars brought death and illness to the Goodwood dynasty but, unlike other aristocratic families who were destroyed by the social upheavals brought by war, the Goodwood dukes managed to hold on to the estate.

★

The following morning we joined Lord and Lady March at 8.30 for breakfast in the circular dining room. Fresh fruit, yoghurt, cereals, bread, honey and jams were laid out before us with pots of tea and coffee to hand. Lady March, dressed in a vivid green wool designer suit, was obviously a fit, health-conscious woman and this spread had clearly been designed by her; her husband, who had exchanged his suit of the previous night for black Levis and a black cashmere sweater, tried to look enthusiastic but, I suspected, would have preferred a good, old-fashioned breakfast. After two cups of tea, a bowl of cereal, toast and honey, Eddie pronounced himself ready for work.

Eddie had sensed a presence in the library the previous evening and decided to start there. Lady March remained with us while her husband went to his office for a business meeting; he promised to join us later. Eddie sat in a hard-backed chair and closed his eyes. As his breathing got heavier Lady March exchanged a worried glance with me. I assured her this was normal. Then Eddie began to speak.

There's someone here. I got a fleeting impression of madness, mental instability and irrational behaviour. It has been lingering here for a long time. I think it's someone who's trapped here, but I'm not sure whether it's specific to this room. I would place this person's personality somewhere between extremely eccentric and slightly mad – very unpredictable, anyway.

This man is rather proud – and he's never escaped from his earthly personality. He felt constricted by too much clothing and preferred to dress very lightly – he had to feel free. He had an interest in the sea. I get the impression of large sailing ships. I think at one time he had ambitions of a naval life, but his eccentric behaviour prevented this: I don't think he ever achieved any responsibility in his career.

He also has an interest in farming – cattle especially. He used to buy strange and odd breeds of cattle. He seems to have been driven by an urge to break away from conventional attitudes. This was his dilemma: to be successful he had to conform and make himself acceptable to people, but he also had a very strong desire to shrug off convention. This resulted in terrible tensions throughout his life. As he grew older and more established he allowed his eccentricity to show itself in very strange ways.

I think he died a very painful death, but not a lingering one. It may have been poison – he went into a paroxysm and his head was thrown back. I think he suffered severe muscular spasms. He says: 'Drugs.' I'm not sure whether they were self-administered or not. Perhaps it was an overdose.

He seemed to be clinging very strongly to life at the end. There was terrible fear around him; a fear of madness, I think. He carried this with him and it made him very reluctant to let go. I think this is why he was trapped. I am keeping him quiet and waiting for the next stage of his release. There's a lot of light round him; he's generating it from within himself. He's feeling the burden of his old personality falling away and the real man – the man he should have been – is beginning to show himself. The beam of spiritual light from him is reaching out to make a union with a light from another level. This is unique in my experience. An angelic being is escorting him into the light.

The date is early Victorian. He lived in this house. There was something deeply significant about this man's life; he veered from the conventional to the eccentric and back again to the conventional. But there was a very highly developed soul underneath. When he was released, it was as though all the power that had been hidden in this twisted personality was released. He seemed to be radiating light.

Lady March was convinced that the spirit was that of the fourth Duke, who had died in 1818 in Canada after being bitten by a rabid fox. Lord March, who had quietly slipped back into the library while Eddie was speaking, was now looking distinctly uneasy. After several reassurances he agreed to join in a prayer ceremony to cleanse the library. Each of us stood in a corner of the room and listened to Eddie, who asked us to imagine a sphere of light rising in the middle of the library and shedding its light into the four corners of the room.

Lady March then led us into the Long Hall which, she said, had always felt cold and unwelcoming. The Long Hall is the core of the original Jacobean house, built by the ninth Earl of Northumberland, also known as the Wizard Earl because he was very interested in the occult. Under the third Duke, the architect

Sir William Chambers had converted the hall into three rooms, the outer two framed by white Ionic pillars. The decorators had removed the paintings from the wall and scattered the furniture around the room. As I sat down with Lady March, Eddie walked around the room.

I sense a great ego – power and arrogance. It's coming from one corner. The presence here draws energy from all who enter it. We all feel cold because we're being drained. The influence extends from this room throughout the house. This is where we need to do the most work. I must be careful how I start this work. I'm getting the message: 'The clinging of powers long past their time; their reluctance to be moved.' There's a strong psychic imprint here allied to something that is still active; it's more on the dark side than the light. I'm going to walk round again and ask for a cordon of light to be laid around the perimeter; then everything unpleasant here will be forced into the centre and dissipated.

Eddie sat down and continued:

The room is being divided into quarters by a line running down the centre of the room, by two lines running longitudinally and transversally. At the centre a torch has been lit. It seems that the geometric centre is important in this operation. I see the light flowing in from two of these quadrants towards the centre and they are now being cleansed. This operation relates to the dark practices that went on in the room. The cleansing is somehow turning the tables on those evil practices; the dark powers will recognize what I have done.

I'm still waiting to see what will happen with the other two quadrants. The light is now coming inwards from them and everything that is remaining from the past is being forced into the torch. It will be consumed by the fire. I now see the flames spread from the centre, out towards the perimeter of the room. It's done. The cleansing is now complete, but there's one more stage to come. I see a sphere coming down

in the centre of the room and a searing white light is
emanating from it. In the centre of the sphere is a cross as
high as the sphere itself. I think this will remain to ensure that
the room is not infested again by dark forces.

The room will feel different now. The ego I sensed when I
entered the room left a very strong imprint here. He used
dark forces and left the stain of his personality here. That
part of him was being sustained by the energy of people who
came into the room. The bad influence lasted for centuries; it
was a debilitating feeling that sapped the energies of anyone
associated with the house. Now you can be assured that it has
gone.

Eddie asked Lady March, who confessed that the atmosphere in
the room had been so bad that she never went in, to imagine the
sphere every time she came into the Long Hall. 'If you reinforce the
symbol of the ball of light you will continue to cleanse the room and
ensure that the evil forces will never return,' he said.

The Long Hall had taken its toll on Eddie. As Lady March
bounded ahead with a list of other places she wanted us to see,
Eddie asked if we could stop for coffee. Lady March frowned and
glanced at her watch; it was 11 a.m. and elevenses were, apparently, just in order. Back in the library a large pot of freshly brewed
coffee arrived, with, to Eddie's relief, a plate of Marks and Spencer
luxury chocolate biscuits. Eddie munched his way through them as
he told Lord March about the morning's events.

Thus refreshed, we set off on a tour of the house, including the
Marches' private apartments. We visited the Queens' double
bedroom, the beautiful yellow Tapestry Drawing Room, Lady
March's office, the nursery, the dining room and the sumptuous
ballroom, which Lord March was restoring as the picture gallery.
Eddie stopped us in the room which Lord and Lady March were
planning to use as a bedroom and said:

I feel a strong feminine influence here. I'm picking up the
psychic imprint of a woman who used this room and is now
showing great interest in what is happening here. She says:
'This room brings back old memories to me – old mistakes,

55

old loves, but good things as well.'

She is someone who loved life, enjoyed meeting lots of people and formed bonds with people very easily. She was warm, but could be critical; she liked everything to be correct. She heartily approves of your efforts to put things right, Lady March. She says: 'You're doing a lot of things which I would like to have done, but couldn't, for reasons that you understand.

'You are a good balance for Charles; don't let him work too hard,' she laughs. 'He needs a tight rein sometimes, otherwise he goes galloping away. He's not been happy of late, but things will improve now the house has been cleansed. He's got to come to terms with his own sensitivities; they're very real and he must not push them away. I think he will do this, but that doesn't mean he needs to force the pace; they will develop into useful accessories for his life in the course of time. He is not to be afraid, he is well protected. My love to you both. That love is always with you. Thank you.'

I think this is Lord March's grandmother. She brings a very motherly feeling with her. A very strong personality. She is watching over the house but she is not trapped here. I think she is a revenant.

Lady March confirmed that her husband's grandmother, to whom he had been very close, had died in 1991. She said: 'Charles was very fond of his grandmother and used to love coming to Good-wood as a child because she was always such fun.'

On our way down the grand staircase to the dining room for lunch, Lady March again showed us the painting of the third Duke which had caused previous psychics considerable consternation. A greying, steely-eyed man dressed in military uniform stared at us coldly from the canvas. Lady March wondered if this had caused the bad feeling in the house. Eddie said:

This was a man who would brook no opposition; I see him thumping the table. The picture is imbued with a lot of his characteristics; whoever painted it did a very good job – he's really captured the spirit of the man. I don't think he's a very well-developed soul and he hasn't gone very far, although he isn't earthbound. It would be best to put this picture well out of the way – he's not a very pleasant character. He did a lot for the house, but he did it at great cost to himself and those around him. If people didn't do as he wanted he would simply get rid of them.

Lord March was waiting for us in the dining room where another superb meal awaited us. Lady March asked Eddie polite questions about his work. Unfortunately, the answers took rather longer than she expected; but she was a perceptive woman and realized that she could not come between a ghosthunter and lunch.

As we prepared to leave Lady March remembered one more place that she felt we had to visit. Underneath Goodwood is a maze of corridors linking storage cellars for the house. The previous week, said Lady March, she had wandered down into the cellar to fetch some extra china and on her way back she had felt someone or something leap up at her at she walked by.

'It was as if something was trying to claw at my back. I had to stop and tell it to get off me and leave me alone. "No, no, no you don't," I shouted and quickly left. I've been rather afraid of going down there ever since,' she said.

She led us down into the cellar and showed us the stretch of corridor where it had happened. As I approached the spot I felt an icy chill whip round my ankles, as if I were walking over an ice floe. When we stopped I felt the cold rise through the soles of my shoes and spread up my legs towards the knees. Eddie had closed his eyes. 'Yes,' he said, 'something has to be done here. But first we must pray.'

There's something very ancient here – it may be Celtic. I think it has something to do with a burial ground. I have a strong sense that something was disturbed here when the foundations of the house were built. Whoever it was that was affected resented the building and is still very disturbed by it. It's primitive; I'm not even sure that it's human. It goes back

57

several thousand years. The person needs to be released; they stayed near their dead body after death and have been unable to move very far away from it. I think the person is upset by the manner of the burial.

The person is pagan, perhaps even prehistoric. Now I'm getting the impression of singing; it's a rejoicing for the release of this soul who suffered. I think this person was ritually sacrificed and died with the belief that he had to remain with the body. I think it's a man, though I'm not absolutely sure. I think he was heavily drugged in order to desensitize him before being sacrificed at a temple nearby. There are a lot of souls who are anxious for his release. We must say a prayer for his release. Now it is done; he is being carried away by some other souls in a state of sleep. My work is done.

Lady March, Eddie and I returned to the library. The housekeeper brought tea on a large silver tray, returning a few minutes later with a plate of the same excellent biscuits we had enjoyed that morning. Everyone, it seemed, was happy – Lord and Lady March because, they claimed, they had already noticed a distinct lightening in the atmosphere of the house, and Eddie because tea was on its way.

Before we left Lady March said she wanted to tell us about a dream she had had before our visit. 'I saw my grandmother [Nancy Astor], who stood behind me and put her hand over my face; she then pulled my face towards the back of my head – but it was her face superimposed on mine. My grandmother had a very powerful personality and I have been told that we share many of the same characteristics – the better ones, I hope. I wonder if she was in some way drawing herself out of me.'

Eddie had no answer to this, nor did I. It was very strange, we all agreed, but most probably a good thing. Lord March pressed several tickets to the Festival of Speed and a guide to Goodwood into our hands as we said our farewells. As Eddie swung out of the car park and into the drive, I looked back at the imposing façade of the house. Externally, it had not changed in three centuries, but inside was a couple determined to make their

58

mark on the house and estate. A split second later I realized the significance of Lady March's dream: her grandmother had graphically demonstrated that Lady March must shed the old face of the aristocracy and reveal a new, modern approach. The Marches had a responsibility to take the house, and what it stood for – duty, humility and vision – into the next century. It was crucial that, for once, the lady of the house should take charge.

Chapter 3

Guests at Number 10

How much I wish that the public could see beyond that famous front door . . . How much I wish, too, that they could share with me the feeling of Britain's historic greatness which pervades every nook and cranny of this complicated and meandering old building.

Rt Hon. Margaret Thatcher, MP, July 1985

Number 10 Downing Street has been the official residence of Britain's prime ministers for more than 250 years. Behind its famous black door, in the rooms leading off its maze of corridors and staircases, the nation's leaders have debated and schemed, through peace and war, and have entertained the world's most influential heads of state in its magnificent reception rooms.

Sir Robert Walpole, Britain's first prime minister, moved into the house in 1735 at the invitation of King George II. The house was originally intended as a personal gift from the King to his first minister, but Sir Robert would only accept it as the official residence of the First Lord of the Treasury.

Downing Street takes its name from Sir George Downing, one of King Charles II's chief ministers, who built a street of houses on the site. Today, only three of these original buildings remain. The development was a seventeenth-century example of what would nowadays be called 'jerry-building': the houses were poorly constructed, using inadequate materials. The fact that the development stood on Thorney Island, a piece of marshy ground between two branches of the River Tyburn, meant there was a substantial risk of subsidence. Over the next 300 years Number 10 needed constant repairs and rebuilding. The front of the house is part of Downing's original building work, but behind the façade is a long history of repairs and extensions.

Before Walpole took up residence in 1735, Number 10 had been enlarged by linking the building facing on to Downing Street with a much larger house in the garden at the rear, and the interior had been almost entirely reconstructed, possibly under the direction of William Kent, who became Deputy Surveyor of Works in 1735. The house which Walpole left in 1742 has remained essentially unchanged apart from a few additions, such as a State Dining Room and Breakfast Room in 1825, and restorations in 1963, which included the conversion of the basement into offices for secretarial staff.

The most famous room at Number 10 is the Cabinet Room on the ground floor, looking out over Horse Guards Parade and St James's Park. It has eighteenth-century wall panelling and Corinthian columns, with a communicating door to the private secretaries' offices. One of the basement rooms under the Cabinet Room, which overlooks the garden of Number 10, was used by Sir Winston Churchill as a dining room during the Second World War, and a plaque on the wall records that King George VI was often entertained there during the war years.

The private living quarters for the prime minister, his family and staff are situated at the rear of the house, on the floor above the state rooms.

Throughout the spring and early summer of 1994, I had tried to arrange a visit to Downing Street. I had read an account of a ghost in Regency-style clothes who had been sighted on several occasions at Number 10. He gave the appearance, it said, of a man of authority, perhaps even a prime minister. The ghost was benevolent and had showed itself only during national crises. The last recorded sighting was in 1960, when workmen who were carrying out renovations saw a figure in old-fashioned clothes drifting across the garden.

Despite numerous letters to the Prime Minister and calls to his private secretary, I received no reply. I had given up when I received an invitation to a private party at Number 10 on 16 June from a friend who was marking her departure from the press office there. Eddie had not been invited to the party, so I had no choice but to become a lone psychic detective.

As you walk past the policemen through the heavy iron gates that now guard the entrance to Downing Street, the short walk to Numbers 10 and 11 is redolent of the triumphs and disasters of thousands of political careers. The street itself is narrow, unprepossessing and devoid of trees; the only suggestion that this is 1994 and not 1894 are the gates and tank-trap defences to deter suicide bombers. A single policeman guards the famous heavy black door marked simply '10' and framed in an elaborate arch of wrought iron below a glass lamp.

The door opens on to a different world. The entrance hall, decorated in red brocade and deep pile carpet, is a hive of purposeful activity. Office staff with top-security clearance carry important papers. Senior civil servants look grave. Politicians are concerned but confident. Policemen busy themselves at the door, being friendly, while other police stay out of sight, monitoring closed-circuit screens which show pictures from the street outside. A narrow hallway in rich old gold, framed with huge antique mirrors which seem to double its size, leads to the foot of the main staircase, in front of the door to the Cabinet Room. As I climbed the stairs, I looked at the portraits and photographs on the wall; every prime minister in British history was there, gazing down at me, starting with Sir Robert Walpole and ending with John Major.

The reception was held in the Pillared Drawing Room, the biggest and most formal of the entertaining rooms at Number 10. With its polished wooden floor, gold silk wall covering and rich Persian carpet, a copy of a tenth-century original in the Victoria and Albert Museum, the room exuded unexpected warmth and intimacy. A glittering crystal chandelier hung in the middle of the high ceiling, and above the marble fireplace was a portrait of

William Pitt the Younger by George Romney, flanked by portraits of Master Newman and Master Coates. Against the far wall was a side table bearing a display of silver trophies.

The guests that day were drawn principally from the media and the Foreign Office. My host said that she was not convinced about the Downing Street ghost or ghosts, but one of her colleagues said that he had heard about a 'presence'. After much cajoling and mutterings about security risks, I persuaded him to take me to a security officer who apparently knew the full story. I had always thought that a building which had been the scene for some of the most remarkable events in modern history – and which had been the home of such extraordinary men and women – would have a psychic dimension. That day I was fortunate that the security guard, who asked not to be named, confirmed my suspicions.

He told me about three ghosts that had appeared over the last thirty years. The first was the Regency figure I had read about who had appeared in the gardens. The last sighting of this person was a few years ago, he said, when a policeman had been checking the garden for intruders one night. He had felt something rush past him and although he had not seen the figure very clearly, he sensed that it had been a ghost and was too terrified to go into the garden again. Next, he told me about a fair-haired woman who had been seen by a security officer in the security section's kitchen and mess room underneath the main entrance hall. The guard had walked upstairs and asked his colleague whether the woman had a right to be there; when they returned five minutes later she had disappeared.

However, it was the security guard's third story that intrigued me most. Late one evening in April 1994 a policeman had seen a man in a dark frock coat stride through the main hall and disappear just as he was about to stop him. A similar figure had been seen climbing the stairs outside the administrative offices by several members of staff who worked in these offices off the main hall.

The security guard told me staff at Number 10 thought that the figure on the stairs might have been the ghost of a former prime minister. Then he added: 'I don't know whether this counts but I have noticed some terrible cold spots in the Pillared Drawing Room and the White Drawing Room. I always feel a chill when I walk into these rooms.'

The White Drawing Room, originally Lady Walpole's boudoir, was out of bounds during my few hours in Number 10, but I decided to test out the security guard's theory in the Pillared Drawing Room. He was right: in one spot I could feel my feet growing cold and a chill spreading up my legs as far as my knees. When I moved aside, the chill subsided. There was no rational explanation; it was a sultry summer evening and my fellow guests were feeling the heat. I wished that Eddie was with me; but then I had a brainwave.

Eddie has often used photographs or plans of houses to locate trapped spirits. The best example of his ability to work long-distance is the case of a Sicilian doctor, who sent Eddie photographs of her house which she believed was haunted. Although he had never visited Sicily or met her, Eddie had managed to locate and free two trapped spirits in the house who were later identified from local newspapers. (The full story is given in Chapter 9.) If Eddie had contacted those spirits, there was no reason why he should not link up with Downing Street's ghost without actually entering the house.

When I returned home that evening I drew a rough plan of 10 Downing Street – the hall, staircase, offices, basement, state rooms and grounds – indicating where there had been an incident without going into detail about what had happened. The next day I faxed the plan to Eddie and sent him a book, *No. 10 Downing Street: The Story of a House* by Christopher Jones, for him to study.

A week or so later I called Eddie to see if he had picked anything up from either the plan or the photographs in the book. But he had not sensed anything, he said. I persisted over the next few weeks, but still he received no impressions. I decided there was probably nothing there at all. But I was wrong. On 23 August Eddie called me to say that a spirit voice had told him to read as much as he could about George Downing, as this would enable Eddie to help him. 'I had been reading the Downing Street book for about ten minutes this morning,' he said, 'when I felt a very strong presence. I closed my eyes and I saw a picture of Downing Street as it must have looked in Downing's time – very run-down and dirty. Then Downing spoke to me.'

'I keep trying to prop up parts of these buildings, but they keep on falling down. I would be grateful for some help – I do not understand why I have to do this all on my own. It was not like this before; it is so dilapidated. It is all I can manage to do to stop the whole lot falling down. I have invested my fortunes in these houses and I cannot afford to see them collapse; I am not able to find any builders, or anyone else. Would you not think that someone would be glad to rent one of these houses? They could be made habitable, but I cannot do it on my own.

'I just cannot understand what is happening. The place is so deserted. I know I have my faults, but surely I do not deserve this. The loneliness is hard to bear. What has happened to London? If I walk outside this group of houses there is nothing else – it is all barren. Even the Thames has dried up. Could this be the end of the world? Am I to face judgement on my own? I feel at times that I am losing my mind, though if I did, it would likely not be worse than this.'

I can see him covered in dust and dirt from the buildings and his clothes are in tatters. He says:

'You gaze upon me in my wretched state, but it was not always like this with me. I have looked for a change of clothing, but everything has gone. I do not understand. Oh God, help me.' He looks a sorry sight, but now I can see that the dull sky behind him is starting to grow light. It faintly illuminates a path which leads away from the area; he is beginning to understand what he has to do.

'Would you advise that I take that path?' he asks. 'Where does it lead, I wonder?'

He wanders off now, looking a very sad and bedraggled figure; it's going to be a very long road for him, I fear, but if he responds to the promptings of his heart and conscience, it will gradually improve.

In spite of giving his name to one of Britain's most prestigious addresses, George Downing was one of seventeenth-century England's most infamous figures. The poet Andrew Marvell called him 'Judas' and Samuel Pepys described him as a 'perfidious rogue'

65

for his shameless career as Oliver Cromwell's spymaster and Charles II's fawning chief minister. He was born around 1624 in either London or Dublin – his birthplace is uncertain – the son of Emanuel Downing and Lucy Winthrop, the sister of John Winthrop, the first Governor of Massachusetts. Both his father and his uncle were Puritan barristers. When Winthrop could no longer tolerate England, he set sail in 1630 for the New World, exactly ten years after the *Mayflower*.

Downing's father was keen to join Winthrop, but his wife refused to leave England. She was eventually persuaded to emigrate in 1638 when her brother extolled the virtues of the schools in New England, particularly the new university that John Harvard had plans to establish. In 1640, at the age of sixteen, George Downing became the second graduate of the new Harvard University, having studied divinity. After a series of posts as a chaplain, Downing returned to England in 1646 to seek his fortune. He became an itinerant preacher, but the Civil War was raging and he decided to join the Parliamentary forces. By the end of the war, he had been appointed Scoutmaster General of Scotland – Oliver Cromwell's master spy.

In 1654 Downing married Lady Frances Howard, a descendant of the fourth Duke of Norfolk. Her brother, Viscount Morpeth, was the first of three peers created by Cromwell after the war. By now extremely well connected and wealthy, Downing became a Member of Parliament and then a diplomat in Paris – where he was sent as a reward after arguing that Cromwell should accept the title of King – and the Hague.

Downing's real role was in fact to spy on the Royalists, especially Charles, later King Charles II, his family and followers. Charles's sister Mary had married William, Prince of Orange, and brother and sister often met in the Hague to plan his restoration to the monarchy. Downing blackmailed his brother-in-law Thomas Howard, a member of Charles's inner circle, to give him intelligence and used his position to extort money from Dutch merchants sailing to England. He soon amassed a huge fortune.

Cromwell died in 1658 and Downing, realizing that Charles was likely to be restored to the throne, performed a swift, self-serving volte-face. He offered his services to Charles as an agent who could feed him intelligence on what was happening in Cromwellian England. Downing's policy was shrewd; as well as saving his fortune and his head, it eventually earned him a knighthood when Charles was restored to the throne.

One of Downing's most shameful acts in Charles's service was to trap those responsible for trying Charles I and condemning him to death in 1649, including Colonel John Okey, who had helped Downing when he had returned to England from America. Downing returned from the Hague in 1665 and resumed his political career. In 1667 he was made Secretary to the Treasury. In 1671 Charles II decided to send Downing back to Holland; but the Dutch loathed him and he was forced to return to England. The King imprisoned him in the Tower for two months for this act of cowardice.

Downing then settled down to a quiet life on the proceeds of his shameful career of extortion and duplicity. He managed to persuade Charles to relax his building laws around Whitehall and in 1683 began work on the houses in Downing Street. Downing did not live to see them finished; he died in 1684, leaving Downing Street to the youngest of his three sons.

★

Less than a week after his message from Downing, Eddie made three further contacts at Number 10: the psychic imprint of a nineteenth-century statesman; the ghost of a Regency man who had been murdered after a gambling argument; and a kitchen maid who returned as a revenant. Eddie told me that he had been studying the plan of the house I had sent him and had tried mentally to walk through all the rooms that I had marked. For some reason, he said, he had found the tuning-in process much more difficult than usual. Then a spirit voice had said:

'Hold your horses. Do you want a conducted tour, my friend? Now don't forget, it takes two to see a ghost.' I followed his suggestion and mentally entered the front door and moved into the hall. I asked myself who the man was that had appeared there. My guiding friend said: 'He is not here for us, let us pass by and go up the stairs [by the offices].'

Then I made contact. It was the psychic imprint of a man who had used this staircase in the past. He belonged to the very early nineteenth century, around the time of the Napoleonic wars. I think he was connected with the navy, a minister perhaps. He had been greatly troubled as he walked up the stairs – his grave thoughts were clearly imprinted there.

He said: 'Nelson, will he be able to find the French fleet, and if he does, will he be able to defeat them? If he doesn't, and he loses the sea battle, what then? He and the country need much good fortune – it is some comfort that he is the best man for the task.'

He is wearing buckled shoes, white breeches, a colourful coat split into tails at the back and a long, embroidered waistcoat. I think he is the man that has been seen in the entrance hall.

I let go of this man and moved on to the Pillared Room, where the security guards had sensed cold spots. I got the feeling that these areas were associated in some way with the man who was said to be wandering around the gardens of the house. I soon made contact with a trapped soul; in life he had had serious financial problems – he was heavily in debt through gambling losses. He was very concerned about the future of his wife and daughters and, knowing his weakness for gambling, he had heavily insured his life while he had some money; he had hoped to make sure that there was something to pass on after his death. But the policy excluded suicide or death in a duel.

He had thought about hiring a villain to shoot him, making it appear like a murder, but he was afraid that the truth might just come out. In the end, he decided on a clever plan. He deliberately provoked a quarrel with some ruffians in a nearby inn which had a bad reputation. He stayed late and drank a lot, knowing the men would be waiting for him when he went out. They were, and they bludgeoned him to death. Then they robbed his body and heaved it over the wall into the garden.

I can see his spirit still pacing the garden, tormented by the memories of his desperate gambling debts. He goes over it all constantly, asking aloud for God's forgiveness. But the light is at hand and shines down on him, giving him a feeling of joy and hope. The light disappears and he wonders what has happened. Then an old friend approaches him and says:

'You have a journey to make; if you can bear my company I would be glad to accompany you – I know the way and can help you. First, we must pass through this gate; it is called the "Gate of Good Hope". Are you ready?'

The other man nods his assent, weeping now with joy and relief, and they begin their journey.

Eddie was then drawn to the area beneath the entrance hall used by the security guards as a mess. As he studied the plan, Eddie had the impression of a revenant. The communication was not clear, but he felt that it was a woman who had spent a lot of time in the room. She told him that it had once been the kitchen of Number 10 and that she had worked there during the war. She had been killed in her home by an enemy bomb. She said:

'I would have been better off if I had been in the shelter here, but I couldn't leave my old mum, could I? She was all of ninety years. I used to like coming here, bringing the food to the kitchen. Sometimes I sat and chatted, but not for long else the cook would send someone after me. I come back now and again to wake up old memories – it's better when there's someone sensitive about. I can get a better idea then about what things are like now. I know I shouldn't hold on to these memories, but they were exciting times for someone like me. Ta-ta for now, it's been nice talking to you.'

Although it is unlikely that we will ever identify the Regency man and the woman in the kitchen, my research suggests that the eighteenth-century statesman was William Pitt the Younger, son of the Earl of Chatham. He had become an MP in 1781 and Britain's youngest prime minister in 1783; gaining a substantial majority at the following year's election, he held office until 1801, when he resigned because of George III's unwillingness to grant Catholic Emancipation. In his second period of office, from 1804 to 1806, Pitt negotiated an alliance with Russia and Austria that made possible the War of the Third Coalition against Napoleon. He died on 23 January 1806, his enlightened liberalism, in the slavery and criminal justice debates, sadly overshadowed by his repressive measures designed to prevent revolution in Britain.

★

Eddie had been concentrating on Downing Street since eleven o'clock that morning. Now it was 12.30 and he was late for lunch. His friend Sheila Green had been waiting in the cafe by Lincoln Cathedral for ten minutes when Eddie arrived. 'I'll explain later,' he said as they ordered their food. Sheila had been going to Eddie's development group for years and was a clairvoyant and healer.

'The reason I was late,' said Eddie, 'was that I'd been reading a book on Downing Street when . . .'

Sheila interrupted him: 'Do you sense someone here with us at the moment?' she asked.

Eddie closed his eyes. It was a man.

He says: 'Don't be worried or anxious. I had a few of your gifts and used them discreetly to help me and the country during those fateful years. I was extremely fortunate to have played the part I did. During that time I often felt the spirit of the nation supporting me – almost pouring through my veins. I knew about the afterlife before I died and have since found that it is how I imagined, but also much more than I could ever have imagined. I like to think that I played my part in preserving the foundation of the country for what will be a burgeoning of its spiritual life.

Eddie was taken aback. He knew instinctively that the message was from Sir Winston Churchill, the Conservative prime minister who had guided Britain to victory against Hitler. Yet the nation rejected him at the 1945 general election. He became leader of the opposition and was prime minister again from 1951 to 1955. He

died in 1965. The contact with Churchill was, said Eddie, so strong
that his identity was undeniable. 'Of all the people I have encountered,' said Eddie later, 'Churchill was the one who gave out the
most warmth and human kindness.'

Staff at Downing Street still sense the presence of Churchill in
the house, even fifty years after the end of the war. It is his portrait
on the staircase, they say, that immediately catches the eye, and
every prime minister is aware that he or she is sitting in Churchill's
own seat during meetings in the Cabinet Room. Outside the
Cabinet Room, a portrait of the great man gazes down over the
country's most senior politicians as they gather for their regular
meetings.

Churchill did not in fact spend much time at Number 10 after the
German campaign of bombing London began in 1940. The old
house was in no condition to protect the prime minister and his
staff, who moved to secure accommodation in nearby Storey's
Gate. However, Churchill had the ground-floor Garden Room
strengthened with massive beams and the windows were covered
with heavy steel shutters. It was here that Churchill liked to
entertain his guests: war workers, mayors, council officials and
even King George VI.

Number 10 was extensively bombed during the war, although
pictures of the damage were never released as they might have been
used by the Germans as propaganda. In his personal account of the
Second World War, Churchill writes how during one bombing raid
he had had a strange premonition that his staff were in danger.
Perhaps this is what he was referring to when he told Eddie that he
'had a little of your gifts'.

> Suddenly, I had a providential impulse. The kitchen of
> Number 10 Downing Street is lofty and spacious, and looks
> out through a large plate-glass window about twenty-five feet
> high. The butler and parlourmaid continued to serve the
> dinner with complete detachment, but I became acutely
> aware of this big window, behind which Mrs Landemare, the
> cook, and the kitchen maid, never turning a hair, were at
> work. I got up abruptly, went into the kitchen, told the
> butler to put the dinner on the hot plate in the dining room

and ordered the cook and the other servants into the shelter.
I had been seated again at table only about three minutes
when a really loud crash, close at hand, and a violent shock
showed that the house had been struck.

We went into the kitchen . . . The devastation was
complete . . . the blast had smitten the large, tidy kitchen,
with its bright saucepans and crockery, into a heap of
black dust and rubble. The big plate-glass window had
been hurled into fragments and splinters across the room,
and would of course have cut its occupants, if there had
been any, to pieces. But my fortunate inspiration, which I
might easily have neglected, had come in the nick of time.

Chapter 4

A Private Affair

London clubs were, and are, an epitome of the high
civilisation which produced them; a civilisation which,
within living memory, appeared as solid as their mahogany
tables, as comfortable as their leather armchairs, as brilliant
as their crystal chandeliers; a civilisation now under siege
and in decline.

Anthony Lejeune and Malcolm Lewis, *The Gentlemen's Clubs
of London*

Private clubs are a quintessentially English institution. Other
countries have tried to copy them – the Jockey Club in Paris, the
Caccia Club in Rome, Brook Club in New York – but without
success. English clubs are a closed world of eccentric characters,
bound by petty rules; the membership lists and records of any
London club would provide a fascinating history of the English
upper classes over the past 250 years.

All these clubs have one thing in common: to provide like-
minded people – usually men – with a meeting place. The adage
'you can judge a man by his friends' could be equally well applied to
his clubs. London has more clubs than any other city in the world.
One of the first recorded English 'clubbes' met at the Mermaid
tavern at Blackfriars, where its members, who included Shakespeare, Sir Walter Raleigh, Beaumont and Donne, would gather to

discuss poetry. Another club, founded by Ben Jonson, met at the Devil Tavern near Temple. The next generation of clubs, formed in the late seventeenth and early eighteenth centuries, were more political and membership was usually a matter of hereditary privilege or connections. By the mid-nineteenth century a new crop of clubs had sprung up in London to meet the demands of the rising middle classes. Today most clubs continue to have a common denominator.

All of London's clubs – the Berkeley, the Reform Club, Pratt's, The Travellers, Boodles, the Turf Club, the Devonshire, to name but a few – can boast members who have shaped the country in crucial ways. Phileas Fogg, Jules Verne's fictional nineteenth-century explorer, for example, began his epic journey around the world on the steps of the Reform Club. Political rivals William Gladstone, the classicist, high churchman and great Liberal who dominated British politics for many years, and Benjamin Disraeli, the flamboyant Conservative politician and author and prime minister from 1874 until 1880, used to meet regularly at the Carlton Club after their spectacular jousts in the Commons.

Arguably London's most prestigious club, the Athenaeum's reputation for gravitas and respectability is built on the intellectual and establishment figures it traditionally draws – ambassadors, judges, bishops and cabinet ministers. White's has a similar membership, although it also attracts figures from less public walks of life, notably from Britain's intelligence services. At the more Bohemian end of the social spectrum comes the Garrick in Covent Garden, founded in 1831 by the dilettante writer and art collector Francis Mills, with the Duke of Sussex as patron. Their idea was to establish a society in which 'actors and men of distinction and education and refinement might meet on equal terms'. Its most notable members were Thackeray and Dickens, who once had a famous argument over the treatment of a young journalist: he had broken the gentleman's code of conduct by reporting something he had overheard at the club and Thackeray had wanted him disbarred. Today the Garrick still attracts actors, lawyers and journalists. The Carlton Club and Brooks's, both in St James's Street, are probably the most politically oriented clubs today. The Carlton, formed in 1832, was a rallying point for opponents of the Reform

Bill and still has strong Tory connections; neighbouring Brooks's was also political, but Liberal.

The Naval and Military Club at 94 Piccadilly – better known as the In and Out Club, after the two pillars marked 'In' and 'Out' at the entrance to the club – is the newest of London's general service clubs. Formed in 1862, it had two homes, in Clifford Street and Hanover Square, before moving to Cambridge House in Piccadilly in 1864. Once called Egremont House, this building had belonged to the Duke of Cambridge and then Lord Palmerston, the buccaneering Whig foreign secretary and prime minister of the nineteenth century, whose former bedroom is now the club reading room.

As well as absorbing property in neighbouring Half Moon Street, the club has amalgamated with several small clubs over the last hundred years, including the Portland, founded in 1816 and the most famous bridge club in the world; the Royal College of Nursing; the Junior Army and Navy; the Albemarle; the Royal Thames Yacht Club; the Cowdray; the Canning Club; the Goat Club; and, in 1976, the Senior. Unlike many other London clubs which have a strict men-only rule, the In and Out has extended its membership to women, making it one of the few genuinely integrated clubs in the capital. Officers of the women's services have long been eligible to join, as have wives, daughters and granddaughters of members. This family principle has meant that its military origins are now rather clouded. By 1994 the club had over 4,000 members and nearly 100 staff; it has forty-six bedrooms and nine function rooms and covers an acre of priceless London land.

On 10 March 1994 a small article in the diary pages of the *Daily Telegraph* caught my eye. Under the headline 'But have you paid your subs, Major?', it reported the appearance of a new ghost at the In and Out Club. 'To the names of Lady Hamilton and Lady Caroline Lamb can be added that of Major W. H. Braddell,' it said. Braddell, a Royal Northumberland Fusilier who had been killed during a bombing raid on London in 1940, had been spotted in the early hours of the morning by the night porter, Trevor Newton, who was making his rounds. Mr Newton had been trying to find out why the security lights outside the building had suddenly gone on at 3 a.m. when he had glimpsed a tall, trench-coated figure with flowing silver hair in the Egremont Room. The figure vanished through the wall and the lights went out.

I was intrigued. If I could arrange a visit to the club, perhaps Eddie could confirm the presence of Major Braddell and even some of the other ghosts that had been sighted. Eddie agreed to a visit, on the understanding that he was told nothing about the haunting. Captain John Cuninghame, a retired army officer who knew the club secretary, Commander Anthony Holt, arranged an appointment for us. He advised us to tread carefully at the club, as the press had seized on the story and were ringing constantly for more information. Our appointment was fixed for 3 p.m. on 26 April 1994.

Captain Cuninghame decided to accompany us. A small man in his early seventies, with reddish hair and determined eyes, he had retired to the West Country after a long career in the Grenadier Guards. He had got to know Eddie through hauntings in the west and had become totally absorbed by the psychic world. However, Captain Cuninghame's passion for the paranormal seemed distinctly odd in a character who could otherwise have stepped out of a P.G. Wodehouse novel. At times he talked like the impressionable acolyte of a New Age guru, which sounded strange since he had a clipped military accent. His most recent passion was for ghost-hunting and he seemed determined to carve out a niche for himself. He certainly had enthusiasm. He followed Eddie around, terrier-like, hanging on to every word and voicing endless explanations and interpretations into his hand-held tape recorder. Captain Cuninghame was out to learn as much as he could.

As we walked up the drive to the imposing eighteenth-century house I noticed the pillars marked 'In' and 'Out' and pointed them out to John and Eddie. Neither seemed to notice what I was saying. We had just walked through Hyde Park from Notting Hill Gate, where we had enjoyed an excellent lunch at a small Italian restaurant. It was unusually hot for a spring day and both had eaten heartily, but perhaps unwisely, of bread, pasta and crème brûlée. Now both seemed sleepy.

In the oak-panelled reception area the Captain gave our names and asked for the club secretary. We were ushered into a comfortable sitting room overlooking Green Park, furnished with two chesterfields, an expensive Oriental carpet and several battered old armchairs. The sun was blazing outside, but a log fire crackled in the grate as I sank down into an exquisite leather armchair. I glanced at Eddie, who was staring absent-mindedly into space as usual; John, meanwhile, seemed hard-pressed to contain his anticipation of the ghost-hunting ahead.

I turned my attention to the comings and goings of the club – people departing after a late lunch, arriving for an early tea – and saw that there was a good mix of people, young and old, men and women, formally dressed and casual. I was glad that there were some women about – the thought of wandering around a crusty old gentlemen's club with Eddie and Captain Cuninghame was not appealing.

After five minutes or so the deputy secretary of the club, Lieutenant John Stevens, a retired naval officer, strode into the room to greet us. He was about sixty years old, but was tall, muscular, steely-haired, and had piercing blue eyes. He was elegantly turned out in a well-cut suit, snappy tie and tasteful shoes, but he did not seem to impress Captain Cuninghame, who was visibly irritated that we had been left in the hands of a mere deputy secretary. However, he cheered up when Lieutenant Stevens offered him the best seat in his office behind the courtyard as he began to tell us about the latest haunting at the club.

'The porter was doing his rounds as usual when, just after 3 a.m., he noticed a light shining into the Egremont Room. When he looked into a room, he saw a figure in a trench coat and . . .'

I stopped him in mid-sentence; Eddie must not know anything about the haunting or any history about the club, otherwise we would not know if Eddie's communications were wholly instinctive and original. The Lieutenant looked deflated at not being able to tell us the whole dramatic story, but brightened when I said we would be delighted to hear his speech later. With a spring in his step, he led us from his office up the deep-pile red carpet of the impressive central staircase to the first floor. We turned into the Cambridge Room and walked into the adjoining Egremont. Both rooms have floor-length windows overlooking Green Park and are used as private dining rooms. The Egremont Room, decorated in rich shades of crimson and terracotta, was dominated by a huge, polished dining table that could seat fifty. As I sat down the Lieutenant explained to me that this was the room where Major Braddell had appeared to the night porter.

Eddie began to pace around the room, with Captain Cuninghame and his tape-recorder following closely behind. Eddie stopped by the window. 'There's definitely somebody here,' he said. 'I'm not sure who it is yet.' He walked to the far end of the room and then back to me. The Captain was fumbling with his tape-recorder and then bashed it on the wall – it was not working. He looked across the table at me, his face a picture of frustration. But it was too late; Eddie had already started speaking.

> This is an old person. He had a tendency to pant when he walked; I think he was short of breath. It's a man who worked here as a servant. I think he went on working here right to the end of his life, or very close to it. He was very reluctant to leave the club on his passing. I think he may have been a footman. I'll try to see what happened to him. I caught a glimpse of a man in a black tail coat. I think he lived in the second half of the last century. I see mutton-chop whiskers.
>
> The overwhelming feeling he gives me is great fatigue; he grew very old here and I think he had to leave because he couldn't get around in the end. He did not live long after his retirement. When he died, all he had in mind was to return here – it was his security and the only home he'd known for many years. There was a lot of affection at the club for him. His breathing became very difficult towards the end of his life; I think he caught a cold and it turned to bronchitis – he was worn out.
>
> He says: 'I wasn't sorry to go.' He's still experiencing some of the heaviness of his earthly life. I think if we can get him to shed that he will immediately feel a lot better. Then we can release him properly.
>
> There is a growing sense of joy. He's shedding memories of his death and the latter part of his life. He gives me the impression that he came originally from a farming background; he's wearing casual country clothes, a shirt

with sleeves rolled up, coarse, tweedy trousers and boots.
He's standing much more upright now that the weight has
been lifted from his shoulders. I think we now have to wait
for him to be escorted away.

I don't think he was ever married. A sister is approaching;
I can't see her, but I sense her. She's accompanied by a large
long-haired dog which he was very fond of. The two of them
lead him away. They're taking him away slowly along a path,
but not into the direct light at this stage; I think that will
come later. He looks back at the scene and the memories he
has discarded and turns his head and goes with them, very
joyfully.

As Eddie slowly recovered, I asked the Lieutenant whether any of
this had made sense to him.

'It's highly likely that the club would have had trusty old
servants; before the club took over in 1867 the house was Lord
Palmerston's private residence, and we inherited a lot of his
servants. We have an archive, which I will check – there should be
some note of the servants there,' he said.

'I get the feeling he died around 1880, when he was in his
mid-seventies,' said Eddie. 'He worked on well after his retirement
age and became part of the institution. He had a good life and
enjoyed the comings and goings at the club. I think he looked on
this place as the only home he ever had. Most people make the
transition to the next world very easily, but if a person has a strong
affection for a place – as this man evidently did – that would be the
dominant feeling when he died. Nostalgia carried him back here.'

Lieutenant Stevens was charming and courteous and was even
managing to ask the odd question to show he was being open-
minded. But I sensed he was rather confused by the whole
procedure and perhaps also a little embarrassed. I could understand this; after all, it is not often that we are asked to suspend our
rational faculties and listen to a ghosthunter.

He led us briskly to the next stop on our tour, the Regimental
Room. This, and the adjoining Octagon Room, had been the scene
of ghostly activity over the last few years. Both were used as
informal reception and conference rooms. 'A couple of years ago, a

member of staff settled down in the Octagon Room to watch a football match on a TV left there from a conference,' he said, as Eddie began to pace the room. 'Five minutes after the man settled down to watch the game, something in the room frightened him so badly that he ran out screaming – and gashed his arm badly on the door.'

Something made me turn towards Eddie. He was behaving very strangely: he was hugging himself and swaying around the room in what looked like a state of ecstasy, a huge grin on his face. This really was a transformation; in fact, I have only ever seen him look like this at one other time – at the Adelphi Theatre in London, when he made contact with Jessie Matthews, another light-hearted spirit, who we will come to in Chapter 11. I moved closer so that I could listen to him.

I feel a lightness and sense of gaiety. I'm a young girl. I sense brightness and excitement. This young woman has a strong sense of humour. I ask her how old she is and she says: 'Don't give away my age!' When I insist, she says: 'Oh come, now, be generous.' I will be generous – she's trying to give the impression that she's in her early twenties, but I suspect she was nearer her thirties! She's so full of *joie de vivre*; I'm sure she was very attractive to men. I can see her now going round the room, giving the occasional twirl. She's wearing a long-sleeved dress, with lots of petticoats and a rather elaborate hairstyle under a little bonnet. I think she loved her social life – the parties and the flirting; she made lots of conquests, but none of them meant very much to her. I don't think she was a bad or calculating person.

I get the feeling that she is not haunting this place. She is a revenant; she comes back here and clings to the memories that she had of this place. I think she may well show herself occasionally to people who are sensitive. She's projecting herself back, reactivating her memory. She says: 'And for why should I not, for they were very happy times and I am loath to let them go.' I think she belongs to the early part of the nineteenth century. She says: 'I haven't learnt much, have I?'

Captain Cuninghame had been whispering to the Lieutenant while

Eddie was talking. I had not managed to catch what he was saying, but he was clearly excited about something. 'What's the matter?' I asked.

'I knew it, I knew it,' he said breathlessly, his eyes darting between Eddie and the Lieutenant.

'Knew what?' I asked, puzzled.

The Captain looked straight past me and in a loud voice barked at Eddie: 'Does the name Byron or Wyndham ring a bell?' Suddenly, it made sense; Eddie had contacted Lady Caroline Lamb, lover of Lord Byron, the nineteenth-century poet and radical hero who died in his thirties, and Lord Palmerston's sister-in-law. Eddie took the question in his stride. He paused for a moment and, with a vaguely petulant shrug, replied:

She says: 'Oh, I knew them all, I knew them all . . .' The Duke of Wellington? 'I was with them all, but they passed me by long ago. 'Tis the memories that I cling to, not the people, for they were not so important to me as my sheer joy in living. I will trouble no-one, but 'tis my fancy that brings me back and if this causes concern, I ask for forgiveness. I have so much happiness in my life now, but I still cannot let go of those wonderful times.'

The Captain – who could not include subtlety among his virtues – was still not satisfied. He wanted more proof. 'Does she react to the name Caro?' he asked, his voice quivering with anticipation, since he knew that Caro was Lady Caroline Lamb's nickname. Eddie snapped back:

She says: 'You know jolly well who I am.' I think she could be skittish and rather haughty at times. 'Think of me in your prayers and help me to lose this anchor, for anchor it is. I know I need to do this to let it go, but the pull is strong and, after all, I am still quite human, you know. Thank you for your patience and your recognition. May God bless you and me also, for I need it.'

★

Anyone who has studied the extraordinary life of Lady Caroline Lamb – born in 1785, died 1828, aged just forty-two – would recognize her from Eddie's communication. She was vivacious, mischievous, irreverent, headstrong, vain, emotional and passionate; a deeply flawed woman, certainly, but one who had an undeniable, and saving, passion for life. She is best remembered today for her outrageous adulterous affair with Lord Byron, which shocked early nineteenth-century London society. But it was her own character that won her the most notoriety – an impulsive, promiscuous and unstable woman, she defied all the rules by which upper-class Englishwomen lived. Caro (as she liked to be called) simply would not behave herself; in fact, she liked nothing better than creating a scandal, whether it was dressing up in boy's clothes in public or baring her breasts at society parties. Many of her contemporaries concluded that she was mad.

She had shocked polite society from the moment that she made her entry as a debutante in 1803 and she soon became notorious as an immoral flirt. In 1805 she married William Lamb, the second son of Lord Melbourne, but it was an unhappy marriage. Lamb devoted himself to politics as a Whig MP – he was prime minister from 1835 until 1841 – while his wife simply became bored. In March 1812 she met Byron at a party and was immediately infatuated by this beautiful and brilliant poet and revolutionary. The affair, however, destroyed Caroline's health and, so many of her contemporaries believed, her sanity too.

'Lady Caroline Lamb would definitely have attended functions here while Lord Palmerston lived at the house,' said Lieutenant Stevens. 'Lady Palmerston was a great party-giver and there was always a very sociable atmosphere in the house. There is a story that Byron and Lady Caroline came here once and he, furious that she had bared her breasts to the guests, dragged her into the library and hit her. She fell and struck her head on the fireplace. Very soon afterwards, Byron left the country.'

The Lieutenant ushered us into the library where the incident was supposed to have taken place. It takes its name – the Octagon

Room – from its shape. A beautiful, oak-panelled room with an ornate raised ceiling decorated with four concentric bands of octagons, it was once the private library and study of Lord Palmerston, the bombastic and crudely patriotic politician who had become a popular hero during his years as a bluff foreign secretary and prime minister.

In December 1839 Palmerston, then fifty-five and renowned for his womanizing, married Lady Cowper, widow of Earl Cowper and sister of William, Caroline Lamb's husband. Lady Palmerston was an asset to her husband as a society hostess; her Saturday evening parties were the toast of London, attracting the most glittering array of guests. After their marriage, the Palmerstons lived in Carlton Gardens in a large house overlooking St James's Park. In 1857 they moved to Cambridge House, now the In and Out Club. Palmerston leased the house, which had been renamed Cambridge House in 1827, from Sir Richard Sutton and used it as a private residence, even after he became prime minister for the second time in 1859.

As soon as Eddie entered the Octagon Room his face became animated and he walked around in a very agitated way. He asked me to accompany him, his hands clasped prayer-like in front of his nose. He paused by the window overlooking the courtyard, where Palmerston once kept his desk. Although Eddie did not know it, Palmerston had done most of his paperwork in the Octagon Room, and had been visited there on several occasions by Queen Victoria; Palmerston had also died in the room, leaving a half-finished letter on his desk. Eddie then began to speak:

There is a strong imprint of a man walking around this room. He wants me to walk with him. An older man, his memories are crowding the room with people, but it's him I must reach. He says: 'I enjoyed the company here.' I think he is a political man – his concerns are matters of state. He has a very powerful personality, but he's rather restless. He's making me feel restless, so I think I'll sit down now and see what I can pick up.

He had considerable power and charisma, aside from any political position he may have held. He could persuade people easily – even overawe them at times. He's confident in his power and capacity, but fair. He's pleased with that comment about him being fair; he prided himself on giving the other man a fair hearing.

I have a feeling I am picking up Lord Palmerston. I sense that he was essentially a good man; he had a very strong ego, but he didn't abuse his power. He carried a lot of political weight and he was highly regarded by . . . the Queen, he tells me. I think he took pride in guiding the young Queen, almost in a fatherly way. He's not earthbound, but he definitely appears here at times. His personality was so strong that he left an imprint here. But he's not like Caroline Lamb who appears because she's casting her memories back to happy times here.

He says: 'A measure of my personality and earth life still rings here and will continue to do so for a long time yet. But I hope it is for the good and will harm no-one.' I'll have to let him go now.

'Right, anyone for tea?' asked Lieutenant Stevens briskly when Eddie had finished speaking. The Lieutenant looked as if he needed something stronger as he strode ahead of us into the sitting room by the courtyard. 'Teacakes or biscuits?' he asked as we sat down in a cosy alcove. 'Biscuits,' replied Eddie and the Captain simultaneously. 'Biscuits it is,' said the Lieutenant, and gave the waitress our order. I could see that Eddie was in need of a cup of tea. Performing so many releases in an afternoon had drained him; normally, he would stop after one release for a break and a cup of tea. Captain Cuninghame, on the other hand, who had somehow managed to keep quiet during the Palmerston communication, was now fizzing with excitement.

'But what about Major Braddell and Lady Hamilton?' he asked. 'Why didn't they appear?' I had been wondering about this myself. Eddie, of course, had not known anything of the club's hauntings, so I asked the Lieutenant if he would tell us about the latest incident, the sighting of the ghost of Major W.H. Braddell, which had provoked our visit. The Lieutenant had been waiting all afternoon for a chance to tell his story and launched into it with relish.

The night porter, Trevor Newton, he said, had noticed that the lights at the front of the building had switched themselves on at three o'clock one March morning. They were timed to go off automatically at midnight; he was puzzled, and went upstairs to investigate. He walked into the Cambridge Room, swiped the switch and as he turned to go, something made him look into the Egremont Room. 'He saw a chap standing by the door wearing a long, dark trench coat. He was six feet tall, slim, slightly stooped with long, silver hair down to his collar,' said the Lieutenant. 'He walked towards the man, asking if he could help him, when the figure moved across the room and disappeared into the wall by the window.'

When the Lieutenant interviewed Newton the following morning, he described the ghost in detail. 'Fortunately, I remembered that one of the stewards had a father, Peter Brabbs, who had worked there in the 1940s,' he said. 'As soon as I mentioned the trench-coat, he said: "Braddell. He never took off that bloody trench-coat – he lived in it." '

During an air-raid on 5 November 1940 the Egremont Room had taken a direct hit, killing two officers, Colonel William Gordon VC and a Major Crozier, who had been dining there with Braddell. Braddell had left the room for five minutes to take a telephone call when the bomb struck; he was killed a week later when a bomb hit his anti-aircraft battalion in Kensington. Perhaps, we speculated that afternoon, he had come back to the club to look for his two friends who were killed that night.

Eddie had not said a word during the Lieutenant's story. He had looked on thoughtfully, systematically munching his way through a plate of biscuits. The Captain, in contrast, had interrupted at every opportunity with anecdotes about the war and his own life in the services. Eddie poured himself another cup of tea and looked around the room. He had obviously forgotten our question, so I prompted him: 'Why didn't Major Braddell appear, Eddie?'

'I'm sure Major Braddell is not haunting the club,' he said. 'I think what the porter saw was a psychic imprint – a re-run of events from the past. The apparition may have been a revenant, but it's unlikely,' he said.

It was a lot to absorb in an afternoon, I thought, as I looked at the contrasting expressions of Lieutenant Stevens, Captain Cuning-hame and Eddie. In between tea and biscuits, the Captain had been asking Eddie complicated questions about ghosts; Eddie had nodded and said very little, evidently exhausted. The Lieutenant, meanwhile, was flushed; he had obviously heard enough for the day. But, polite as ever, he asked if we would like another pot of tea. Eddie and John looked up with interest, but my expression stopped them in their tracks. 'Er, no thanks,' said the Captain. 'We really must be on our way,' echoed Eddie.

What was important, of course, was not the Captain's ambitions to develop a name as a psychic researcher to rival Eddie, but the three spirits we had encountered. We had spoken to the trusty footman, who had spent his whole life in service at the club; the society beauty who, in the early nineteenth century, was castigated for being unstable and promiscuous when today she would be considered merely feisty and independent; and, finally, the elder statesman, who had led his country with such vigour. Three contrasting personalities in life, but in death they had all chosen to return to the In and Out, where they had seen their happiest days.

Chapter 5

The Linton Secret

They went through the air and space without fear
And the shining stars marked their shining deeds

Tribute to squadrons based in the Vale of York,
1939–45

It was nine o'clock on a sharp November morning in 1988 when
Eddie drove through the gates of RAF Linton-on-Ouse in north
Yorkshire. With him was Martin O'Collins, a BBC producer who
was there to film Eddie for a BBC2 documentary. Martin had
arranged the visit and had kept the location secret until that
morning; he had told Eddie nothing about the haunting at the
airfield.

Eddie had spent his early career working on airfields within
the Air Ministry Works Department and Linton-on-Ouse was
one of the few airfields in the north-east that he had not visited.
As they got out of the car, he looked at the windswept runways
and the flight tower and its glass control room and memories of
his youth came flooding back. Walking across the snow-covered
grass towards them were two figures, a man and a woman,
muffled against the biting east wind. Squadron Leader Michael
Brooks, a burly, distinguished man in his late thirties, introduced
himself and his companion, Brenda Jenkinson, an Assistant Air
Traffic Controller. Brenda, a shy woman in her early twenties,

had seen the ghost of a man in the control tower on two separate occasions and wanted to show Eddie where the incidents had occurred. 'Follow us,' said Michael as he led them to the control tower.

Although Eddie had not been aware of it, RAF Linton-on-Ouse had attracted a great deal of publicity the previous summer. As the RAF's main centre for basic flying training, the base received around fifty new recruits each year for instruction on Tucano turbo-prop jets before moving on to advanced training. The base had around 500 personnel, both RAF and civilian. A ghost in the control tower was, of course, not just curious; it was potentially hazardous as it could distract the air traffic controllers.

Local newspapers had seized on the story that a ghost had appeared there. Their reports had soon been picked up by the *Daily Express*, the *Daily Mirror* and the *Sun*. Speculation about the identity of the ghost had reached such a pitch that Michael Brooks, who also acted as the station public relations officer, had called a press conference on 16 August to set the record straight. He had taken the unusual step of issuing a full statement about the ghost, under the title 'Tower of Fear'. The RAF had also taken a rather controversial decision to endorse Brenda's story – an admission that they believed the ghost really existed. They had even flown Brenda in for the day from her new post in Anglesey to tell her story.

Brenda remained seated as Michael introduced her at the press conference. The audience waited, hushed; they knew that what they were about to hear would make wonderful copy in the following day's newspapers. Brenda took a deep breath and began to speak.

'We were night flying in the control room and just before 10 p.m. I came out of the switchboard room to go down to the met. office. As I walked out of the door, I froze; before me was a black shadowy figure – a broad-shouldered man, about six feet tall, wearing a flying jacket. I could see right through his shape. He moved slowly towards the approach room and then disappeared. Nobody else was around, so I screamed: 'I've just seen a ghost.' They thought I'd gone mad. One of the officers came out and asked

what all the noise was about, and I told him what had happened.
We checked to see that no-one had come into air traffic control,
and no-one had.'

For three nights, Brenda said, she waited by the doorway at ten
o'clock hoping to catch another glimpse of the mysterious figure.
Nothing happened and she forgot about the incident. Two months
later the ghost reappeared. She said:

'I was coming down from the glass tower with Flight Lieutenant
Mark Byrne behind me. I quickly glanced into the tea room off the
first-floor landing and I saw the shadow again by the door. I said to
Mark: "Did you see that?" He nodded. It seemed to stare at me
and then just vanished. I was shaking; I ran back into the
switchboard at a rate of knots and put the lights back on. It felt very
spooky.

'What I saw was a ghost and nothing will convince me otherwise.
I was petrified, but no-one believed me. They treated it all as a
joke. Then two of my colleagues also admitted they had seen it and
suddenly it didn't seem so daft after all. I was sceptical about ghosts
before, but now I believe in them completely.'

When Brenda had finished her story the TV, radio and newspaper reporters fired questions; they wanted to know who the ghost
was and whether they could see it for themselves. Michael Brooks
said he could not guarantee an introduction, but he did have a
theory about its identity; he thought it was the ghost of Warrant
Officer Walter Hodgson, who had flown from Linton-on-Ouse
during the war.

'At the same time as the first sighting last summer,' he said, 'we
moved a plaque which was donated by Hodgson's family from the
outside of the tower to inside. It was to his memory and perhaps the
moving of the plaque upset his spirit. We have no records for him
after the war, but we do know that he came from Hull and that his
family gave the base a commemorative plaque in 1959 when he
died. I hope his relatives will now come forward.

'We've accepted that something inexplicable has happened.
Brenda was so sure about the ghost that she has convinced many of
us. Other people have apparently seen a ghost but failed to report it
officially because they were too embarrassed. We could be dealing
with a restless spirit, but at this stage we have no plans to call in a

priest to conduct an exorcism, as no harm has come from the presence.'

Michael Brooks's theory about Walter Hodgson was spotted in the newspapers by his widow, Audrey Hodgson, who lived in Ilkley, west Yorkshire. She too was convinced that the ghost was her late husband. 'Don't be afraid,' she told the air traffic controllers, 'he won't harm you. He just loved the place so much.'

Warrant Officer Hodgson, a flight engineer on Lancaster bombers, was decorated for his wartime bravery. He was shot down over Holland in 1943 during a bombing raid and captured by the Germans. He was one of seventy-six British and Allied airmen who succeeded in tunnelling their way out of Stalag Luft 3, the Luftwaffe's top prisoner-of-war camp, an escape which generated wartime Germany's biggest ever manhunt. He had walked halfway across Germany before he was recaptured. His story was later immortalized in the epic war film *The Great Escape*. Hodgson died in 1959, aged thirty-eight, from tuberculosis. His ashes were scattered on runway 22 of his old base.

With such evidence, Martin O'Collins was sure that the story would make a good TV documentary. All that he needed now was for Eddie to corroborate the story on camera. Eddie took up his position on the first-floor landing by the tea room, where Brenda had seen the ghost on the second occasion. Martin checked the lighting, microphones and recording equipment and nodded to Eddie that he was about to start filming. Brenda and Michael watched as Eddie began to walk around the landing. 'Yes, I have someone with me,' said Eddie. 'I think I'll have to sit down on the stairs.'

> I think this man was killed out on the airfield. It was an ordinary accident; he was knocked down by a vehicle at night. His back was broken and he was in a lot of pain. He was put on a stretcher and brought into this building for a while. Then he died. It was after the war, in the late 1950s or early 1960s.
>
> There's a great weight on his mind. I think he feels that he had not prepared himself and his family for his sudden demise. He doesn't seem to understand that a lot of time has

passed since his accident. That's why he keeps appearing; he has unfinished business on his mind.

Someone is saying: 'Thank you, Brenda, for your help in bringing this to the attention of others. For your courage in coming back and waiting to make contact.'

There's a feeling of light and lightness coming through now. A team of spirits is coming forward and taking him into their care. They say: 'God bless, leave him to us.' He's free now.

Brenda and Michael had been transfixed by Eddie as he spoke. Brenda had been visibly moved when Eddie thanked her for the courage she had shown in waiting for the ghost and was fighting back a few tears. Michael, too, was speechless. Finally, he said: 'What an extraordinary experience. Did you really feel his injuries?' Eddie explained how a trapped spirit often impressed the experience of its death on him, and that often meant physical discomfort.

Martin, however, was uncertain what to make of Eddie's story. It had been completely different from what he had expected – there had been no mention at all of Walter Hodgson and the story did not tally with other accounts. He wondered how he could use it. He was working to a very tight budget and was not sure that he could spare the time or money to film another encounter. Eddie had warned him a few weeks before the visit to Linton-on-Ouse that he could not guarantee to deliver exactly what Martin needed for the programme and he had accepted that risk. But he also remembered that a few minutes later, Eddie had blurted out: 'There won't be a problem. A little voice has just told me that it's all been arranged.' All he could do now was to trust in that and hope for the best.

Both Michael and Martin were keen to discover whether there were any more ghosts at the station. Shortly after Brenda's experience, a cleaner called Betty Fenwick claimed to have seen an apparition in the Officers' Mess building. Mrs Fenwick, who had worked at the station for fourteen years, had seen the shadowy figure of a man dressed in RAF uniform and a Biggles-style pilot's helmet sitting on a chair in one of the first-floor bedrooms. She called the ghost 'Old Fred' and believed he was just one of a number of ghosts that haunted the station. 'You can often sense them,' she said. 'Several people have felt them. It's often as though someone is watching you. It's nothing to be scared of, though, it's quite a nice feeling.'

Michael led Eddie and Martin to the room and sat down in one of the armchairs. Eddie was shown to the chair where the pilot had been seen by Mrs Fenwick. As soon as he sat down, Eddie made contact with the pilot.

I can sense him with me. He was a very extrovert, likeable man who was completely dedicated to his flying. He was the sort of man who could have joined the Red Arrows – he loved the excitement of aerobatic flying. I don't think he is earthbound; he's at an intermediate stage between the earth state and the spirit world. His love of flying and the glamour of his life in the RAF made him loath to leave it. He is still gazing back towards his earth life, whereas he should have been looking towards the spirit world.

I shall leave him to a team of spirit helpers who will try to persuade him to leave. I can do no more for him now.

'Lunch?' asked Michael, to Eddie's relief. He had always enjoyed his food, but he found that, more and more these days, he needed to keep up his energy levels. Eddie and Martin followed Michael into the Officers' Mess dining room, where a buffet lunch had been laid on for them: sandwiches, cold cuts, salads and wine. Michael brought Eddie a glass of wine and urged him to help himself to some food. When they were all seated, Michael asked Eddie how he could be so sure of what he picked up.

'I tune in,' said Eddie, 'and after a time the person comes through clearly. When they do, my own thoughts are pushed aside and the communication is quite definite.' Michael looked a little puzzled, but decided not to push the matter further. He had, he said, been very interested in the paranormal as a teenager; the mother of one of his friends had been a medium and he had often called at the house to talk to her about the subject. 'But you tend to develop a lot of scepticism in an institution like the RAF and I suppose I just lost interest,' said Michael. 'I do believe there is something out there, but I just can't understand it.'

Eddie was interested in Michael's revelation. 'I often find that ghosts appear when there is someone around who has some understanding of the spirit world,' he said. 'In this case, it was Brenda who was psychic enough to see the ghost, while you let her speak without ridiculing her. You may not think that on the surface you are sympathetic to the spirit's plight, but it was drawn to you because, underneath, you had that understanding.'

Martin then told Eddie the story of Walter Hodgson's plaque and how the RAF had assumed that he was the spirit behind all the disturbances.

'It's a nice theory,' said Eddie, 'but I can't guarantee who will come through to me. All I can give you is what I get.'

Michael had no idea who the first spirit might be, but he had an idea that he could trace the name of the pilot Eddie had contacted. 'There have been six fatalities on the base since the war,' he said. 'In September 1966 an aircraft crashed on a navigation exercise and in May the following year, an aircraft crashed soon after take-off. Then nothing happened until March 1971 when there was a mid-air collision above the base. There were two in the early 1980s – but I'm pretty convinced that the one you referred to happened in June 1978, when a young pilot crashed into a hangar during a flying stunt.'

Eddie decided it was his turn to ask some questions. 'You must understand', he said to Michael, 'my fascination with airfields – I spent many years after the war building them.' Michael was happy to fill him in.

RAF Linton-on-Ouse was opened on 13 May 1937 and was part of No. 4 Group Bomber Command, whose headquarters were at Mildenhall, Suffolk. The following month, HQ were moved to Linton under the command of Air Commodore A.T. Harris – later known as 'Bomber' Harris: Sir Arthur Harris, Marshal of the RAF and Chief of Bomber Command. During the war years, Linton-on-Ouse hosted many squadrons from both the RAF and the Royal Canadian Air Force and participated in many of the night bombing raids on Germany and Norway. As in all Bomber Command stations, losses were high during the war years.

When Germany was defeated in 1945, the RAF had a further

role to play in providing air transport in the war against Japan, and Linton-on-Ouse was made HQ for Transport Command. After the bombing of Hiroshima ended the war, Transport Command concentrated on repatriating servicemen from the Far East, and when No. 4 (Transport) Group was disbanded on 2 February 1948 Linton settled down to a peacetime routine as a station of Fighter Command. No. 264 Squadron moved there, followed by Nos 64 and 65. Fighter Command stayed at Linton for ten years, followed by one of the first ever Coastal Command helicopter squadrons (No. 253). In 1957 the station became home to No. 1 Flying Training School which has been there ever since, training both RAF and Royal Navy personnel.

Eddie, absorbed in Michael's words, had not noticed the time passing; it was nearly three o'clock and Martin was keen to get back to London. Before they left, Michael asked Eddie to inspect a corridor at the end of the building, which he thought might also be haunted. 'The cleaning lady who works in that corridor says she always feels strangely happy when she works there,' he said. 'She tells me she often feels like singing.' To start with Eddie felt nothing, but when he was about halfway along the corridor, he stopped and said:

I have a strong urge to run. There's someone here – a woman, I think. She ran past me to the far end of the corridor and embraced a man who came out of the end office. There's a great feeling of joy and excitement here.

She was the man's wife. He had been on a flying mission not long before the war ended and she lived just off the station. Staff at the base had told her that he hadn't returned. She decided that he must have been killed and stifled any hope of ever seeing him again. Then several days later they told her that he had turned up and was being debriefed. She had come up here to meet him.

I don't think this is a haunting – it's a psychic imprint caused by the strong emotions that were expressed here. These two people could still be alive today.

Michael took Eddie back to his office before he left. He wanted to look up the newspaper cutting relating to the pilot's death. He lifted the large scrapbook off his top shelf and, after dusting it down, flicked through the large pages back to 1978. 'Look at this,' he said. He showed Eddie three cuttings from the *Yorkshire Evening Press*, dated 1 and 2 June and 4 October 1978.

Eddie read the headline: 'Pilot may have misjudged Linton stunt', it said. 'During aerobatics over RAF Linton-on-Ouse, near York, a Jet Provost failed to recover from a barrel roll, hit the ground at more than 300 mph, and crashed into the corner of a hangar 400 yards away and caught fire. The pilot, Flt. Lt. Robert Arthur Hatton Rogers, aged twenty-nine, a married man, ejected shortly before the impact, but was killed. He had multiple injuries.'

The inquest had recorded a verdict of misadventure. The jury was told that the RAF board of inquiry had revealed no evidence of mechanical failure and the most likely cause of the crash was pilot error. The York Coroner, Mr Anthony Morris, said that the pilot had been performing a dangerous aerobatic manoeuvre that had gone wrong. According to an eye-witness, the Jet Provost Mk 5A had completed some manoeuvres, then went into a dive and hit the ground. 'The aircraft began to break up, the wings fell off, but the fuselage travelled towards a hangar in a cloud of dust and came to rest in the corner of the building. The pilot was not in the cockpit, but on the grass, some distance away.'

A few days after Eddie's visit, Michael went to the York reference library to see if he could unearth any information on the young man who had been killed by a vehicle on the airfield. He began scanning through local newspapers from the early 1960s on the microfiche. After an hour of this, his eyes had started to ache and he had decided to call it a day. But before he returned the films to the desk, he decided to have a look at what was happening in the world around the time of his own birthday, 26 July 1949. Something caught his eye as he scanned the microfiche back towards 1949: 'Airman killed at Linton-on-Ouse' in bold capital letters and 'Airman's death theory' below. He read the two stories in amazement.

AIRMAN'S DEATH THEORY

A verdict of 'Accidental death' was recorded by the York Coroner (Col. Innes L. Ware) at a resumed inquest held in the York Law Courts on AC1 T. Davies (21) of the RAF Linton-on-Ouse.

Aircraftman Frederick Lyles, also of the RAF station at Linton, said he was driving a petrol wagon and had just finished refuelling an aircraft when he asked Davies, who was attending to the next aircraft, to guide him round. He felt a slight bump and stopped.

Corporal W. Baker said he saw Davies directing the lorry, which was turning round on the perimeter track, but he did not see the accident.

LAC Patrick Holden said he saw Davies stagger round from the right-hand side of the vehicle and collapse behind the rear wheel of the petrol wagon.

'There is very little evidence really before me,' said the Coroner. 'Nobody actually saw the accident. I think that Davies was caught by his clothing and then staggered round to the rear of the vehicle.

'I know from long experience in these matters', he added, 'that there was no need for a lorry of this weight [nine tons] to go right over him to cause the injuries he received.'

Davies died from internal haemorrhage due to multiple injuries, including a fractured pelvis, it was stated.

Yorkshire Evening Press, 3 August 1950

AIRMAN KILLED AT LINTON-ON-OUSE
Error of judgment was possible

A verdict of accidental death was recorded by the Coroner Colonel Innes L. Ware at an inquest on Wednesday on AC1 Thomas Davies, aged 21, of RAF Linton-on-Ouse, who was killed at the aerodrome on July 27.

Cpl. W. Baker said that Davies was assisting a refuelling vehicle to turn round. He did not see any accident, but saw Davies afterwards lying on the ground near the rear wheel. A Meteor plane was being attended to at the time and there was considerable noise.

The Coroner said that probably what happened was that Davies had been caught or had tried to get behind the vehicle and there had been an error of judgment. The cause of the death was said to be internal bleeding from multiple injuries.

York Gazette, 5 August 1950

Michael immediately told Martin O'Collins about his research. It was enough to convince him that he had sufficient evidence to broadcast the documentary, and in December 1988 his programme *Ghost Train* went out on BBC2.

Chapter 6

The Royal Connection

It is important for people to believe in something, even if
it is not the established Church.

HRH Prince Charles, 1 July 1994

On the afternoon of 10 March 1988 Prince Charles narrowly
escaped death on the ski slopes of Klosters, Switzerland, after he
had led a group of friends off-piste. Charles and his party –
Major Hugh Lindsay, a 34-year-old former equerry to the
Queen, Patti and her husband Charles Palmer Tompkinson, a
former Olympic skier, and a Swiss guide called Bruno Sprecher –
were all accomplished skiers and the snow off-piste seemed
inviting and challenging.

Minutes later tragedy struck. A huge avalanche engulfed them
near the 5,000-foot-high middle station on the Gotschnagrat mountain high above the village of Klosters. The Swiss authorities had
warned skiers that blazing spring sunshine meant avalanches were a
threat, but Charles ignored the advice. As the snow swept into the
royal party, Charles somehow managed to dive out of its path. He
missed death, literally, by inches. Major Lindsay, however, was not
so lucky; he took the full force of the avalanche. He was killed
instantly, when a huge lump of ice fractured his skull, and was
buried in twelve feet of snow. Mrs Palmer Tompkinson suffered
severe leg injuries.

Distraught and weeping, Charles, helped by Bruno Sprecher, scrabbled through the snow with his bare hands, in a desperate effort to rescue the major. But it was hopeless. Numb with shock, Prince Charles was led away from the scene, weeping as he climbed into the rescue helicopter. Members of the royal party said that they had never seen the prince so distraught. Later that day there was a short official statement: 'The Prince of Wales and the whole party are naturally extremely distressed by this tragic accident which resulted in the death of their close friend, Major Hugh Lindsay and the injury to Mrs Palmer Tompkinson.'

Princess Diana insisted that the holiday had to be cut short; Charles could hardly return to the slopes as if nothing had happened. So, the morning after the accident, dressed in black, their faces pale from the strain, the royal party emerged from the Kulm Hotel and headed for the airport and the flight back to London.

Major Lindsay's wife of eight months, Sarah, had met him at Buckingham Palace, where she had worked as a press officer for twelve years. By now seven months pregnant, she met the royal party at RAF Northolt, Middlesex, and watched as the flag-draped coffin bearing her husband was carefully unloaded. Then, devastated, she withdrew to the seclusion of Major Lindsay's family home in Budleigh Salterton, Devon.

Charles had been deeply disturbed by the accident, as royal aides admitted. They said privately that he blamed himself for the major's death, because he had encouraged the party to head off-piste, though many press ski commentators thought that the guide of the day, Bruno Sprecher, who knew the dangers of an avalanche in those weather conditions, should have exercised more authority. But Charles could not be consoled; it was, said one aide, 'the biggest tragedy in his life since the assassination of his great-uncle Lord Mountbatten'. Sarah Lindsay also tried to persuade him that there was no question of blame when she asked him to be godfather to her daughter Alice, who was born in May 1988.

As a personal tribute to Major Lindsay, Diana said that she would never again ski at Klosters. Charles, however, returned there in February 1989, less than a year after the accident and the highly critical report on it by the Director of Public Prosecutions for the District of Graubünden. This concluded that Prince Charles and Mrs Palmer Tompkinson had led the way on the steep slope and waited for the others at what they thought was a safe location; but the movement had loosened a vast mass of snow.

Conditions in Klosters in 1989 were almost exactly the same as the day of the accident a year earlier, but again Charles defied warnings and skied off-piste with his party. Ironically, it included three people who accompanied him on that fateful day the previous year – a Swiss policeman called Domenic Caviezel, the guide, Bruno Sprecher, and Charles Palmer Tomkinson.

Friends of Charles insisted that his visit was meant 'to lay the ghost of his friend's death', but the timing was condemned by many commentators as extraordinarily insensitive. His determination, some said sheer stubbornness, to pursue this dangerous sport was questioned by members of his own household; they suggested that the Prince's thirst for adventure revealed a disturbing immaturity.

But, in retrospect, the accident at Klosters was a turning point for the Prince. Since his schooldays at Gordonstoun, the tough Scottish public school, Charles had been attracted to high-risk sports. After Cambridge, when he became a lieutenant in the Royal Navy, he experimented with deep-sea diving and parachuting, among many similarly risky activities. He refused to renounce polo, a sport which he loved, despite chronic back problems and a broken arm which took over a year to heal. The avalanche at Klosters, however, confronted him with his own mortality and he was forced, perhaps for the first time, to weigh up a sport's adrenalin-packed thrills against his responsibilities as heir to the throne. And those responsibilities became painfully apparent to Charles in the next six years, as he watched both his marriage and his place in the public's affection crumble.

At nine o'clock on 31 October 1988 Eddie was sitting in the dining room of his farmhouse in Lambley, near Nottingham, chatting with his second wife Pat and their teenaged son, Christopher. They had just finished dinner when Eddie became aware of a pain at the back of his head. He was aware that this was a signal that someone was approaching him for help. At this moment he was drawn into the unfolding drama of Prince Charles's private life. Eddie relaxed and let the ghost of Hugh Lindsay, who had died on the ski slopes that March, come forward:

I am feeling a lot of pressure on the back of my head and neck. This man was separated from his body; he couldn't see anyone he knew on the slope and didn't realize what had happened to him. I can't hold on very clearly to him at the moment – I get the feeling that he is a very private person, not keen on sharing his feelings. He asks: 'Where the hell am I?'

As he became engulfed in the snow he started to choke – he tried to move his arms and legs, but couldn't. He told himself: 'Don't panic, don't panic. Mustn't let go, mustn't give in, got to get out of here.' Suddenly he felt himself out of that situation and wandering around. He was in a terrible muddle. He thought he was wandering around on the lower slopes below the snow line, unable to find his bearings. He thought he would make his way to the hotel, but it wasn't there.

I have to try to hold him steady, but he won't stay still for very long. He cannot accept that he has died and won't allow himself to think that for a moment. What happened to him on the ski slopes – the avalanche – is confusing him terribly; he managed to get out, but he doesn't understand how. The big problem is to get him to understand his situation now.

A clergyman is approaching him; I think he may have been an army chaplain. They are sitting down together and talking; the chaplain is being very gentle. Major Lindsay is asking about his wife – he doesn't know about the baby yet. He asks if he can be taken to see his wife, as he says she will be worried about his absence. The chaplain assures him that he will be taken to see her. He realizes that he will have to be very careful with Major Lindsay, as he could become very angry when he discovers what has happened.

I must let him go now and trust that he will be helped gradually to understand his situation. It is going to be very hard for him to accept it at first; I must try to get back to him in a few days' time to see how he is.

Three days later, Hugh Lindsay returned to Eddie:

> He's among friends now. The chaplain took him on a journey and introduced him to other people who had passed over. This was done very cleverly, so that the weight of evidence would suggest that he, too, was in the same situation. He has been shown his wife and baby, but has not actually visited them. He is filled with sadness, so his friends are now supporting him. I understand that he will be taken closer to his wife and child when he is better able to stand the emotional impact. He is slowly learning how to appreciate the beauty of his surroundings. He is quite safe now.

Eddie respected and admired the royal family but, like many people of his background and age, that was as far as it went; he was just not interested in the stream of scandalous stories about the royals which were splashed over the front pages of tabloid newspapers. Perhaps he was chosen by the spirit world precisely because he was so innocent; if he had known more about Charles, Diana, Camilla and the others, whom the media portrayed as figures in a soap opera, then his mind would have been filled with the images of publicity.

Major Lindsay's message was the first in a series of inspirational messages over a six-year period which were designed, it seemed, to encourage Charles during the most testing phase of his life. They show that Charles receives vital support from people who once loved him – such as his mentor, Earl Mountbatten, and Hugh Lindsay – as well as from highly evolved spirits who act as guardian angels to the nation as a whole. These spirits believe in Charles's ability to take the monarchy into the next millennium; after six years Eddie was left with the impression that, far from being an amiable eccentric who had lost touch with reality, the view of many newspapers, Charles was a man of vision.

The royal family is no stranger to the paranormal. Queen Victoria employed a court clairvoyant. More recently, to the delight of the tabloid press, the Princess of Wales and Duchess of York have consulted psychics, either to help them with personal problems or to contact deceased relatives and friends. Prince Charles has been more discreet, but has also had private, informal links with clairvoyants.

Eddie did not expect to hear any more from Major Lindsay, but on the morning of 25 November 1988, as he was travelling by train from Doncaster to Leeds, the major returned, this time with a message for his widow, Sarah.

'Dearest, you may find this difficult to accept, but I'm absolutely safe and secure now, thanks to the efforts that have been made on my behalf. It has been an extraordinary experience and I've learnt a lot about the need to be prepared before the event. One never knows when this is going to happen and one can get caught unawares – as I was – without a route map.

'I've been shown you and the baby and I'm pretty grateful for that. I'm going to do my utmost to make you aware of my presence. Don't let this frighten you – you know I will take every care not to alarm you. There are ways, I'm told, that will not cause you distress. Try not to blame Charles. I know you find this hard, but it really wasn't his fault any more than mine – we can all make mistakes. A single misjudgement can lead to disaster.

'Don't withdraw from life – you know that's not the way we lived. I want to see you put the pieces together again and I'm going to do as much as possible to help you. My love for you is as strong as ever and will always be with you.'

In the years that followed Hugh Lindsay's communication the royal family suffered a series of public relations catastrophes which threatened its entire future. The 'fairytale marriage' of Charles and Diana, which had been collapsing visibly for years, was exposed as loveless and acrimonious in June 1992 when Andrew Morton's book *Diana: Her True Story* was published. The book, which was allegedly written with Diana's cooperation, was hailed as the biggest royal scoop since the abdication of Edward VIII in December 1936. Morton described, using the Princess's own friends as sources, a marriage in which a young, vivacious woman was shackled to a cold, selfish, middle-aged man.

Two months after Morton's book was published, the *Sun* published a sensational transcript of a telephone conversation between the Princess and her friend James Gilbey, a member of the famous gin dynasty. In the conversation, which had been mysteriously recorded by a radio ham who claimed that he had tuned into Gilbey's mobile phone, Diana complained bitterly about the royal family and whispered intimately to Gilbey.

On 13 November 1993 the *Daily Mirror* published extracts from a similar tape, this time incriminating the Prince and his long-time confidante, Mrs Camilla Parker Bowles, the wife of an army brigadier. The conversation, also allegedly picked up by a radio ham, revealed that the Prince had had a long and serious relationship with Mrs Parker Bowles. An unedited transcript of the tape was published in Australia the following January, which proved beyond doubt that the two had been – or still were – lovers. The revelation that the Prince had been unfaithful to his wife shocked the nation and fuelled the debate about whether he was fit to rule. Charles himself made no comment.

The Palace did not comment on either of these two tapes, popularly known as 'Squidgygate' and 'Camillagate', but official silence could not save the marriage: the separation was announced on 9 December 1992.

★

On the evening of 5 April 1994 Eddie held his spiritual development group in Lincoln; for no particular reason, he asked the group whether he had told them about the communications he had received from Major Lindsay. When Eddie wondered whether it would be possible to pass the Major's message to his widow, one of the group suggested that Eddie should write to the Prince's private secretary, Commander Richard Aylard. Perhaps Charles could then pass the message to Sarah himself?

As soon as she finished speaking, everyone felt a cold breeze swirling around them. It was, said Eddie, as if Major Lindsay was bringing with him the conditions he had experienced in the last moments before he died on the ski slopes.

He [Major Lindsay] says that the suggestion is a good one.
   'Thanks for all the help you gave me. I know that Charles still worries about the incident, so if you can get the message to him that I gave you before, you'd be doing him and me a great favour.
   'I see it all in a different perspective now, of course. It had to be one of us that got caught in that slide and I'm glad it wasn't Charles. I know it was a horrible blow to my family, but there have been some major improvements there lately. Naturally, it made me very sad at the time – and it still does when I come back to it all – but time does heal, as we all know.
   'Over here, you know, we pick up the grief that is felt for us. It's a great relief to us when the grief dies down. We don't feel sorry for ourselves at all – we're the lucky ones. I'll leave it with you then. Do what you can. God bless you all.'

Charles did indeed receive reports of Lindsay's message, but told Commander Aylard to reply that he did not wish to take the matter further. Eddie showed me the Commander's letter, concerned that he might have embarrassed the Prince. I assured him that he had not; I told Eddie that Charles had long been interested in the paranormal, but that in his role as future head of the Church of England he could not risk contacting psychics.
   Charles had a very personal reason for being interested in the psychic world. Since his beloved great-uncle, Earl Mountbatten, had been killed in 1979 by an IRA bomb planted on his boat in Ireland, he had worried whether Mountbatten's spirit had been laid to rest. After the murder, which also killed Mountbatten's grandson, Nicholas, and a boatman, Paul Maxwell, many psychics had contacted the Prince, concerned that the Earl's violent death might have trapped him spiritually. Locals also reported seeing a ghostly figure pacing up and down the shore by Mullaghmore harbour, County Sligo, where Mountbatten was killed.

105

It would be difficult to exaggerate Mountbatten's influence on Charles. At the memorial service held for him at St Paul's Cathedral Charles said: 'He was the centre of the family, a patriarchal figure. I adored him and I miss him so terribly.' Charles's loyalty was admirable; but to historians who had studied Mountbatten, Charles's unequivocal affection showed a worrying naïveté. One historian, Andrew Roberts, claimed that when Elizabeth became Queen in 1952 Mountbatten boasted to his German cousins that 'the House of Mountbatten now reigns in Britain'.

Mountbatten's position was unassailable, despite his legendary vanity. His great-grandmother and godmother was Queen Victoria, and his mother's youngest sister was the last Tsarina of Russia; but noble birth had not stopped him from developing a colourful private life. His infamous 'open' marriage to Edwina Ashley was unpopular with the Queen and Queen Mother, who were also concerned about his relationships with bisexual and homosexual men. Yet Charles had gravitated to him. Mountbatten knew it was vital for the Prince to marry well, by which he meant a young woman who was wholly chaste, but in the meantime he encouraged him to court as many upper-class girls as possible. By the time Charles was thirty, though, a royal bride had become a matter of urgency. Rejecting, among many others, Lord Mountbatten's granddaughter Lady Amanda Knatchbull, Charles became engaged to Lady Diana Spencer on 23 February 1981. Unfortunately, it was the royal wedding, on Wednesday 29 July 1981, that marked the beginning of Charles's problems. Whatever the experts think now about Mountbatten – and many condemn him as a pompous fraud – he was a supreme politician, who understood that the monarchy needed to be carefully nurtured if it was to survive. If he had lived, then Charles might well have avoided the traumas of later years.

★

After his contact with Major Lindsay in November 1988, Eddie gave no more thought to the royal family until 8 June 1994, when he received an extraordinary communication from Mountbatten himself in the sitting room of a cottage in Sussex owned by Lady Mary Mumford, sister of the Duke of Norfolk. She had invited us back

106

for a second visit to Arundel Castle.

After lunch Lady Mary and Lady Winefride Freeman, Lady Mary's aunt, said that they had to pop out for a few minutes before taking us to the castle. Eddie and I were chatting when he said that someone was present, who has a very pressing message to deliver:

It's Thomas Howard [the fourth Duke of Norfolk, whom Eddie had contacted at Coutts Bank]: he's bringing Louis Mountbatten forward. I think he's doing this in return for the help I gave him. Mountbatten is a little reticent – he says: 'I'm not used to this sort of thing, you know.

'I understand that Charles is in a rather delicate and sensitive position with regard to the things you call the paranormal. He is walking a bit of a tightrope, but he has a lot of courage and will not be put off easily by sneering comments. As far as I am concerned, he need have no fears. I am all at peace, well in control and busy exploring this extraordinary life. But I still have an interest in the affairs of the country, particularly Charles's own fortunes. I have come to admire his integrity and motivation and feel sure that he has moved a long way since my death. So I am torn between old interests and the prospects that are offered by my new life. I think I shall know when I can no longer be of service to the country I loved – and still love. When that time comes I shall be free to turn my face upwards to what lies ahead for me.

I then asked whether Mountbatten was still close to Prince Charles.

I still take some interest in his affairs and offer him some intuition about likely problems. But, as you know, I cannot interfere in his choices, nor would I wish to. His is a lonely path, more so than I ever realized; this is why I continue to keep watch and offer him my support. We are, and always have been, close in interests and affection and it is for this reason that contact has always been easy. I will leave now. Farewell.

Mountbatten had always been sympathetic to the more sensitive side of Charles, unlike Prince Philip, who regarded interest in anything vaguely spiritual as a sign of moral degeneration. His communication to Eddie suggested that the Prince's struggles to find a truth beyond the immediate demands of power were an essential part of his development as a future King. Indeed, the more enlightened Charles became, the more he opened his mind to new ideas, the greater the monarchy's chances of survival in the twenty-first century.

★

Throughout his domestic difficulties in the early 1990s, Charles had maintained a dignified silence. Then, in 1993, he was approached by the respected broadcaster Jonathan Dimbleby, who asked if the Prince would cooperate in a documentary on his life, to be broadcast on 1 July 1994, the twenty-fifth anniversary of his investiture as Prince of Wales.

The two-and-a-half-hour documentary, *Charles: The Private Man, The Public Role*, attracted an unprecedented number of viewers. Charles would not speculate on the possibility of divorce, but two of his comments were seized on by the media. His statement that he had been a faithful husband until the point where he considered the marriage had irretrievably broken down was his first public admission that he had, indeed, been unfaithful to his wife. His second admission, that as monarch in a multi-racial society he wished to become Defender of [all] Faith rather than Defender of *the* Faith, provoked a fierce debate among Britain's religious leaders. It is important, the Prince said, 'for people to believe in something' even if it was not the established Church. 'I happen to believe that the Catholic subjects of the Sovereign are as important [as the Protestants], not to mention the Islamic, Hindu and Zoroastrian,' he said.

Although Charles did not talk directly of the disestablishment of the Church of England, he clearly wanted to open a debate on the relationship between the Church and the monarchy. Privately, he confided in friends that he felt the Church of England had become a minority voice in a multi-racial, multi-faith

Britain: in these circumstances, it was potentially divisive for the monarch to be seen as head of such an institution.

While leaders of Britain's Jewish, Hindu and Muslim communities applauded him, some influential Anglicans voiced their displeasure. In the *Sunday Times* Lord Coggan, a former Archbishop of Canterbury, said: 'This is a hornet's nest of problems. If he's saying Christianity is equal with other religions, we should differ profoundly from him.' David Bryce, grand secretary of the Grand Orange Lodge of Scotland, was more forthright: 'There is no place for Charles imposing his woolly religious beliefs or disbeliefs on the United Kingdom.' Roman Catholics were divided, although the Catholic church teaches its members to respect all faiths.

Despite the uproar he provoked in some quarters, Charles did emerge with a positive image and was fêted by many for his stance. 'I take my hat off to him,' said Hesham El-Essawy, chairman of the Islamic Society for Religious Tolerance, in the *Sunday Times*. 'It shows the vision of a man who recognises that there are only two religions: belief and non-belief.' Rabbi Jonathan Romain, spokesman for the Reform synagogues of Great Britain, echoed this sentiment: 'The enemy today is not religious difference, but religious indifference.'

Dimbleby followed his documentary with a biography of Prince Charles, published in November 1994. In it, the Prince admitted that his affair with Camilla Parker Bowles had spanned more than twenty years and that he had married Diana under duress from his father. Far from consolidating his role as the future monarch, the book led to more battering and bruising of the Prince's image. Some commentators argued that Charles, a self-confessed adulterer, had proved himself unfit to rule; others went further and proclaimed that the book would be the final death blow to the monarchy.

★

Throughout the very public trials and tribulations of her family in 1992, the Queen had maintained her usual dignified silence. But on Friday 20 November 1992, the eve of her forty-fifth wedding anniversary, a terrible disaster confirmed her view that the year had truly been her *annus horribilis*. Late that morning, a thin plume of white smoke rose above the grey towers and walls of Windsor Castle, the oldest inhabited castle in the world; within minutes the smoke turned from white to black and began to billow violently above the ancient castle's ramparts.

Minutes later ten fire engines and several hundred firemen from five brigades were on the scene, frantically trying to control the blaze that had rapidly swept through the castle after starting in the Queen's Chapel near the base of the Brunswick Tower. Refurbishing and restoration work, including rewiring, had been under way there since 1989 and was only months from completion. Giant flames leapt through the roof and glass came crashing down as the lead in the priceless stained glass windows began to melt. The fire, which raged well into the night, also threatened Windsor Castle's treasured art collection as flames engulfed the north-east corner of the Upper Quadrangle. The state apartments housed many of the world's greatest works of art, including portraits of Charles II by Van Dyck and Queen Charlotte by Benjamin West, and the adjoining Royal Library contained thousands of precious drawings by Leonardo da Vinci and Holbein. The Queen herself oversaw the rescue operation as Prince Andrew joined castle staff, workmen and an army detachment in a human chain to pass the national treasures to safety. Fire-fighters battled heroically, but every time they seemed to come close to controlling the blaze, it flared up again with renewed vigour. Next morning, the damage was clear: seven state apartments were gutted and St George's Hall, where the Queen holds state banquets, was destroyed, its fine timber roof largely collapsed.

At first the public were sympathetic, but that mood swiftly changed when the government said the taxpayer would have to pay for the repairs, estimated at around £60 million. There was national uproar; even staunchly monarchist commentators thought it was outrageous that such a stupendously wealthy family as the Windsors did not want to dig into their own pockets but expected ordinary people to refund repairs to what was, so most argued, their family home. In an attempt at damage limitation, the government said that the Queen and Prince Charles would pay income tax in the coming tax year. But this was not enough to stem the tide of debate about the nature of the monarchy in modern Britain, an issue that had been rumbling on for at least a decade. The newspapers were full of damaging facts about the royal family, notably that they cost British taxpayers almost double the combined cost of the monarchies of the Netherlands, Sweden, Spain, Denmark, Belgium and Norway. Opinion polls showed that four out of five people wanted a monarchy that was more in keeping with the status of the country on the world stage.

The world had changed from the days when the Crown embodied the spirit of Britain's far-flung Empire. By the 1990s the country was a minor player in the European Union, its industries challenged by the fast-growing economies of the Pacific Rim and its people wearied by years of recession and high unemployment.

Eddie was not, of course, thinking in such terms as he strolled through the grounds of Windsor Castle one blazing hot day in July 1994. He had decided to take a trip to Windsor to inspect the progress of restoration work since the great fire nearly two years earlier. He walked through the milling crowds of tourists past St George's Chapel towards the North Terrace. As he took in the splendid view of the Home Park and Eton College with its manicured playing fields, he was approached by the spirit of a man dressed in white livery, decorated with the royal coat of arms. Eddie made his way to a bench and sat down. The man then began to speak.

'I was a footman to King George II and in time became his valet. I found him to be a kind, sensitive man sadly treated by fate. He seemed to find the weight of his duties too much at times and in a moment of confidence told me that he envied the simplicity of my life and would even have exchanged lots if that were possible.

'He once said: "How does God choose his servants? The burden he places on them can exceed their strength at times, but perhaps that is good for their eternal souls." He dearly loved his Queen – I never saw a man so grieved as when she died. Because of my station I could do little to comfort him but pray, which I often did. I died in his service and felt he missed my attendance on him.

'I come to you not as a trapped soul, but to say that he was not a vain and cruel sovereign as some have been. I can say this for in some ways I knew him better than any courtier. Farewell.'

As Eddie made his way towards the Round Tower, he felt another entity approach: not a ghost this time, but a more evolved, almost angelic spirit who had come, it seemed, to explain the importance of Windsor Castle in the nation's life. A communication like this was rare; Eddie knew, therefore, that it was vitally important and probably was the reason for his visit. He made his way to a grassy verge and sat down, waiting for the communication to come through more clearly. He took a notepad and pen from his bag and began writing a few minutes later. He concluded afterwards that this spirit was the guardian angel of Windsor Castle. This is what he wrote:

'Windsor Castle is an outstanding example of the way time, usage and deference can cause a place or building to take on a psychic imprint that reflects special qualities – in this case the pomp and glory of the monarchy. But the advance of tourism is diminishing the quality and effectiveness of the angelic protection the castle once had.

'Royal majesty is undergoing great change. It may have to rise, phoenix-like, from the ashes of the devastating fire that swept through Windsor Castle. In the early years of this century, Britain possessed a great and far-flung Empire, but by the 1950s it had divested itself of most of these territories. In doing so, it was responding to the tide of history. The resulting loss of world power and influence has been difficult to accept. We are still coming to terms with this great change. Nevertheless, it had to be, so that a new kind of leadership could develop.

'Throughout history, individuals with the qualities that a nation needs are thrust forward to bring about change. The signs are that Prince Charles is such a one. He has shown himself willing to present controversial ideas which challenge aspects of national life. There is no doubting his courage and the sincerity of his views.

'The monarchy has to move away from pomp and show and towards spiritual leadership. It has to draw from the past that which is highest in the spiritual sense, creating a national focus for these values and the understanding that flows from them. This has no more to do with the established Church than any other, yet it will draw from them all, since spiritual truth is not the exclusive possession of any of them. Such changes will meet with much resistance, but they will gain ground because they are carried on a rising tide of enlightenment which is taking us into the new millennium.

'This new outlook will not be divorced from physical reality, but will add a much-needed dimension to life – one that will bring about changes in the way we view our society and the world at large. A keynote of the new outlook will be responsibility for the welfare of our fellow men and women and for all life on this planet.

'These islands have always responded to history's challenge, absorbing many new races, from the Celts to the Normans and, more recently, peoples of the Caribbean and Asia. This nation, perhaps more than any other, has had to come through a great deal of trauma to have arrived at the state of religious tolerance which generally prevails, although that still has to be carefully guarded. This is one reason why it is well placed to foster a broader spiritual outlook throughout the world.

'We are in the early stages of this process; inevitably there will be struggles and tensions, but out of the gradual national metamorphosis will come a caring, loving people with a growing spiritual awareness. This country will then attract a different sort of visitor. People from other parts of the world will come to absorb and take back with them some of this new understanding, an understanding which can solve some of humanity's most pressing problems.

'This is not a chauvinistic vision. There will be nothing selfish nor self-protecting in this, only a desire to give to

113

others – no matter from where – something precious and essential for the growth of humanity. It will not be forced, nor come about by force, but will grow naturally out of an enlightened appreciation of the true meaning and purpose of our lives. That this can be focused and led by a transformed monarchy is surely a glorious vision for us all to behold.'

When he returned home Eddie pondered the messages that had come through to him at Windsor. He wondered whether the great fire had been a dramatic warning from the spirit world that the monarchy ought now to begin the long overdue process of reform. Eddie's mind went back to King George II's valet who had approached him at Windsor. A servant all his life, the man had observed at close quarters the tremendous burden of responsibility that went with the enormous privileges of being sovereign. In a moment of rare introspection the King had confessed that he would have exchanged his position and all his worldly goods with his servant for a life that was simple and uncomplicated. 'The burden [God] places on [his servants] can exceed their strength at times, but perhaps that is good for their eternal souls . . .'

Eddie had also been moved by the Prince's views on the universality of religion and the importance of protecting the environment and helping the weakest in society. He was especially heartened by Charles's spiritual quest – despite the ridicule heaped on him by sections of the media who had often portrayed him as nothing more than a New Age dilettante.

'Whatever his destiny, I would not swap places with Prince Charles,' Eddie said. 'I could not live with the weight of his responsibilities. But he will guide us, with the help of his guardian spirits, safely into the next millennium.'

Part II

The Human Drama

Chapter 7

Evil in the Beacons

. . .facilis descensus Averno;
noctes atque dies patet atri ianua Ditis.

(The gates of hell are open night and day;
Smooth the descent and easy the way.)

Virgil, *Aeneid*

A dim light flickered through the trees around the graveyard by the old manor house. From a distance a faint humming sound could be heard, rhythmically rising to a crescendo and then fading away into the dark winter night. Ten or twelve figures dressed in hooded cloaks clustered around a tomb in the clearing, where a woman dressed in black lay motionless. The scent of burning myrtle, thorn-apple and nightshade hung heavy in the night air, its smoke billowing around the group. As the chanting stopped a man dressed in a dark red cape and scarlet cap stepped forward, lifted a triangular bowl above his head and shouted:

'Lord Satan, the just God, master of slanders, administrator of luxurious sins and great vices, cordial of the vanquished, suzerain of resentment, accountant of humiliations and treasurer of old hatreds, king of the disinherited, the Son who is to overthrow the inexorable Father . . . Lord, grant thy followers glory, riches and power. Help us drive out the impostor Jesus, breaker of promises,

117

who was to appear in glory and did not, who was to intercede for man with the Father and did not. Lord, let me be thy instrument to bring this coward God down into the host before us so that we may violate her body.

'*Hoc est enim corpus meum, his est enim calix sanguinis mei; sanguis meius super nos et filios nostros*,' he chanted ['This is my body and this is the chalice of my blood; may my blood be on us and our children']. As he drank from the bowl, a man stepped forward and tore the young woman's robe from her thin body. The leader poured the remains of the chalice over her naked body and smeared a mixture of blood and faeces over her face. Then he knelt before an altar at a nearby tomb where two black candles were burning and said:

'Our father, which *wert* in heaven . . . Thy will be done, in heaven as it is on earth . . . Lead us into temptation, and deliver us not from evil . . .' On the back of his cloak was embroidered a triangle and a black goat with silver horns. On the tombstone hung a picture of Jesus, his face twisted into a cruel smile. The man turned and nodded to the congregation, who fell upon the writhing woman like a pack of starving wolves. They grabbed handfuls of her hair, sank their teeth into her neck and lacerated her legs and abdomen with knives.

Thomas Edwards felt his stomach lurch as he fled into the woods. He ran at full speed for twenty minutes, then fell to the ground exhausted, vomiting into the grass. Shivering and panic-stricken, he lay immobile on the ground, not daring to remember what he had just seen. A fine drizzle began to fall and as it washed away the sweat and grime from his forehead, he slowly came to his senses.

Earlier that autumn night in 1848, at around eleven o'clock, Thomas had wandered across the fields from his home at Cwmgwdi Farm, where he worked as a stable-hand, for a secret rendezvous with a serving-girl who worked in nearby Brecon. She had arranged to meet him around the back of an inn at midnight, but after an hour had still not appeared. By then it had grown wet and windy, so Thomas had decided to return to Cwmgwdi, hoping that nobody had missed him. On his way home he had taken a short cut past Heol Fanog, an old barn and farmhouse attached to a manor house of the same name. Seeing a light flickering in the woods nearby, he had drawn closer, trying to see what could be going on there in the

Eddie Burks outside Coutts & Co., the Queen's bank, which, until Eddie intervened in August 1992, had been haunted by Thomas Howard, the fourth Duke of Norfolk (*Gillian Cribbs*)

St Philip Howard, Thomas's son. His refusal to denounce Catholicism led to his imprisonment and eventual death in the Tower of London in 1595. He told Eddie 'I did right at the time as I then saw the truth' (*Peter Newark's Historical Pictures*)

(*Left to right*) Gillian Cribbs, Lady Mary Mumford, Georgina, Countess of Arundel, Eddie and Lady Winefride Freeman at Arundel Castle (*Christopher Johns*)

Goodwood House, the home of Lord and Lady March (*Christopher Johns*)

Eddie, Gillian and Lady March in one of the many corridors that link storage cellars under Goodwood House. It was here that Lady March felt something 'trying to claw at my back' (*Christopher Johns*)

Lord and Lady March (*Christopher Johns*)

Lady Caroline Lamb. She said of her spirit's presence at Cambridge House, now London's In and Out Club, '. . . 'tis my fancy that brings me back . . . but I still cannot let go of those wonderful times' (*Mary Evans Picture Library*)

Lord Palmerston. His very strong personality left a psychic imprint on Cambridge House, his former home, where he appears from time to time (*Peter Newark's Historical Pictures*)

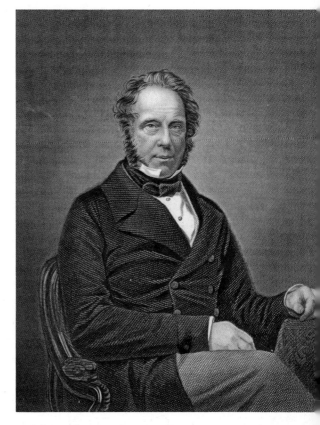

Number 10 Downing Street
(*Syndication International*)

The insignia of RAF Linton-on-Ouse, where Eddie released the spirit of a young aircraftman who had been killed by a vehicle on the airfield. Research by Squadron Leader Michael Brooks was later to reveal the man's identity

Prince Charles with his beloved great-uncle, Earl Mountbatten, and Prince Philip (*Syndication International*)

Right: A rescue helicopter at the site of the avalanche that killed Major Lindsay at Klosters (*Popperfoto*)

Major Hugh Lindsay and his wife Sarah (*Press Association*)

Heol Fanog, the home of Liz and Bill Rich, which had been the source of a series of terrifying psychic disturbances (*Gillian Cribbs*)

Bill Rich (*Gillian Cribbs*)

Bill's painting of the cross that now protects Heol Fanog from evil. It was completed three years before Eddie and Gillian's visit (*Christopher Johns*)

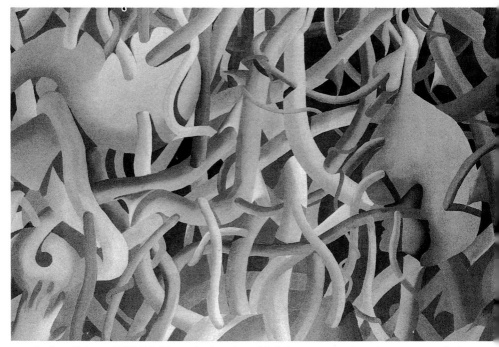

A detail from Bill Rich's painting in which he unconsciously expressed the feelings of the spirit of a young man who had been murdered near the house. Through Eddie, he said: 'For God's sake, help me . . . When I passed over, I found myself in a thicket from which I could find no release' (*Christopher Johns*)

Eddie with Joanne Silverwood. She has repeatedly acted as a magnet for lost souls (*Christopher Johns*)

early hours of a November morning.

Suddenly, the full horror of what he had witnessed came flooding back to him, and he ran across the muddy fields with the piercing, pleading cries of the victim still ringing in his ears. Forty minutes later Thomas fell into his bed, numb with exhaustion. His room-mate, James Griffiths, another stable-hand, snored on, oblivious to the disturbance. Thomas then fell into an uneasy and fitful sleep. He was awoken at five the next morning by James tugging at his bedclothes; they were supposed to muck out the stables at five and they were already late. Thomas quickly pulled on his clothes and boots and tried to remember what was causing him such a feeling of fear. By the time they had reached the stables, he was ashen-faced and dripping with sweat. As soon as their master, John Powell, was out of sight, Thomas collapsed to the ground and sobbed out his story to James.

Wide-eyed, James listened as Thomas related the tale; he was sure that his friend, a simple country boy of eighteen, had neither the intelligence nor the imagination to make it up. When he had finished, James said nothing and they worked in silence for the rest of the day. That same evening, still shaken, Thomas went to the local inn for a pint of ale. An hour later he was reeling, plied with drinks by the curious crowd that had gathered around to listen to his extraordinary story. At midnight he was carried home in an alcoholic stupor.

On 25 March 1849 David Powell, son of the owner of Cwmgwdi Farm, stood in the witness box before Mr Justice Erle at Brecon Assizes. He had been called as the first witness in the trial of James Griffiths, who was charged with the wilful murder of his fellow farm-hand Thomas Edwards on the morning of 17 November 1849. Griffiths, a simple and trusting boy of nineteen, had pleaded not guilty and stood undefended.

David Powell said: 'I am the son of Mr Powell, farmer of Cwmgwdi. On the 17th November the prisoner and deceased, who live in the house, got up around five o'clock. I got up at 5.15 and went to the stables where I saw both the deceased and the prisoner with the horses; they appeared to be quite friendly. I went off to the blacksmith, about half a mile away, and on my return I went back to the stables and nearby dung-heap, and called for the servant-men. There was no reply, so I went back to the house. Shortly afterwards I returned to the dung-heap with Elizabeth Phillips, the servant maid; it was getting lighter by then and I saw someone lying there. It was Thomas Edwards. I called my father who tapped the man on his thigh, but he was insensible. We took him to the house and sent for Mr North, the surgeon, from Brecon.'

The next witness to appear was the servant-girl at Cwmgwdi: 'My name is Elizabeth Phillips and I have been in the employ of Mr Powell for five years. On the day in question I got up at 5.45 and lit the fire. I saw no-one but noticed that the door had been opened. I took my pail to fetch some water from the brook and saw James Griffiths standing by the dung-heap. He made no reply when I asked him what he was doing there. On returning to the house I heard the sound of groaning, but it was too dark to see what was there. James was at the house when I returned and I asked him what he thought the groaning was. He left me to fetch a lantern. I did not see him again until he appeared before the magistrates in February.'

John Powell then came forward: 'On Friday, November 17, I was called up at about 6.30 a.m. and with Elizabeth Phillips, my son, daughter and wife, I went to the dung-hill, where I found Thomas Edwards. He was nearly doubled up with his head near his knees and, assisted by the others, I carried him into the house. He was in a dreadful state, his head and face being covered with blood. Seeing that he was dying I immediately called for Mr North, the surgeon, and the deceased's father. Mr Probert, the blacksmith, and I later went out to search for evidence; we found a pitchfork with blood on it in two places, corresponding to where a man's hands would have held it, and looked for the lantern, which was not in its usual place. The next day I went to examine the dung-hill with Constable Richard Beard. It had been stirred, as if a man had been trying to climb up it, and there was some blood at its base. I also found a piece of human skull. At the time of the murder I kept an axe in my house, which was used for chopping wood; when my wife showed me the axe I could see blood near the handle and on the iron.'

John Powell's wife Mary said that she remembered helping to carry Thomas Edwards into the house. She attended him from around seven that morning until he died at 6.20 the same evening. She had found the head of an axe lying in a pool of water in the gutter at 8 a.m. the same day. The deceased had been wearing a calico shirt and brown trousers, marked with his initials, T.E.

During the testimonies Griffiths had remained in the dock with a blank expression on his face. The judge then asked him if he had any observations to make to the jury. He replied: 'I do not know what to say. I leave the case in your hands, my Lords.' The jury retired; after an absence of ten minutes they returned to the court to deliver a verdict of guilty.

Shortly after dawn on Wednesday 11 April 1849 a large crowd gathered in front of Brecon county gaol. At five minutes past ten, James Griffiths appeared and was marched to the scaffold. As he approached the place of execution, he was asked if he wished to address the 1,600 spectators before him. He declined and did not even lift his head to the crowd. The black cap was placed over his head and, after a brief service, the bolt was drawn and he was hanged. Griffiths struggled for four minutes and then hung limp on the scaffold. His body was cut down and buried within the precincts of the gaol.

★

Annie MacDonald, a freelance film producer, was intrigued when she read my story about Eddie Burks and Coutts Bank in the *Sunday Telegraph*. She decided to contact him to see if he would agree to be filmed. She mentioned the idea to her husband, Robert, a scriptwriter; by chance, he had heard about an artist and his wife, Bill and Liz Rich, who had been troubled by disturbances at their farmhouse, Heol Fanog, in Brecon, south Wales. Annie and Robert visited Eddie on 8 March 1994 and told him about them. Then Eddie said:

> There is much confusion in this situation; it must be approached with care. Some of it is rather dark, but we will help you with this and give you the necessary protection.

There are many layers of influence here which have unpleasant overtones. Start by appraising the area around the house and garden. We will lead you, so keep your sensitivity sharp. There will be much of interest in this. That is all.

After a short interval Eddie began to speak again:

I have someone with me in a very agitated state who is connected with this house. He says: 'For God's sake, help me. I am in a great tangle, as though I have been wrapped up by a spider. I have managed to break free in order to contact you, but I have a nasty feeling that I am going to be ensnared again.'

I think this is a man who was murdered at the farm. I think he died in the last century. He says: 'You are right. The real story of my death has not been properly told. I came across something that I was not supposed to know, and I was murdered to keep me quiet. I was a fool – I should have kept my mouth shut. When I passed over, I found myself in a thicket from which I could find no release; every time I tried to get out something would ensnare me again. For God's sake, help me.'

I think he was fair-haired. He says: 'I was not of this breed, you know.' He's wearing trousers that are cut off at the knee, a short-sleeved brown calico shirt and an old pair of boots with no socks. I think he was killed with a blow to the head; he was definitely hit more than once. The first blow paralysed his arm and his knees gave way under him, but he still showed signs of life so they struck him again. Only one man did the evil deed, although there were others around. I am getting the impression that he had witnessed the practices of a Satanic group and had let it be known.

His young sister is coming for him now; he was very fond of her and he is growing excited. He has got to let go of the pain he feels in the back of his head – it is part of his memory of his death. His sister is calling him now; he can hear her voice but he cannot yet see her. I think her name is Annie. The light is growing and she is standing there in the light; she has

122

appeared as a little girl – as he would have remembered her. She says: 'Come on, come on.' He kisses her and they walk off together into the light.

Later that day Eddie called the Riches. Bill and Liz could make no sense of Eddie's communication; they only knew that the previous occupant of the house, a young woman who had lived there for seven years with her small son, had left because strange things had happened – her dogs would cower and howl and her spinning-wheel would start working by itself. The mother of their landlord had also lived there during the 1950s and had held seances there, using a ouija board. Eddie promised to visit the following Sunday, 13 March 1994.

★

Heol Fanog stands in the rolling green countryside above Brecon, south Wales. Originally a barn attached to a sixteenth-century manor, the farmhouse was built in the early 1950s from stone taken from the ruined house. Locals believe there was once a graveyard on the site of the barn.

Bill Rich met Eddie and myself, with Annie and Robert Mac-Donald and their cameraman, at the Wellington Hotel in Brecon at 11 a.m. We set off up the winding country roads to Heol Fanog. Bill, a tall, bearded man, the image of actor Richard Burton, had evidently been shaken by the disturbances. After five minutes we turned into a muddy drive in front of a pretty, whitewashed stone farmhouse. It was a wet and blustery day and I was not looking forward to tramping over Welsh fields in the driving rain, but Eddie was well prepared, as usual, in a rain cape and wellies.

Bill's wife Liz, a fair-haired woman of about thirty, welcomed us into the kitchen. It was small and cosy, with a heavy pine table, chairs and dresser and a huge Aga blasting out welcome warmth. Bill and Liz's young son and daughter knelt on the window seat, trying to coax a passing squirrel with titbits while Liz brought coffee and biscuits. I asked Bill to tell us what exactly had been going on at Heol Fanog. It was obvious that they had been through so much that he did not know where to start, so I asked him to tell us what had brought them there in the first place.

'I had been working as an artist in London, where I met Liz, and was becoming quite successful. Mick Jagger was one of my clients and I had been commissioned to make a wedding chest for the Duchess of York. Things were going really well for us, but I decided I needed some fresh inspiration away from London. Liz is Welsh, so we decided to look for a cottage around Brecon.

'There was something about this place that immediately attracted us; it felt as though a dome of happiness hung over the house and I felt very inspired by it. We moved here in August 1990 and our first months here were quite magical. We did notice a few strange things when we moved in. One very odd thing was the way the number 666 kept cropping up: the rent turned out to be £699.66; we saw a car with the registration CNT 666; our supermarket bills were £66.66 and lunch at a bar one day cost £6.66. Of course, 666 is the number of the Antichrist, according to Revelation.'

After six months the atmosphere in the house suddenly changed, according to Liz: 'It would suddenly grow dark and a sweet, acrid smell – like incense mixed with sulphur – would fill the kitchen. Then we all felt unwell with exhaustion, headaches, colds, terrible night sweats and cracking skin. I had the feeling that something was drawing on our energy. I didn't know what to do or say, I was so worn down by it.'

Two incidents convinced them that the house was haunted and that they should seek help from an exorcist. In January 1991 Bill was woken up by the sound of heavy snoring in their bedroom. The noise seemed to be coming from a spot in front of the back wall.

'I went into the centre of the sound and it stopped. It would start again the minute I went back to bed; I couldn't understand it, but I knew I had no control over it. Liz was terrified and refused to sleep in the bedroom again. The worst time for me was a few weeks afterwards. I began seeing terrible black shadows in the house that looked like people and strange birds of prey. I thought I was losing my mind.'

They looked everywhere for help. Over the next eighteen months Anglican and Catholic exorcists, psychics and dowsers came to Heol Fanog and performed various cleansing rituals, but with no success. A local exorcist, David Holmwood, told them that the snoring in the house was probably the sound of Satan himself, and that the shadows were the evil spirits that Bill had unwittingly drawn in by keeping books on the paranormal in the house. At the time Bill was working on a religious painting and had been using a book on sixteenth-century engravings of devil worship for reference.

'He told Bill that he'd found something terribly evil here and banished it,' said Liz. 'We were desperate at that stage, so we allowed him to take away our books, pictures and ornaments, which he later burnt. We believed him, because he'd worked in Brazil for seventeen years, helping victims of black magic.'

Holmwood and his assistant also told the couple that Jesus was testing them spiritually. They became Christians in a desperate attempt to ward off the feeling of evil that was seeping into the house. 'He told us that the experience would make us so spiritually aware that we would eventually learn to recognize the devil and cast him out through exorcism ourselves,' said Bill. 'Holmwood believed that Heol Fanog was a Satanic stronghold from which Satan could take over the world during the rule of the Antichrist.'

Bill admitted that the story sounded far-fetched, but at that stage they were prepared to believe anything. Bill was unable to sell any of his work in his regular outlets in London, Bath and Bristol and the couple had to sell their furniture to pay the rent and feed their family. The entities had also begun to interfere with the electricity supply to the farmhouse. One morning Bill discovered that he had been charged £700 for electricity for the quarter. The electricity board insisted the bill was correct and threatened to cut off the Riches if they did not pay.

'We just couldn't live in the house for a lot of the time,' said Bill. 'We stayed with Liz's parents nearby, but the problems followed us. We found huge pools of water on the bedroom floor when we got up in the morning and the baby alarms picked up horrible, garbled sounds in the children's bedroom which sounded like the devil himself.

'I went back to the house every day to feed our animals. But our cat ran away and the pig – which we kept as a pet – went mad and died. I hated going there, but on one occasion I had to get something from a box in the living room. The atmosphere was less oppressive and reminded me of the happy days when we first moved in. Then a voice said to me: "Sit down, Bill. How are you feeling? What's all the fuss about? Why don't you just relax and stay here?" Then I saw a set of kitchen knives laid out neatly on the table and the voice was telling me to use them, use them . . . I ran out as fast as I could and drove away. I nearly crashed the car on my way home.'

Bill was clearly an intelligent man, yet this house had brought him and his family to the brink of destruction. Eddie then asked us to be quiet. He was being given instructions on how to clear the house of its evil presence. Annie and Robert MacDonald began filming. His first task, Eddie said, was to walk around the outer edge of the grounds and lay a circle of light around the site; he repeated the same process walking around the house.

But the cameraman had noticed that his portable power unit had run flat, even though it had been fully charged when he set off, so filming was impossible. (Annie and Robert later discovered that their recording equipment had also failed.) Bill asked Eddie if he would like to inspect the house, but he shook his head and sat down at the kitchen table. He sat for a while with his head in his hands. Then he said:

> There is a concentration of energy here and it is not benign. This house must be filled with light. I am aware of the figure of Christ and I am getting the words: 'There will be nowhere left for them to go. So they shall lose hold and fall away and the light shall prevail. Praise be to God.'
>
> I am aware of a cross manifesting. First it shows itself as dark, but now it is becoming illuminated from within. Now it is radiating great power and protection. I am told that this cross will be your protection in this house from this point on. The cross is connected to the Christ spirit which is hovering directly above it; Christ is shedding his light upon the cross. I am getting the words: 'And so shall I leave my mark and my protection upon this place. There shall be no more fear and no more darkness and all will be safe within.'

We immediately noticed a lightening of the atmosphere. When we had arrived the weather had been cold, dark and blustery, but

126

sunlight was now streaming into the kitchen. Over lunch, Bill and Liz asked Eddie whether the house itself was haunted or whether they had attracted the entities.

'Liz is psychic,' he said, 'but I think in this case you simply walked into a black hole. The Satanic practices performed near here have left a dark stain on the area and have affected the house. They attracted the young boy who was murdered and since then there has been a build-up of evil forces which have started to work their way into your lives. In these situations, it's normal for people's lives to break down completely.'

I asked Liz about Eddie's first communication, when, before visiting the farmhouse, he had contacted a young man who had been murdered nearby after witnessing a black mass. She said that local records at Llanryddnoch had revealed that a farm-labourer called Jones was freeholder of a nearby house in 1849 and had lived there at the time of the murder. He had three unmarried sons, a daughter named Annie and two grandchildren. The family originally came from Llanhamlych, four miles away. Eddie had said the murdered boy was a farm-labourer who 'was not of this breed' [not a local]; he was killed by a sharp axe blow to the head and was escorted away by his younger sister, Annie.

Bill now returned from the sitting room with a large canvas, about five feet by three. 'I painted this three years ago,' he said. 'Now I understand what it means.' We all looked at the painting, an ugly abstract picture of a white cross on a dark brown background; the base of the cross was dark, lightening to the top which was a pure, bright white. Above the cross were small arrows shooting upwards. I was astonished: the picture was a mirror-image of what Eddie had described when he drew the darkness into the kitchen.

I suggested to Bill that we should see if there was any more evidence of psychic inspiration in his art. In the corner of his workshop stood a huge painting, apparently unfinished. It could not have been more different from Bill's other work, which included a gilded portrait of a Byzantine icon, pop art studies and a traditional landscape. The eau-de-Nil, pale blues and dusty pinks gave it an ethereal, dreamlike quality which belied its ugly, disturbing theme: shaved heads with fluid features; tears dropping from watery eyes; outstretched hands; random teardrops and – entwining everything – tangled, twisted branches studded with sharp thorns.

It was a strange work, yet the mood of the colour was dreamlike and soothing. If El Greco had painted it, I thought, he would have used vibrant reds and blacks to convey the violence of the subject; yet these gentle colours confused the mood. There was only the suggestion of humanity – the profiles were vacant, amorphous and, yes, ghostly.

Eddie's words suddenly came back to me: 'For God's sake, help me. I am in a great tangle . . . When I passed over, I found myself in a thicket from which I could find no release; every time I tried to get out something would ensnare me again . . .' The young man who had been murdered near the house had evidently been trying to communicate with Bill and the artist had interpreted this in a painting. He said:

'I painted this in the autumn of 1991, when our problems were just starting. I was at an exhibition in London when Heol Fanog came to mind; and a very peculiar picture started to emerge. It was a web of closely entangled thicket with thorns and faces peering out of it, crying, yelling and screaming. I immediately began work on a painting. I wasn't aware of what I was doing when I painted it. It's only just made sense to me.'

It was late in the afternoon and we had to leave. Eddie told Liz and Bill to call if they had any more problems. I asked Bill whether he thought any good had come out of their ordeal.

'Until Eddie came here, no-one could do anything to help us. It's not like having squatters – at least you can try to get them out with a court order. We had to rely on ministers, priests and psychics. Our family, friends and neighbours abandoned us and we felt completely helpless. We just prayed to God for help. Eddie has brought the light back here.'

The day after our visit to Heol Fanog, Eddie called me to say that James Griffiths, the young man who had been hanged, had also been in contact with him. Bill Rich had called him and said that the atmosphere in the farmhouse had changed overnight and they were concerned that something else was amiss. As soon as Eddie heard

Bill's voice, he realized that he would have to fit one last piece into the jigsaw.

Griffiths told Eddie that he had, in fact, been duped by the Satanists; they had told him not to be afraid of going to the scaffold as they would use their magical powers to rescue him before the trapdoor was opened. So he had said nothing in his defence, and up to his final moments had waited for them to rescue him. No help had come and he was trapped by the injustice of his death. Eddie sensed his fear:

I am beginning to feel pressure on my larynx as a rope is put round my neck. This is the young man who was hanged for murder. He is terribly upset. 'I didn't know which I feared most, those people threatening me or the hanging,' he says. 'I'd seen what they could do. They told me that if I said nothing they would use their magic powers to free me from the hanging. I believed them right up to the moment I dropped. They tricked and betrayed me – they sacrificed me. I didn't realize how wicked they were.'

He is wringing his hands in grief and anger and he is starting to cry. I am aware of his parents, who are invisible as yet to him, and they, too, are weeping. Now the father says: 'Come with us, you need to be away from this place.' The light begins to grow in front of the young man. His father is trying to calm him, but he can't hear him. Now he steps across the threshold of light and see his parents. There is a great outpouring of feelings and his father says: 'Now let's move out of this place,' and the three of them walk off into the light. Let's wish them Godspeed and let them go.

A few weeks later, I called Bill. He said the oppressive atmosphere had lifted and that life was slowly getting back to normal. Best of all, he had started to work on a new painting and had sold another to an art dealer in London. The phone was ringing again. Bill cut our conversation short as he had to dash out to meet someone. At last he could look forward to happier days at Heol Fanog.

Chapter 8

Repeated Nightmares

Lead, Kindly Light, amid the encircling gloom,
Lead thou me on;

The night is dark, and I am far from home,
Lead thou me on.

John Henry Newman, 'Lead, Kindly Light'

For most people, ghosts are inextricably linked with haunted houses. Imaginations can run riot in a deserted house or an eerie place where the atmosphere is highly charged. Who has not felt a shiver run down their spine as they walk alone through a derelict house or an overgrown graveyard? But sometimes it is not the place, but *the person living there* that is the trigger for supernatural activity.

In his work as a ghosthunter Eddie has come across many ordinary people living unexceptional lives who have suddenly found a ghost in their midst. Slowly, the ghost has alerted them to its presence and, having realized that something is wrong, they have sought help. In most cases, that was the end of the matter. Once the ghost had been cleared from their lives, they returned to their normal routine. In rare cases, however, another ghost arrives to fill the vacuum left by a departing entity. Sometimes ghosts follow the people who attracted them to other houses – even in different countries – in a desperate effort to be recognized and

130

helped. Eddie has met people who have attracted ghosts like a magnet. In a few cases, the original contact was made when the person visited a particular place or house; once it was released another ghost simply took its place. It seems that some people act as temporary 'hosts' for entities, offering them a safe haven until he arrives on the scene to release them.

I have termed this phenomenon 'serial haunting'; in the two cases in this chapter Eddie was recalled time after time to release spirits haunting the same people. Both cases feature ordinary individuals, living busy lives; none wanted to deal with a string of unwanted ghosts in their houses. But they now realize that they attracted them because they were themselves psychic – although at the time they did not know this.

Joanne's story

Joanne Silverwood tried to look enthusiastic when her husband, Simon, showed her their new three-bedroomed house in May 1987. Number 9 Riverside Walk was one of the biggest houses on the new estate in Bottesford, near Lincoln, but Joanne felt uneasy as she walked up the drive and through the freshly decorated rooms. It was unusually dark for a new house, she thought, and it felt cold, even though the sun was shining outside. Perhaps she was imagining it; perhaps it was just that she was annoyed with her husband, who had bought the house for cash at auction, without consulting her. She would just have to accept it. Three weeks later, on 12 June, Joanne and Simon moved in with their two-week-old baby son, Nick.

Joanne was twenty-two years old; small and dark-haired, she had been born in Lincoln and had worked as a secretary and part-time hairdresser until her baby son was born. Her friends described her then as warm and extrovert. Today she says she is nothing more than a shell of her former self. Divorced, with two small children and shattered nerves, she only just managed to sell the house in spring 1994.

At 11 p.m. on their first night in the house, Joanne and Simon sat back and surveyed the mountain of boxes in their living room; it would take days for them to sort everything out. At midnight they decided to go to bed and Joanne popped her head around her son's bedroom door; Nick lay there sleeping, his tiny hands clutching a teddy bear. Then she went to bed, where her husband was already asleep. Five minutes later she was lost in a confusion of dreams. Suddenly she awoke; she felt as though her breath was being sucked out of her body and a dark, heavy body was pressing down on her, suffocating her. 'Someone is suffocating me!' she screamed aloud to her husband. He tried to comfort her and said she was just exhausted by the move. After an hour or so, she fell into an uneasy slumber.

In the following months Joanne noticed other strange things about the house. It felt oppressive; her son's bedroom had cold patches which no amount of heating could warm up; the light-bulbs often blew when she walked past; and she heard footsteps upstairs when no-one else was in the house. She also had the unmistakable feeling of someone unseen watching her as she went about her daily routine. Joanne tried to ignore all this. She now had more pressing concerns: a new baby daughter and a husband she strongly suspected of being unfaithful.

Simon left her a year later, and it was only when her baby son's life was put in danger that she was forced to confront the reality of the haunting. 'I had to take in ironing to make ends meet,' said Joanne, 'and I would do this late at night when the children were asleep. One night I felt a hand touch my shoulder as I walked downstairs to the living room. Seconds later, all the light-bulbs in the hall blew and I heard the sound of a man rushing downstairs.

'I ran into the living room, picked up a poker and searched the hall for an intruder. I prayed to God that he would not harm me or my children, but when I looked I could find no sign of a break-in. Then Nick walked out of his bedroom and stood at the top of the stairs; a moment later I saw him tumble down the stairs, as if an invisible hand had pushed him. He lay there, crying, his head bleeding and bruised. I decided then that things had gone far enough.'

The next day, Joanne called a friend who suggested that she perform an exorcism. The two women, both Catholics, sprinkled water from their local church font in every corner of the house and held a crucifix above their heads, declaring: 'A curse on you, evil spirit. Leave this house. I cast you into the dark regions of hell.' For a while, the atmosphere improved; but after two weeks, she sensed a presence again. The next day, the figure of a man materialized before her eyes in the living room.

'I was terrified. I am very down-to-earth, but this really did scare the life out of me,' said Joanne. 'I realized that he was angry; there was a nasty, oppressive feeling in the house which I'd never felt before. I think our attempts at exorcism – calling him an evil spirit – had done this. Then the local spiritualist church told me about Eddie.'

Eddie arrived at Joanne's house on 1 September 1989. As soon as he entered it, he realized that he was dealing with a very angry spirit. He silently asked the entity to come closer and let him help. A second entity approached, who was concerned to help the earthbound spirit on his way.

I have an intermediary here who is anxious to move someone trapped at earth level. A man is trapped, someone who suffered a lot during his life and who is very bitter about the experience. He seems to have been attacked a number of times during his life, but I don't know why. I've got to gain his confidence; he's not evil, but he is misguided.

You [Joanne] have tried to exorcise him. This drove him away for a while into the darkness and then he found his way back here again. He suspects that I, too, am going to drive him back into the darkness again.

I think he was something of an outcast; he lived on the outskirts of the village and was blamed for everything that went wrong there. He had a rather strange manner and the villagers suspected him of practising witchcraft. He was pinioned to a piece of timber attached to a long pole and dumped in the river. He drowned. I get the year 1270.

In his life no-one would listen to him. He was stoned a number of times and the only way he could fend off his attackers was to pretend he really did have the supernatural powers they thought he possessed. He had an ungainly way of walking which set him apart from others from an early age.

133

He has tried to stay in this area, but he resents the houses that have been built here – he wants you to move away. He has learned to manipulate your [Joanne's] psychic energies to cause disturbances in the house.

I'm getting a glimpse of him now; he's wearing very ragged clothing and a dull brown hat. I can now see the hovel where he lived; I think he used to light a fire in the winter just outside the door – this also helped him see who was approaching. Another thing that angered the villagers was the fact that he befriended stray dogs – they were his only companions in life. He never went to church – he was not allowed in – so people regarded him as an evil man. His life was devoid of any love or affection.

He is recalling his mother now and remembering her calling his name. 'Thomas,' she says. The voice has stopped for a moment and he is wondering if he has imagined it, but it has set him thinking about the only time when life was tolerable – while she was alive – and for the time being he is laying aside his bitterness. Now he is becoming aware of a growing feeling of love. Two men are approaching him – friars, I think. They stand a little way off until he is ready to accept them. One of them says: 'Come, Thomas, it is time.' He is not sure what to make of this. 'Come, Thomas, you remember me,' says the other. His mind is going back to the time when a passing friar stopped to speak to him when he was a little boy. His mother had given the friar a drink and he had spent a little time talking to Thomas, telling him about the world beyond the village. Thomas had said: 'I'd like to be like you and go to other places.' He'd forgotten this until now.

He is now willing to trust. He goes forward and the friar embraces him, saying: 'Thomas, you have a long journey to make, but we will go with you.' He's gone now and he will never return here.

Eddie advised Joanne to pray regularly and ask God to bring a purifying light into the house. 'He warned me never to be complacent,' she said. 'I could act as a magnet for other trapped souls, so I had to make sure that the atmosphere was always clear and pure.'

134

For a couple of months Joanne followed Eddie's instructions and the atmosphere remained calm. At the time, she was working as a secretary in an estate agent's office during the day and singing in clubs during the evening. In November, two months after Eddie's first visit, she felt the familiar touch of a hand on her back while she was singing her last song of the evening. During the period of Thomas's haunting, she had become accustomed to the hand tapping her; it was a warning that something was about to happen.

The following day, Joanne felt unwell at work. She decided to take the evening off. At 10 p.m. she sat down to the watch the television; she dozed off and was then woken at midnight by the burglar alarm. She checked for intruders, but found none; puzzled, she went to the kitchen to make herself a snack. She returned to the living room and was about to take a bite when the ghostly figures of a man and woman materialized before her eyes.

'The woman sat on the sofa and the man stood next to her. They were young and dressed smartly; he was wearing a dark blazer and slacks and she was wearing a pale dress,' said Joanne. 'A few seconds later they disappeared.' Joanne got the impression that they were full of fun. 'My father practised the occult and I grew up thinking that all spirits were evil. Yet I did not pick up any bad feelings from this couple. They seemed to be laughing and joking and urging me to join in their pranks.'

Joanne called Eddie the next day. Contrary to popular belief, it is very rare for a spirit to materialize in front of someone, as this requires a great deal of energy which the spirit has to draw from its host. Eddie was intrigued; he had never come across a case where two entities had materialized at the same time.

At 6 p.m. on 12 November, 1989, Eddie again pressed the doorbell of 9 Riverside Walk. Joanne, dressed in a pink jumper and leggings, opened the door, flanked by Nick and Victoria, her two children. Eddie settled into a chair, closed his eyes and waited for a contact.

I get the feeling of someone who was very extrovert in life, who indulged in innocent pranks at times, but who is now very frustrated. He feels as if he has gone down a cul-de-sac and can't get out at the far end; he can't go back, either. He has someone else with him, a woman, I think. He has been up to some mischief here; he was showing his companion a few tricks and amusing himself. The more frustrated he became, the more mischievous he got; that was intended to make you [Joanne] take notice of him. These two people are not earthbound, but nearly so; I need to find out why they haven't moved on yet.

I think they are fairly contemporary; I am getting the impression of the late 1920s or early 1930s. I think they died in a car accident. He lost control on a bend and the car crashed into a tree; the front of the car is badly crumpled. They were very close in life and I think that is why she has stayed with him. I don't think that either of them realized what had happened at the time. They died instantly and wandered away from the car, hand in hand, to find someone to tow the car away. But after a while they forgot their original intention and started to explore the area surrounding the crash. They discovered that they could make contact with living people; I think they have come here to seek help from you [Joanne].

If I can get the man free his companion will go with him. We have to hold them in the light and project love towards them. Good God, the car is here – it's gleaming white and polished. The man knows that he must drive it away and he's very excited about this. Both of them get into the car; it starts by itself, which delights them. He can see a road stretching ahead of him, wide enough to take the car, with a fence on the left and a stream to the right. The road leads off to a plain and then winds into the distance. Somewhere along the road a group of people is waiting for them; when they reach that, they will no longer need the car.

★

Joanne managed to keep the hauntings at bay for the next five years. Several times she felt the warning touch on her arm, but she managed to avert any further intrusions by regular prayers. During that time she divorced her husband and found a new boyfriend,

Gary, a policeman, who came to live with her at Riverside Walk. For a time it seemed that life was finally working out for her. She enjoyed her job as a secretary and was happy in her relationship. The last thing she wanted now was to have to deal with another haunting. In spring 1994, however, she recognized the familiar signs. She felt a pair of invisible eyes watching her every move in the house; her son had again complained of cold spots in his bedroom; and the lights in the house were regularly going on and off by themselves.

On the evening of 11 May 1994, Joanne felt a hand touch her shoulder-blade. She tried to ignore it and carried on with her housework, tidying the kitchen and preparing he children's packed lunches. But an hour later she felt an excruciating pain course down her back and legs. 'I just fell to the floor in absolute agony,' she said. 'I could not bear the pain – I just begged God to take it away.' When the pain finally subsided, Joanne staggered to the living room, wondering what was happening to her. 'Then I noticed two light-bulbs blow and the television screen flickered and the hand was on my back once more.

'I suddenly got a strong urge to call my sister, Rosemary. I don't know why; we're not close, in fact we rarely speak, but I felt an overwhelming need to talk to her. When I rang she told me she had just received some very bad news. A close friend of hers, a Greek man, had just been tragically killed in a car crash; his wife and child had also been injured,' said Joanne. Shortly after this conversation Joanne called Eddie, who agreed to meet her the next day. He sensed that the spirit needed urgent attention and would grow angry, and even violent.

At 10 a.m. the next day, Eddie visited Joanne for the third time. She was a normal, busy, young mother, yet she seemed to be plagued by troubled souls more than anyone else he had ever met. She was undoubtedly psychic, but there had to be another reason for these repeated disturbances. Eddie closed his eyes and rested his hands on his knees, palms upwards; his breathing settled into a regular, deep rhythm and he urged the spirit to approach. 'I am here. Let me help you in the name of God,' he said silently. A voice in his head told him to ask Joanne to join him as she could be of help, so he beckoned her to sit down with him.

I have a man with me who wants to be helped. I think it is the man you were talking about, the Greek. He's asking for reassurance that I can help him; he says: 'I don't want to be hanging around like this any longer. I don't want to be stuck, I want to get away, but I don't know how to.'

I'm going to ask him to stay calm and tell me about his death. He doesn't remember much about the accident, just the terrible impact and then nothing. His first thoughts were for his family; he didn't want to leave them the worries of his business. He couldn't understand what had happened at first, but then he realized that he was in the next life. He didn't take the opportunity to move on; he stayed behind because he was worried about his family and his business. It shouldn't be too difficult to move him on, but he has got to let go of the anxiety he's feeling – and the frustration.

He's asking: 'What's happened to my child?' I think the child is recovering, but I don't want to focus on the child too much or I'll lose contact with him. I have to ask him to be patient. Somebody is trying to reassure him that he will be taken to see his child if he will only relax. A man is approaching who says: 'I will show you the child, then you must leave. This is not the right place for you to be.' The man is taking him along a path and after a while they sit down. He helps the man see his child, who is playing quite happily. They are now going on an upward path towards the light – I think we can let them go now.

Eddie watched the spirit of the young man leave for a few moments while Joanne telephoned her sister. Rosemary told her that although the father went straight through the windscreen and died instantly, the child hit the dashboard and broke his jaw; he was recovering slowly, but he would be all right. When Eddie was confident that the young man had finally gone, he turned his mind to Joanne. Before he opened his eyes, he asked his spirit guide why he had been drawn to her so repeatedly. Slowly, the answer filtered into his consciousness: Joanne's role was to act as a magnet for lost souls and maintain them in a spiritual holding position until Eddie could release them. He was impressed by her sensitivity and help in the release they had just performed. Was she perhaps, he wondered, to be one of the next generation of ghosthunters?

Joanne admitted that this thought had crossed her own mind: 'I am sure that I have been chosen to do this work myself one day,' she said. 'But at the moment I am happy to watch and learn. What strikes me most strongly about Eddie is the way he has no fear. I worry that I may not be able to protect myself from evil.'

In June 1994, a month after Eddie's last visit, Joanne moved to a house on an estate not far from her old home, which had taken nearly three years to sell. In 1994 Joanne was visiting her local spiritualist church regularly and studying books on the spirit world; she believed that an opportunity to release troubled souls would come to her one day. She was also sure that she had to build up her psychic protection through regular meditation and prayer. 'After all, Eddie may not be there to help me with the next ghost,' she said.

Neil and Stephanie's story

Eddie has defined a ghost as an 'earthbound spirit', a soul that is trapped close to the earth and is unable to move on to the next world. Earthbound they may be, but they are not necessarily tied to a particular place; they seem to be able to travel freely in their earthbound state. This phenomenon became apparent to Eddie in the summer of 1993, when he received a request for help from a couple in Lancashire.

For eighteen months Neil Barton, an insurance salesman, and his wife Stephanie, a journalist, had had terrible luck. They had experienced repeated break-ins, burst pipes and floods at their home in Preston; most of the electrical items in their house, including the television, video, washing machine, iron and hairdryers, had broken down; their car windscreen had shattered three times in a month, once nearly causing a crash; and they and their teenaged daughter had suffered from impaired memory and depression.

Stephanie Barton had racked her brain a thousand times for a reason for these disturbances. In the end, the only new thing she could identify was the purchase, in 1988, of a holiday home in France. Stephanie and Neil had paid £17,000 for the property, a derelict barn outside Calvados, Normandy. It had never been lived in, so the Bartons had drawn up plans to convert it. Renovations began late in 1991 and were complete by Easter 1992. Stephanie believes now that their problems can be traced to the start of the renovations and that they somehow disturbed an entity there.

However, it was in Lancashire that the family had suffered the effects of the disturbance; the ghost, she deduced, had attached itself to them in France and had returned to haunt them in England. She recalled how their house in Preston had suddenly become oppressive and the family had begun to feel unwell. She said:

'On a few occasions my husband, who is quite sensitive, saw a dark shadow in the house out of the corner of his eye. It's as though something fastened itself on to us and then tried to attract our attention by disrupting our lives.'

Before she heard about Eddie, Stephanie, who belongs to the Church of England, had called a Catholic priest into the house; he had performed an exorcism and asked for the absolution of the entity's soul, but the atmosphere only lightened for a few days. In July 1992 they returned to France, determined to get to the bottom of the problem. They found the door jammed and had to force their way in. 'Inside, there was a heavy atmosphere, and a rancid smell filled every room, even though it had been freshly decorated,' said Stephanie. 'My daughter immediately said it was haunted.'

They feared that they would have to sell the house in Normandy. Then a friend told Stephanie about Eddie. She wrote to him, explaining the circumstances of the haunting and enclosing photographs of the house during different stages of renovation. Eddie received Stephanie's letter on 23 November 1993 and contacted her. He explained that he could only help the entity if he was in direct contact with Stephanie or her husband, and that it was quite normal for him to work over the telephone. He then asked her to write down what he said:

It's the last war. I see images of fighting – German soldiers. It seems to be just after the D-Day landings. There is an entity

140

here who seems desperate to get away. You [Stephanie] offered him some psychic light and he attached himself to you. He's made a desperate effort to make his presence known. On the other side is a woman who is connected with him in some way – a Frenchwoman, she may be his mother.

This man suffered a very unpleasant death. He was suspected of being a Resistance member. I can see a rope around his neck, with a knot on one side – it's awful. I think he was hoisted on a rope by three Gestapo officers and strangled. He's very distressed as he relives this memory. They have also broken his legs; poor devil, he was in terrible pain and just wanted to die. He says they would not believe that he knew nothing.

He's telling me that he's confused; he thinks he may have lived in the house, but everything seems to be in a fog. He tells me they broke his shins with a club. He's growing quieter now, calming down. He's on his feet and feeling relieved already. I think he's going to be put to sleep and taken away – he's gone through so much already. He will be taken to a hospital where streams of coloured light will flood through the windows and heal him.

His mother is waiting for him now. He's very quiet and the light is moving towards him, as though it's pushing back the darkness. She is full of compassion and love. He is so utterly exhausted that he doesn't know what is happening to him. Now his mother is by his side and the angelic beings are coming to take charge, helping him move towards the light. He's gone now.

After the initial contact with Eddie, Stephanie noticed an immediate improvement. 'It was as if a fog had lifted; for the first time in over a year I could think clearly, remember things, plan ahead,' she said. 'I thought that was the end of it. I had enough to do trying to pull the family back together without having to deal with a haunting.' Yet during the next two months Stephanie and Neil had to deal with not one, but four, more ghosts.

★

Less than three weeks after her first call to Eddie, Stephanie again needed help. In early December she had noticed the atmosphere deteriorating once more: her husband was distant and confused, she was irritable, and their fifteen-year-old daughter Alice was becoming difficult. Neil and Stephanie had decided not to tell her about the haunting; Alice had sensed that they were hiding something and had become withdrawn, until neither parent knew what to do with her. Now she was threatening to leave home.

On 13 December 1993 matters had reached crisis point. Stephanie called Eddie the following day, who again asked her to note down what he said. It seemed to him that another ghost had filled the vacuum of the last. The new entity also originated in France; however, this one pre-dated the first haunting. It was as if the Bartons were peeling back several layers of hauntings, like old wallpaper. The entities had attached themselves to the Bartons, whom they saw as their only hope of release. Eddie told Stephanie:

I think it's someone who's been trapped for a long time; it goes back a lot further than the last war. I think it's a gypsy – a man who was shot for stealing a chicken. There's a lot of ill-feeling here; the man who owned a house near yours had had a lot of trouble with gypsies and warned them to keep away. He had no compunction in shooting them. I think he had served as a soldier during the Napoleonic wars.

The entity I have seen with me is a young man; he thought he could get away with it, but the owner was lying in wait for him. He bears no malice towards the man who shot him – he regarded it as a bit of a challenge, a duel, and he lost. What's holding him back is the fact that his wife was expecting a child when he died; the agony of knowing that he had left her at such a critical time is the reason why he's trapped. He seems to be very angry with himself, and remorseful, for taking a chance. He has stayed behind to be with her.

He's beginning to sense that freedom is close and he's getting quite excited – he's jumping for joy and doing a little dance. I'm waiting to see who will come for him; I've got to hold him until we can get him away, but he's got an urge to go wandering again. Wait, I think a brother and sister of his

142

are coming to take him away; they've brought with them a
gipsy caravan and he's walking off now. They're going to
follow a track and this will lead them to their heaven. He'll be
very happy now.

Eddie explained to a baffled Stephanie what had happened. 'Your
house in France has been the scene of at least two murders; a
violent murder can leave a psychic imprint – or stain – on a place
that in time will attract more of the same activity,' he said. 'You
and your husband are drawing the entities to you because you are
both very psychic – next time you visit you will notice an awakening
in the house and in yourselves.'

Three days after this conversation, Eddie became aware of
another presence. He realized that this communication was the
next layer of haunting he had to deal with, as it pre-dated the gypsy
he had released on 14 December. As soon as he sensed the spirit
voice coming through, he picked up his pen and wrote:

Someone is very anxious to make themselves known to me.
It's a woman, I think. She's on the verge of tears and is
asking: 'Why have I carried this sorrow for so long?' She saw
something happen and she had to keep quiet about it. I think
the period is early eighteenth century. She saw a murder. 'I
am wretched, wretched,' she says. I think her brothers
committed the murder and the guilt of not revealing it to
anyone caused her to be trapped. 'Why have I carried this for
so long?' she asks. She is wringing her hands and says: 'They
swore me to silence on the Bible, otherwise I fear that they
could have done away with me, too. So I held my tongue and
paid a heavy price.'

Her brothers enticed a man to their house, killed him and
buried the body nearby. She said: 'It was an evil deed, but my
silence made me party to it. Help me out of this hell.' I see
her now stepping out of the gloom and into the light. She
stretches and is beginning to feel better already. She tells me
that sorrow over the deed prevented her from marrying. I get
the impression that the victim, a gamekeeper, had also
witnessed something. She says: 'May God forgive them, for

he was a good man. They sent me out of the room – I knew
they were going to do it.'

She is wearing a dress with padding and her long, dark hair
is arranged in a bun. She asks: 'Am I to go now?' We have to
tell her to wait, as someone must come for her. It's the
gamekeeper; he is wearing a colourful top-coat and a top hat.
He greets her and holds out his hand. There is great warmth
between them and I think she is very relieved to see him.
They've gone now.

Eddie decided to wait a few days before he told the Bartons about
this latest incident. He felt that more entities were waiting to come
through who were somehow connected with the woman's release
on 17 December. He was right. At 4 p.m. on 21 December the
woman's two brothers – the men who had killed the gamekeeper
and forced her to stay silent – came through to ask him for help.

I have a man with me who is quite confident that we are
going to get him away. His brother is here too. I was
wondering whether this brother was the one who committed
the murder. 'We shared equally in the deed,' he says. 'It's
time the affair was closed. We have suffered enough.' The
gamekeeper is here too: 'Be not afraid, for I have forgiven
all. In our forgiveness we set aside God's wrath.'

One of the brothers is hanging back, out of fear, perhaps.
If we can bring him forward, the two of them will be able to
leave together. The reluctant one is closing in now and their
sister has joined them. She says: 'It is the love of Christ that
you must seek, for through this the wounds between us have
now been healed.'

I'm aware now of a light increasing, almost like the sun
coming up over the horizon. I'm seeing the sister together
with her two brothers and she's urging the gamekeeper to
join them. They are all holding hands. I think they can see
the figure of Christ approaching them. The two brothers are
weeping now, completely overcome by the turn in events.
The figure of Christ is walking towards the light; they walk in
line, following the figure into the light.

144

Happily, the Bartons were not visited by any more ghosts after Eddie's final communication in December 1993. Today, late in 1994, they are rebuilding their lives; they still have the house in France, although they rarely visit it and have not managed to let it for the holiday season. But Stephanie says they have learnt a lot:

'I wonder if our lives will ever be the same. What most people don't understand about this kind of thing is the isolation. It is impossible to talk to anyone – friends or family – about a problem like this. If one of us had been ill or made redundant, we might have got some understanding; if you say your house is haunted everyone thinks you are mad. People should be warned that it can happen to them too – and the effect can be devastating.'

Chapter 9

The Sicilian Job

Lasciate ogni speranza voi ch'entrate.

(All hope abandon, ye who enter here.)

Dante Alighieri, *Divina Commedia*

January 1982

Dr Faustina Raciti unlocked the heavy wooden door of the elegant eighteenth-century house at 199 Via Vittorio Emanuele and walked into the spacious hall. She stood at the foot of the staircase for a few moments thinking about how far she had come since her divorce. Times had been hard then; for years she had put up with her husband's fierce Sicilian temper and jealousy. Alone, she had supported the family by working ten hours a day as a clinical haematologist. Her career had flourished, but her marriage had died. She had left him and found an apartment in town for herself and her two daughters. Now, four years later, she had saved enough money to buy the stone-built house in her home town of Acireale, eastern Sicily. At forty-six, her successful practice had made her a rich woman and her two daughters, Rosaria, twenty-three, and Valentina, five, were happy and stable. Life, it seemed, had turned out well for her after all.

As Faustina climbed the stairs to the first floor, she thought about the hard work ahead; she had planned to convert the first floor into her lab and office and use the top two floors as an apartment. This was the main reason why she had bought the house – for years she had longed to set up her own clinic at home to avoid driving through the congested roads of Acireale. The upper floors had not been used for over thirty years as the previous owners, an elderly man and his two sisters, had been confined to the ground floor.

Suddenly there was a loud knock on the door. Faustina ran downstairs and opened it; her furniture had arrived and was being unloaded off the lorry in the street, causing chaos and confusion in the traffic. Ignoring the blare of horns, she gestured to the workmen and instructed them to take everything to the second floor.

February 1982

Within a few weeks, Faustina and her daughters were settled in the house. The laboratory was functioning and Faustina had begun to receive patients. She had decided to do some building work in the apartment upstairs, and was waiting for planning permission from the local council. Rosaria had joined the clinic as an administrator and their patient list was growing by the week.

But Faustina felt strangely dispirited, as if her life were spiralling downwards and out of control. She shrugged this off and put her feelings down to tiredness.

August 1982

It was late in the evening and Faustina was sitting on a stool in her lab, her head in her hands. She had been feeling dizzy since that morning and now she had a blinding headache; it must be the lack of air, she thought to herself. As she walked to the door, a stabbing pain shot through the back of her head and made her cry out loud.

Upstairs, she took a painkiller and lay down on her bed. She closed her eyes and tried to blank out the pain; black shapes darted across her field of vision and she had the strange sensation of falling into a spinning vortex. Suddenly, she sat up with a start. What was wrong with her? Was this a bad dream or was she going mad? After a few moments, she slumped back and fell into a fitful sleep, full of disturbing dreams.

December 1982

On Christmas Eve, Faustina and her daughters attended Midnight

Mass in the tiny church of Aci Platani, a few kilometres outside the town. Nodding to her neighbours, she sat down in a pew close to the front of the church and knelt down to pray.

'Lord, give me the strength to carry on. I feel so weak and I am anxious about my health. Who will support Rosaria and Valentina if I am struck down? I come each day to church to pray and thank you for all my blessings. Please help me, Lord.'

Faustina crossed herself and rose to her feet. Although she had said nothing to her daughters, she felt that her energy was being drained out of her. She could not understand it; she looked after herself, but still she felt weak and listless. She hoped God would listen to her prayers.

March 1983
Two of Faustina's staff had resigned. At first they would not explain why; but after she pressed them, one had said that he felt uncomfortable in the house. His colleague, a woman, agreed; she had been uneasy from the day she had started work at the laboratory, and in recent weeks she had felt nauseous and depressed. They would not be drawn any further; they urged Faustina to ask her other staff if she wanted to know more.

Faustina watched as they both crossed themselves before they packed up their belongings and left. She had felt the same uneasiness, although she did not admit it to either of them. Curious, she asked a young technician if they had said anything to him. He told her that the previous afternoon, when Faustina had gone into town, they had heard the sound of footsteps on the stairs. One had called to Faustina; when no reply came, he had walked over to where the sound had come from and had found no-one there. A few minutes later they had heard the sound of someone groaning in the lab.

Faustina was shocked. Was it a ghost? Of course not, she reasoned, and immediately got back to work.

November 1983
Valentina had woken Faustina in the early hours of the morning, screaming and shaking. It was only a nightmare, her mother had assured her. But the little girl was convinced that someone was in

her room and she refused to be left alone. Faustina allowed the frightened child to sleep in her bed that night, and as she lay in the dark listening to Valentina's muffled sobs she wondered what her daughter had really seen.

Faustina's health had not improved. She was tired and irritable and her work was suffering. On top of this, another woman had left, unable to cope with the bad atmosphere in the lab. With only three staff, she was unable to process as many tests as she needed to earn a living. The building work on the house was proving difficult; since they had moved in almost two years ago, they had been living in four small rooms.

April 1984

The clinic was not doing well. Faustina's failing health had made it impossible for her to work for more than three days each week and physicians in the town were not referring as many patients to her. It was a vicious circle; without the income from the patients, she could not buy enough chemicals for her clinical tests, and so could treat only a few patients.

She still went to Mass each day and confession on Sundays. Each week she would pour her heart out to the priest, who would listen intently to the story of her declining practice. 'Have faith,' was all he would say. 'You are being tested.'

January 1985

Faustina had obtained as much credit as she could, but she had practically no referrals now and her income had dwindled to nothing. If something did not happen soon, she would have to close the practice altogether.

Halfway through the month, Faustina's close friend Maria died suddenly. Maria had stood by Faustina and supported her, both financially and emotionally. She was devastated by the loss. A few days after Maria's death, Rosaria noticed a strange mark on the front door of the house. She showed her mother, who examined it carefully; it looked like a small cross, and the black marks around its edges suggested that it had been burnt into the wood. Rosaria told her mother that she was sure something was happening in the house that was beyond their control.

149

'Whenever anyone says anything bad about the house, something awful seems to happen,' Rosaria said. 'I think we need an exorcist.' Faustina, a devout Catholic, blanched. 'Never,' she cried, 'say that again.'

September 1985
Faustina had tried over the months to ignore her elder daughter's warnings. It had occurred to her, too, that the house might be at the root of all their problems, but she had always refused to believe it was actually haunted. In the end, her own experiences slowly forced her to accept the truth. She was awoken from a deep sleep one night by the sound of heavy footsteps on the landing outside her door; terrified that it was an intruder, she grabbed her bedside lamp to defend herself and peered into the hall. No-one was there. In a cold sweat she climbed back into bed, wondering if she had imagined it all. The next night, the same thing happened; and again, two days later.

She said nothing to her daughters, fearing it would disturb them, but a few weeks later Valentina rushed, sobbing, into her mother's office. She had just seen a black snake slithering across her bedroom floor and begged Faustina to kill it. Faustina called a neighbour, but they found no trace of the snake in the room, even though the child had slammed the door behind her. Again and again during the next month, Valentina claimed the snake was in her room.

February 1986
Strange things continued to happen. One morning Faustina went into her lab to find an overpowering, rancid smell coming from the sinks. As she got close, she saw that they were overflowing with vomit. She rushed out and was sick. It was impossible, she thought; no-one had set foot in the lab the previous day. It took the plumber three days to unblock the drains.

Faustina knew that she had to do something, but by February 1986 her financial problems were so severe that she was on the verge of a breakdown and bankruptcy. Faustina was terrified; if she were declared bankrupt, she could be struck off the medical list and her career would be over. Time was running out.

July 1987
From being one of the wealthiest and most respected members of Acireale's community, Faustina had become an outcast. Staff who had left the practice had told friends and family about the strange happenings at 199 Via Vittorio Emanuele and rumours began to spread that the house was haunted. Friends crossed to the other side of the street when they saw her.

The humiliation was complete one day in July when she went to the bank in the town. As she chatted to the cashier, she noticed that his calculator had started to tap out numbers by itself; ignoring it, she carried on talking, until it burst into life, punching out a whole list of numbers on the paper roll. Aghast, the cashier threw the machine on the floor. As Faustina left the bank she felt as though every pair of eyes was watching her.

Faustina walked straight to the church and asked to see a priest. She explained her problem and begged him to exorcize the house. The priest agreed and performed the ceremony later that day, sprinkling holy water in each room and asking for any lost soul to leave the house. But it made no difference; after a few days, the footsteps returned and Valentina saw dark shadows in the house again.

December 1987
In December Faustina and her daughters moved out of the house. In desperation, and against her Catholic faith, she had taken several mediums to the house; without exception they had told her that unless she left the house it would destroy her health. The best thing she could do, they said, was to close the door and walk away.

Rosaria, by now twenty-eight, found a small apartment in the town, while Faustina and Valentina moved into a small house near the laboratory. It was not ideal, but Faustina began to feel a little stronger. A month later, as she was flicking through the magazine *Gente*, her eyes were drawn to a small article. The reporter had interviewed psychics in several European countries about their work, including Eddie Burks in England. With growing excitement, Faustina read how he specialized in releasing trapped souls, particularly those who haunted houses. She immediately called the magazine and the next day she posted a letter to Eddie, explaining her story.

★

Eddie pored over the photographs on his kitchen table. Three or four showed a yellow limestone house on a busy side-street with tall, shuttered windows on each of its three floors and wrought-iron balconies. The rest of the pictures showed the interior of a sparsely furnished room: tall ceilings, white walls and three wooden doors. On one wall was a fireplace; facing it, an elegant chaise-longue. Viewed from the other side, three tall windows pierced the room, overlooking the street below.

He picked up Dr Raciti's letter and read it again. There was no doubt in his mind that the house was haunted, but he simply could not spare the time to travel to Sicily. Yet he would clearly have to do something; 'Please, please help me,' she had written. 'You are now my only hope.' He studied the pictures carefully and then closed his eyes; he was getting the impression of a group of men.

I sense a gang of about six men. There's a feeling of intrigue and conspiracy around them. Some are carrying daggers in their belts, with blades of about seven inches. I think they have committed a robbery; they were dividing spoils, but then they had an argument and fell out. There's a lot of shouting going on and violence of some sort. One of them has been stabbed. A feeling of panic ensues – they are wondering how to cover up the stabbing and conceal the body. The victim is not dead; he is screaming and shouting and they have to do something to shut him up. I think they are leaving him to bleed to death and are taking the proceeds of the robbery with them. They hurry out of the house, careful not to attract too much attention to themselves.

I think they had used this room on a previous occasion to plan the robbery. I think they robbed a church of its treasure. It happened between 1922 and 1926, during the Mussolini era. The man they left to die is now haunting the house.

I am aware now of an Italian priest who has come to the

scene to make some observations. He says: 'None of these
men gained from their deeds; they died unhappy deaths
because greed took hold of them. The cause of unhappiness
in that house is the great weight of the guilt centred on it that
comes from their thoughts, fears and remorse. You [Eddie]
must deal with the man in the house. I [the priest in spirit]
will seek out the others and minister to them as well as I can,
for they do not understand your approach. They are still of
the Holy Church in spite of their wickedness. Rest assured
that they will be saved, though it could take a long time. It
was my church they robbed, you see. Thank you for reaching
this far into this sordid situation. It has needed unravelling for
a long time now.'

The priest makes the sign of the cross and bids farewell. He
is wearing a biretta and a black soutane. He has a strong
feeling of piety around him.

A few days later, on 10 March 1988, Eddie received another
message. He had been thinking about the man who had been
stabbed to death in Dr Raciti's house, when suddenly the man was
with him.

He says: 'Can God forgive me? I don't know what madness
overtook me. I am unholy. I was not given the last rites. I will
be consigned to torment. How is it I am still here? I can never
be forgiven.' I see him sitting on a bench with his head in his
hands. He is utterly miserable and without any hope. I must
ask for him to be surrounded with light.

I think he is about twenty-three years old – this is the age at
which he died. The other men quarrelled with him because he
had expressed regrets about his part in the robbery of the
church; he had told them that he wanted to confess. They
tried to dissuade him, but when they could not do this one of
them became very angry, lost his temper and stabbed him.

He is going over the experience now. Finally, he falls
asleep in utter weariness. I cannot hold on to him any longer.
[A few minutes later.] A priest is with him now. He is
sprinkling the man with holy water, saying: 'This will dissolve

153

his sins. I will care for him when he awakes. He has a journey
to make and I will accompany him. Your task is done. God's
blessing be upon you, my son.'

Eddie wrote to Dr Raciti the next day and explained the impressions he had received from the photographs. He was fairly certain,
he said, that the robbery had taken place between 1922 and 1926
and asked her if she would check local church records to see if there
was an account of a robbery then.

'If what I received is correct,' wrote Eddie, 'you should find that
the atmosphere in the house has changed or will begin to change for
the better. It may appear extraordinary to you that such a haunting
may be dealt with at a distance, but I have had some success with
this method. I hope you will now be able to make full use of your
beautiful house.'

Tears spilled down Faustina's cheeks as she read Eddie's letter;
she had long given up hope of anyone believing her. An orphan
from the age of sixteen, she had been brought up by a local priest,
Paolo Castorina, who had died over thirty years ago. Faustina
re-read Eddie's letter; it was formal but sympathetic, and she was
grateful for that. She immediately sat down to compose a reply.
'Dear Engineer,' she wrote, using the formal Italian address,
'Thank you for having written to me. At last I understand the
difficult problems surrounding my house; now I have some hope
that I may get rid of them one day. Thank you for your help. I hope
I can come to England soon to thank you personally.'

On 26 April, a week after receiving Dr Raciti's letter, Eddie was
aware of another presence connected with the house in Acireale. It
was a Catholic priest who had come to link him with the house.

I am aware of a priest; he says his name is Father Ignatius.
He wants me to accompany him [in my mind] around the
house, purifying each room in turn. He is scattering holy
water and the drops are falling on to the floor, producing
shimmering cascades of light. He tells me that the house
cannot be purified at the physical level unless it is also
cleansed at the spiritual level. We continue to walk around
the house. 'Good, the work is done,' he says.

In early June Eddie received a call from Dr Raciti in Sicily. She was excited and this made her English difficult to understand, but Eddie grasped that the atmosphere in the house had indeed improved and that Dr Raciti's clinic was taking off again.

Eddie heard no more from Dr Raciti until early September, when he received a note from her to say that she would be visiting England on 11 September with her daughter Rosaria. Eddie invited them to visit him in Nottingham and they arranged to come on the 24th, the day before they were due to return to Sicily. Over tea, Faustina revealed the reason for her visit. She opened her briefcase and extracted a sheaf of papers which she then handed to Eddie. 'I found these at Aci Platani Church, near Acireale,' she said. 'They are photocopies of church records that say that the church was ransacked and robbed on 26 November 1922. Get them translated – I think you will find them interesting.'

Eddie was astonished; of the many cases he had investigated, he had rarely received such proof of his accuracy. It was often impossible to trace the identity of the spirits he released, but in this case, it seemed, he had been absolutely right. And he had never visited Sicily in his life. Eddie arranged for a friend to translate the material she had brought for him. After lunch the following day, a strong image came into his mind; but this time, he was in the nineteenth century.

There was a fencing school in the house at one time – I think the nineteenth century. I am aware of a fencing master who took great pride in his school. I am also aware of some of his pupils who are showing off their postures. I think they are gathered in the room where the conspiracy and murder later took place. But a bout also took place in this room between two of the students. It got out of hand and turned into a duel. The man who lost realized that he was less skilled than his opponent, but he was too proud to acknowledge this. I think he was killed by a sword thrust through his throat.

It caused quite a scandal at the time and the fencing master was discredited for having allowed it to happen. After a while some rather dubious characters came to his school who wanted to learn fencing for the wrong reasons. The fencing master died a very unhappy and bitter man. I don't feel that any of this resulted in a haunting, but it left a psychic stain on this room.

I can see a horse and cart rumbling by now. It is collecting bodies; I think it is a time of plague, the eighteenth century. A whole family was wiped out in this house and its contents were looted. A pall of sadness fell over the house after this and there was some dispute over who would claim title to it. This is the root of the present atmosphere and we must go right back to this time to cleanse it. It will take time, but it can be done.

Later, Eddie settled down to read the translations of the material from Sicily:

We sadly inform you of the sacrilegious robbery of sacred objects on 26 November in Aci Platani and 27 December in St. Maria Ammalati and another attempt in Capomulini which failed by chance.

S.E. Rev. ma Mons. Vescovo went to the site of the sacrilege to hold a healing mass in Aci Platani on 8 December, and 31 December at Ammalati. Masses will be held in the main churches on the day chosen by the incumbent priest.

The Catholic Newspaper, December 1922

In the brief time since our Lord has sent me among you and during which I have had so much proof of your avowed faith which has edified and consoled me, I have also felt deep anguish in my heart. It is a diabolical premeditated plan that has been perpetrated in the last few days and a sacrilegious act that has intensely embittered every Christian soul . . . it is necessary that the conscience of the faithful shows a full protest in disgust and reparation for this atrocity offered to our Lord.

We invite then all the priests of the Diocese to conduct a Mass for the purpose in the month of January . . . And also we ask that these and other priests of the Church keep a great watch on the sacred objects and ask them to remind the people from the pulpit of the most serious punishments that are inflicted on the perpetrators of such profanities . . . Tremble, O unhappy ones at the thought of the punishment which will befall you if the crime with which you have stained yourselves manages to escape man's justice. It will not escape that of God, who will even more terribly strike you when his tolerance is exhausted, however great this is . . . Forgive Lord, forgive your people.

Sacred News, Acireale, 1 January 1923

Alfio Russo, aged 24, died a violent death on 26 November 1922.

Local records, Acireale

★

September 1992

Eddie looked through the windows of Faustina's dilapidated car as she wove in and out of the traffic on the choked streets of Catania like a madwoman. Huge, ugly buildings of grey volcanic stone rose from either side of the road and grimy baroque churches and palazzi cast their dark shadows over the town.

It was almost exactly four years since Faustina had first visited Eddie in Nottingham. She had been urging him to visit Sicily ever since, but until now he had not taken her up on her offer. As well as not being able to spare the time to go, Eddie had been concerned that Faustina might introduce him to everyone she knew on the island who might need psychic help. But he had never been to Sicily before, and in September he flew to Catania, the eastern part of the island, where he was met at the airport by Faustina, Rosaria and Valentina, who took him to his hotel in town.

Compared with the capital Palermo, with its Arab–Norman churches and Byzantine streets, Catania is an ugly city. Dominated by the soaring peaks of Mount Etna, the live volcano that last erupted in 1983, Catania is widely regarded as Sicily's gloomiest city. In 1669 Etna's eruption, which engulfed the city, the lava swamping the harbour, was then topped by an earthquake that devastated the whole of south-eastern Sicily. Giovanni Vaccarini, the eighteenth-century Sicilian architect, rebuilt the entire city using volcanic stone. Today, most of his churches and mansions are crumbling from neglect.

The coastal road south from Catania to Acireale sweeps down past the blue expanse of the Ionian Sea. A famous spa town, Acireale was rebuilt directly over the old lava streams after Etna's 1693 earthquake. Faustina parked the car outside the Aloha Hotel in town and helped Eddie with his luggage. They joined him for an early dinner and discussed plans for the next few days. Faustina wanted Eddie to visit her house the following morning; she had not lived there with her daughters since moving out in December 1987, although she still used the laboratory and consulting rooms there. Then she had a friend in a village in the foothills of Mt Etna, another in Palermo, and yet another in Catania who would like to see him . . .

At 9.45 the following morning, Eddie heard the sound of a car horn blaring outside the hotel. Faustina's friend Teresa, a South African-born English teacher married to a Sicilian, was waiting outside in her beaten-up Fiat. With a grinding of gears and a screeching of tyres, Teresa drove them off in a cloud of dust, picking her way through the winding streets to 199 Via Vittorio Emanuele.

Eddie recognized the building from the photographs Faustina had sent to him. A tall, yellow building with a small balcony, it stood at the point where two narrow roads joined an open square. A grocery shop filled with baskets of bread, fruit and hanging sausages occupied the ground floor fronting on to the square. Busy traffic screamed past both sides of the house, making conversation impossible.

Faustina welcomed Eddie into the house. The interior had a simple elegance, its walls painted white with the occasional patterned tile; the ceilings were decorated with traditional blue, black and gold designs. As soon as he stepped into the hall, Eddie became aware of a strong psychic imprint. It was redolent of political discussion from the late eighteenth and early nineteenth centuries; Eddie was sure that this imprint was from the period of French occupation which ended when the Sicilians rebelled against the French troops in 1812 and drove them from the island. Suddenly, this feeling was interrupted by a message from a spirit who told Eddie that he should go to a room on the first floor. When he walked inside, he stopped and said:

> I can feel the presence of a young man. He is prancing
> around the room with a foil. He is the man who was killed in
> the duel. I am trying to encourage him to remember his death
> – his alarm and anger when he realized that he was dying. He
> has stopped moving around and is now quiet. He tells me that
> the man who killed him had been his friend. The light is now
> appearing and out of it walks his friend, who is coming to
> take him away. He appears to the young man who greets him
> warmly, telling him all is forgiven. They walk off together
> now into the light.

Despite Eddie's apprehension, Faustina assured him that only one other person wanted to see him before he left Sicily. This man, a pupil of Teresa's, was a wealthy contractor who had made his fortune building the autostrada in Sicily. He was convinced that one of the bedrooms in his house was haunted. He lived in one of the small villages in the foothills of Mount Etna, so Eddie decided to combine a day's sightseeing with the visit.

Wreathed in white clouds for most of the year, the crater rim of Mount Etna is barely visible. At over 6,000 feet, Etna is one of the world's biggest live volcanoes. Some of its eruptions have been disastrous; in 1169, 1329 and 1381, the lava reached the sea and in 1669 Catania was completely destroyed. This century the railway line has been repeatedly ruptured by lava flows and in 1979 nine people were killed on the edge of the main crater. The most recent eruption occurred in 1983.

Eddie walked with Teresa up to the point of the 1922 eruption and gazed up at the great black lava field which is slowly being colonized by clumps of grass. A moonscape of grey and black waves of frozen lava, it is almost 300 yards wide and extends down one side of the mountain as far as the eye can see. On a clear day you can see smoke rising from the crater rim and spitting explosions of molten rock.

On the way back down to the car park, Teresa explained to Eddie that the man whom he was seeing was extremely nervous about psychic phenomena. It was rare for Sicilian men, she said, to admit to a problem like this. Sicilians, she said, were superstitious; if things went wrong for them, they believed that their enemies had looked on them with the 'evil eye' or had paid someone else to do so.

It was a short drive from Mount Etna to the large white house on the outskirts of Randazzo. As Teresa swung the car into the long drive, Eddie noticed a figure standing at the top of the gravel sweep, beyond the heavy wrought-iron gates. He pressed a remote control and the gates slowly parted. Teresa parked the car outside the nineteenth-century white mansion and introduced Eddie to her friend Domingo. A stocky man in his late forties, Domingo held out his hand to Eddie. Inside, the house had been furnished tastefully, with expensive pieces of modern art on every wall. Eddie sank down into a soft armchair and sipped mineral water. But he could not sense anything.

Although he had been reticent to start with, Domingo gradually revealed the story of the haunting. The problem was in the bedroom at the end of the ground-floor corridor. Designed as the master bedroom, he had been unable to use it since moving into the house five years before. Separated from his wife, Domingo had lived on his own for three years and occasionally his teenaged daughter came to visit him. The last time she came Domingo had given her the master bedroom, but something – she would not say what – had frightened her so much that she had refused to sleep there again.

It soon became apparent, however, that it was not Domingo's daughter who was his main concern. Domingo had confided in Teresa that girlfriends did not care for his bedroom either; at the critical moment they would scream and run out of the room. Domingo wanted to know if there really was a ghost there or whether *he* was the problem.

Eddie stifled a smile as he walked into the room while Domingo waited outside in the corridor, reclining on a sofa, trying to look nonchalant. An enormous bed covered in white lace dominated the room and floor-length white lace curtains hung at the French windows. Then Eddie sensed a presence; it was an old woman, and she was angry. She refused to communicate with Eddie, so he decided to leave the room and wait for her to come round. After ten minutes, she indicated that she was ready to talk.

> She tells me she was married young, in about 1870. Her husband was uncaring and he shattered all her romantic notions about life. She was starved of affection until, in an attempt to gain some attention, she feigned illness and took to her bed. After a few years of this behaviour, she grew more and more demanding and irascible. Then her illness became real and she died. Her bitterness over what happened left her earthbound. She says: 'He [Domingo] is a fool. He brings these women here and I SHOUT at them.' No wonder they ran out screaming. A pathway is opening up for her now and she is leaving, no doubt for heaven, as she is not a bad woman.

Domingo had been listening secretly at the door while Eddie had been talking. As soon as Eddie finished, he appeared with a bottle of vintage Sicilian wine. Nothing more was said, but the look on his face showed that he was satisfied with the outcome.

The visit to Domingo's was Eddie's last foray during his trip to Sicily. After two relaxing weeks he flew back home. Faustina watched the tall, lurching figure disappear through the departure gate at Catania airport. As she turned to walk away, she said a few silent words of thanks and crossed herself. Without Eddie she would have lost her business and been struck off the medical register; worse, she would probably have nowhere to live. Now, at last, she could make plans for the beautiful old house that she had fallen in love with more than thirteen years before.

Chapter 10

The Alehouse Dimension

Whoe'er has travelled life's dull round,
Where'er his stages may have been,
May sigh to think he still has found
The warmest welcome, at an inn.

William Shenstone, 'At an Inn at Henley'

In the days before television, the inn, like the parish church, was a focal point of the community – a place for people to gather after a hard day's work and swap stories and gossip. Sometimes strangers passing through would bring news of what was happening in neighbouring villages or far-off cities. The inn was the place where men celebrated their successes, forgot their problems and mourned life's tragedies.

But alcohol is a dangerous drug: laughter and excitement can quickly turn to angry words and fights; threats and jeers to violence or murder. In time, certain pubs build up a distinctive atmosphere, the psychic imprint of the events that happened there. The reputation of many pubs – warm and inviting or gloomy and sinister – is a direct consequence of their history. Many of England's public houses are said to be haunted. Ghost stories about them have been passed down from one generation to another over countless pints, and many are probably the result of too much beer rather than any evidence of psychic activity. Yet many others are undeniably more than that.

During the summer of 1994 Eddie and I visited four pubs in the London area which were reknowned for their ghostly 'regulars'. The most famous of these was the Spaniards Inn, on Hampstead Heath, which Dick Turpin, the eighteenth-century highwayman, frequented. Landlords have often commented on the psychic disturbances there and tourists from all over the world visit the pub in the hope of glimpsing the ghost of one of England's most famous villains.

We also called in at The Grenadier, near Hyde Park Corner, once the Duke of Wellington's Officers' Mess, and the Old Queen's Head, Islington, reputedly haunted by Queen Elizabeth I and a mistress of the Earl of Essex. Finally, there was the Blue Anchor, on the Brighton Road in Croydon, south London. Local newspapers reported that most of the pubs here had recorded some form of psychic disturbance; perhaps because the Brighton Road, like most main roads, had once been lined with gallows where criminals were hanged publicly. Many of the ghosts that haunt these pubs met their end on nearby scaffolds.

As usual, I researched all the cases and led Eddie to each one without telling him anything about the history of the haunting. In three out of four cases this approach worked well since they were, superficially, just ordinary pubs. The Spaniards Inn was different because of its long and famous association with Dick Turpin; even Eddie, who always tried to avoid research that would compromise his integrity, had heard of Dick Turpin, so here I just had to let him work as best as he could. Given that he had failed to pick up some of the ghosts who are supposed to haunt equally famous places, I was quite prepared for Mr Turpin not to grace us with his presence. But we were not disappointed at the Spaniards Inn – or at any of the other locations; in fact, the more we delved into the haunted pubs, the more fascinated we became.

Some of the ghosts who haunt pubs are well-known historical figures, which means that the facts of their earthly lives, the names and the dates, can be checked; others, however, are like most of us and left no trace in the history books; they were remarkable only to their family and friends. Castles, theatres, aristocratic estates and the sites of great battles – ghosts here tend to come from that élite circle, the powerful and the privileged, who shaped Britain. Many

of the ghosts who inhabit pubs left no such mark; but, as Eddie and
I discovered, that makes them no less interesting.

The Spaniards Inn, Hampstead Heath

On the edge of Hampstead Heath stands one of London's oldest
inns. The present building, with its heavy timber beams, open
fireplaces and cosy rooms, dates from 1701; before that there was a
private house on the site, built in 1585 and thought to have been the
Spanish ambassador's residence. The Spaniards Inn has an atmosphere that is quite unlike that of any other pub in London:
boisterous, jolly and – if you are sensitive enough to perceive it –
tinged with danger.

This is no doubt due to the lingering presence of Dick Turpin,
England's most notorious highwayman. He regularly lodged at the
Spaniards Inn and left his legendary horse, Black Bess, in the stable
across the yard. It is still possible today to see the room where
Turpin stayed and the tiny window cut in the stairway wall which
was used to pass supplies out to highwaymen who were saddled up
and ready to ride off into the night.

When we visited the inn in 1994 the publican was David Roper,
forty-nine, a down-to-earth New Zealander who had been there for
eight years. He said that his predecessor in the 1970s had heard the
clatter of horses' hooves in the night and his children had seen
strange shadows in the house. In fact, the publican thought this was
excellent for business and publicized the hauntings to attract
visitors. David told me: 'I like to think I am open-minded about
ghosts. I recently showed someone around the pub who had been
born here and he said that he definitely saw a ghost, a Grey Lady,
on the stairs. He seemed a genuine chap, so I suppose he must have
been telling the truth. Personally, though, I'm not that interested.'
Honest sceptic though he was, David was also a shrewd businessman; ghosts added to the mystique of the inn and helped attract
visitors from all over the world and countless British celebrities.

David led us upstairs, through the Dick Turpin Bar, into the flat
above the pub. The child of a previous publican had seen things
flying around her bedroom; it was next to the staircase that led up

to Dick Turpin's room. Eddie and I walked into the bedroom, then back into the hall. 'There's someone here,' said Eddie immediately, 'but he's being very elusive. I'll have to sit down and wait a while for him to come forward.' After a few minutes, he was ready.

There's a swashbuckling feeling about this person, but he's very guarded. I've got to move around a bit and make him understand that I'm here to help him. Let's see what the stairs are like. Sometimes he stood on the stairs like this, stooped with his elbow crooked. I think he's pausing to revive some of his memories. He's disturbed by the traffic outside – he's aghast at the noise. We'll have to close the window. The noise is disturbing him greatly.

He's an untrusting fellow. That's why he's taking so long to reveal himself. He says: 'I couldn't afford to trust people.' He was a highwayman. He was hanged not far from here. I can feel the rope around my neck and the knot behind my right ear. My head falls over to the left. I've got to go through this with him. He struggled quite a lot at the end; he didn't see why he should make it easy for them. He wasn't dropped to break his neck; he was strung up and choked.

He would come here and listen to conversations and pick up clues about who was going where. He would disguise himself and ride off to a point where he could then intercept the traveller. I think he was in a league with the landlord or one of his assistants, but I think he was captured by soldiers. He keeps taking me back to the hanging; it's still very much in his memory. He's a very defiant and cunning man. He was very good at keeping his own counsel. I think he may have been betrayed by someone at this pub, after a quarrel between him and his contact here.

I've an idea that this man was bad for trade in the end, because people would pass by this inn and go on to others. The inn began to get a bad name. They turned King's Evidence against him. He's stuck because he is bitter over that betrayal. I think he was shot through his right shoulder when he was captured, as I can feel some pain there. He says he himself avoided violence whenever he could.

He's got a journey to make. He's got to be tested quite a lot. But he is willing to go. He doesn't lack courage, so I think he'll accept the challenge. He's opened a gate on to a path; he seems to be unaccompanied – there's quite a lot for him to work out for himself first and he understands that. He seems to offer some gratitude for being released. He says: 'It was not often in my lifetime that anyone did anything for me.' That's an important statement for him. I must let him go.

I asked Eddie whether the name Dick Turpin meant anything to the man.

I'm not getting a response from him but he was definitely eighteenth-century. He had long dark hair which hung in a plait down his back and he's wearing a black patch over his right eye. He dressed quite well – that was deliberate, to avoid suspicion. He's wearing buckled shoes, breeches, a frock coat and a tricorn hat. I think he occasionally had lodgings here.

Although Eddie could not be absolutely certain – since the ghost had been so evasive – everything pointed to Dick Turpin: the dress, the defiance of authority and the suspicion. The most curious thing about Dick Turpin is that, despite being a gangster, thief and murderer, he became a hero in his own time. Indeed, so many legends grew up around him that today it is not easy to sort out truth from fiction.

However, it is thought that he was born on 21 September 1705 in the village of Hempstead, near Thaxted in Essex, the son of an innkeeper and butcher. He attended the village school, where he was taught by a schoolmaster called Smith, who, many years later, helped track Turpin down. At the age of sixteen Turpin was apprenticed to a butcher in Whitehall, London, where he remained for five years. It was there, in the dark alleys and disreputable inns of eighteenth-century London, that he became interested in crime and discovered some of the hiding places that were so useful for him in his later life. In 1728 Turpin returned to Thaxted and married a local girl, Betty Millington.

At the age of 23, with a wife and a small butcher's business of his own, he seemed to have a promising future. But he did not settle; some historians believe that he fell into debt while others say that Turpin was just not destined to grow old peacefully and needed the excitement of crime. Whatever the reason, he left Thaxted in 1729 and began stealing cattle, then a capital crime. He tried smuggling but returned to dry land as a highwayman in Essex and then London. It was not his fearlessness that made him such a hero, but the fact that he behaved as a gentleman thief; even if it could not be said that he robbed the rich to give to the poor, Turpin's robberies were rarely marked by violence. Ordinary people admired him, especially for his ability to slip away from what often seemed like certain capture.

In the late 1730s Turpin established himself in York as a respectable citizen, using the name John Palmer. He might well have lived there quietly for the rest of his life had he not been thrown into prison after shooting his landlord's cockerels. He would have been freed – but he decided, fatally, to write to his brother-in-law. Mr Smith, his old teacher at Hempstead, saw the letter at the post office, recognized the handwriting and alerted the authorities that Dick Turpin, alias John Palmer, was being held in York.

Turpin was tried on 22 March 1739 and condemned to death by hanging. On the day of his execution, 7 April 1739, he dressed himself in a new coat and shoes and hired five men to follow him to the gallows in mourning hats and gloves. He bowed repeatedly to the crowds as his cart passed through them and, as the rope was placed around his neck, presented the hangman with the gift of a small ivory whistle.

★

Eddie and I let ourselves out of the hall and stopped to look at the drawings of Dick Turpin in his bar. Most were caricatures of the great highwayman from contemporary newspapers; the one that caught my eye was a picture of him hanging from the gallows, his neck twisted and his face contorted.

Eddie was sitting down at a table by the open window. He was hunched in concentration, which meant that he had made contact with another ghost. This time it was a barmaid from the Victorian era:

It's a woman, early Victorian. She's saying: 'Never mind him, what about me?' She's in a terrible state. She says: 'For God's sake help me, I can't stand it here. Talk about being in prison. What have I done to deserve this? I ask you. They made me a serving wench – used me and abused me. We used to get some rough ones in here, I can tell you. Landlord said I was to be nice to them – it was good for custom. It may have been for them – it wasn't for me. I started to bear child.'

She says: 'And the heartless bugger threw me out. I had nowhere to go except the heath. And I froze to death out there, child and all, still carrying it. Would you believe it? I can't forgive him. For Gawd's sake, get me out of this place. I didn't want to come back, but there was nowhere else to go in the end.'

She's short, with fair, curly hair and rather buxom. She's wearing long skirts and an apron with petticoats underneath. She had a roundish face with a slightly bulbous nose and wide cheekbones. She had been attractive in her time and the landlord had played on this, using her to attract more customers. I think her mother originally put her into the job.

She's going to go into the light, I feel sure. There's a young man coming out of the light towards her. He says: 'You don't know me, but I was the son you would have had. We must get to know each other.' She leans on him and is crying. She says: 'I even had a name for you. I guessed you were a boy. I called you Jacob.' He says: 'I am Jacob.' They're going into the light. She's so happy, she's crying with joy.

Dick Turpin may never again be seen on the stairs of the Spaniards Inn, but, of course, his name will linger there for ever. As for the barmaid, we will probably never know who she was; but future visitors to the Spaniards Inn can console themselves with the thought that, like the famous highwayman, she, too, has moved on to a happier place.

The Old Queen's Head, Islington

Nestling behind Islington's busy high street, on the corner of Essex Road, is the Old Queen's Head. With its soft lighting and trendy jazz music, it is a fashionable meeting place for young people, who flock there to sit at scrubbed pine tables and sip expensive bottled beer or mineral water. In the corner of the main bar is the only clue to the pub's illustrious history – an elaborately carved Jacobean fireplace.

The Old Queen's Head stands on the site of the house of the Earl of Essex, one of Queen Elizabeth I's favourite courtiers. The Queen is said to have stayed there on several occasions while visiting Essex in London, and many witnesses have claimed that the Queen's Head's resident ghost was Elizabeth herself.

Damien Considine, a tall, dark-haired man in his late twenties, had been the publican there for just over two years when I arranged our appointment in June 1994. Although he was very sceptical about ghosts, he suggested that Eddie should start in the cellar and led us down the cold stone steps. Crates of soft drinks were stacked to the ceiling and the storage room gave off an icy draught whenever anyone opened the door. The cold froze my feet and travelled up to my knees; I shivered, not quite convinced that it was the cold room that was making the temperature so unpleasant. Eddie paced up and down and then spoke:

I'm picking up someone with a sense of humour. There is someone trapped here, but I get the feeling he is playing tricks with me; it's very difficult to maintain contact. It's someone who didn't want to be serious about anything – it takes a little while to get used to his jokey frame of mind.

I think it's a young man. I don't think he's been dead a long time. He feels post-war to me. He died in an accident here; I think he'd been fooling around. It's hard to hold him in a serious frame of mind but he's beginning to reveal himself a little more. He's very, very sad. He's feeling a deep sorrow about his sudden death and blames himself for it. People said to him: you'll do that sort of thing once too often. He did, and now he finds it hard to forgive himself. There'd

169

been some sort of silly bet whether he'd do something. He did – and it killed him.

I'm getting a very intense pain at the top and back of the head; he may have fallen on his head. I think he was jumping over something in a confined space – it may have been here in the cellar. I think this was his local. It was in the 1950s or 1960s. He says: 'Needless to say, we got pissed.' I think he's only got a vague memory of it himself, because he was so drunk at the time. He was doing a balancing act on several chairs piled up together, probably in the pub upstairs. He pitched off it and struck his head on the floor. His mind's clearing a bit now about the event. It was a silly trick; a simple accident, but he was always one for doing silly tricks.

He was in his twenties and unmarried. He was auburn-haired, half Irish, I think. I've got to see if anyone will come for him. He's very upset still. There was never much affection between him and his mother – she's not coming for him. There is an uncle of whom he was very fond. I think this is the man who will come for him – I sense him approaching now. This uncle had the same sort of sense of humour and jokey attitude to life. They're going joyfully into the light now.

When Eddie had finished speaking we made our way upstairs and got a drink from the bar. 'Let's sit by the fireplace and see if you can pick anything up,' I said. I was concerned that the pub was reportedly haunted by a female ghost, yet Eddie had only picked up a young man. Before I could mention this, Eddie began to speak again:

I have a woman with me. She dates from the 1930s, I think. She used to come to this pub quite a lot. She's not trapped in the pub itself, but belongs to the area around it. She was an alcoholic. She says: 'I wasted my life and all I owned on drink.' I think she collapsed on the pavement outside and died there. She's in her fifties and has very untidy brown hair. She's in a pretty miserable condition. She still carries with her a yearning for alcohol, but she can't satisfy that any more.

I think she'd had a family – two children – but the father

took them away in the end because he couldn't stand her drunkenness. She never saw them again. I think she died around 1935. She looks exactly as she did before she died as she's still carrying all the memories. She's pretty ragged, wearing an old shawl with holes in it, and a long, dirty skirt. In the end she just stopped looking after herself and people shunned her. Somebody would occasionally buy her a drink out of pity. It's only because she was so well known in the pub that anyone gave her the time of day.

Her husband is coming for her. She's changed in appearance now: her hair was grey, but now she's a brunette and she's looking clean and bright; and her shawl no longer has holes. She's about five feet five inches tall. I can hear the words: 'The suffering and the degradation are over.' She looks quite radiant and happy – her relief is enormous. He's taking her hand and they turn their backs on everything we've witnessed. They're going off into the light. She's going to be a very happy woman.

Damien could not give us any clues about the identities of Eddie's two ghosts. But he said that the Queen's Head was known as Islington's 'Irish pub' since it was a favourite of north London's Irish community, though he was also anxious to point out that the pub was now very respectable. No expense had been spared in refurbishing the Old Queen's Head, but there was still an uneasy feeling about the place; it was cold and unwelcoming. Eddie agreed. 'You can't wipe out ingrained memories with a quick change of décor,' he said. 'This place has a very bad atmosphere.'

The Blue Anchor, Brighton Road, Croydon

The Blue Anchor was a completely different proposition from the Old Queen's Head. Situated on Croydon's busy Brighton Road, it is a huge, mock-Tudor house dating from the early 1920s. Inside it was cosy and spacious, although perhaps the attempt to recreate an 'olde-worlde' atmosphere had been overdone, with decorative timber beams and imitation inglenook fireplaces. Despite that, it was warm and friendly.

Andrew Wagstaff, the publican, told us to make ourselves at home. He confessed that he did not know much about the haunting, although the previous publican had told him that doors would slam in the night and lights would turn themselves on and off. The barman told us that he had once come downstairs to find all the glasses he had washed and put away the night before standing on the bar, in descending order of size, so it seemed that the ghost there did at least have a sense of humour.

Sitting at a small table near the entrance, I asked Eddie whether he had sensed anything. 'I'm not sure,' he said, 'although I get the feeling that we will achieve something here today.' After a few minutes he signalled to me that a presence was close:

I'm getting a feeling of excitement and I think it comes from the spirit of a man who is approaching. He has a real swashbuckling feeling about him, a man of great courage and daring. He's aware that he's trapped, but says the reason for it is not what people think. He had such an adventurous life that he can't bear to turn his back on it; he simply won't let go. Part of his problem is that he dislikes what he sees around him now.

Now he says: 'I'd rather be away from all this here – if you can point me to a better place.' I think it's dawning on him now that he has to move on. He still does not understand where he's going to, and this needs to be made clear to him. He has a strange sense of excitement about what's going to happen. Somebody else is now saying to him: 'Will you make one last voyage?' I can see a ship anchored at sea and someone is rowing ashore in a small boat to pick him up.

The entity is a tall man, with a dark beard and lots of dark hair. He is dressed in a white doublet and silver buckled shoes; he has a sword by his right side. I can sense his excitement as the boat approaches him. He steps into the prow of the boat with one leg and pushes it off with the other. He doesn't recognize the oarsman. This man was strongly wedded to the sea and you can sense his excitement over this new journey. I think he fought naval battles against the French and the Spanish. A rope ladder hangs over the side of the boat which he proceeds to climb. He's done this before – so he's quite happy.

A whole group of people he once knew are on board the ship. There is much excitement as the old shipmates meet up again. He asks them: 'Where are we going?' and someone replies: 'To shores you've never visited before.' He's very pleased because he's always interested in new destinations. He's greeting the crew now, the sails are unfurled and they're sailing off to a bright new horizon. It's a very exciting time for him as he sails off towards the light. This will not be a short voyage, for he still has much to learn. He has got to let go of his earthly memories and attitudes. Though he does not realize it yet, his crew are his teachers. When he does make his landing he will be chastened by what he has learned. But do not be mistaken, his courage and audacity will prove to be of great value. Within him is a very bright spirit.

The Blue Anchor takes its name from an old pub nearby that was built in the seventeenth century and collapsed in ruins just after the First World War. The area on which both pubs were built was once the property of Lord Charles Howard of Effingham, born in 1536. Everything that Eddie had picked up – and my own historical research – suggested to me that the ghost had been Lord Howard himself.

Charles Howard was cousin to Queen Elizabeth I and played an important role at her court, first as Lord Chamberlain and then as Lord High Admiral. Elizabeth appointed him admiral of the English fleet during the Armada campaign of 1588 in an attempt to reconcile her quarrelsome naval officers, Sir Francis Drake, Sir John Hawkins and Martin Frobisher. In recognition of the subsequent victory – the highlight of a long naval career of brave and daring leadership – Elizabeth made Howard Earl of Nottingham in 1597. He spent the rest of his life in loyal service to her and was at her side when she died on 24 March 1603; Howard himself died at home on his estates in 1624, aged eighty-eight. He had been a brilliant, dashing commander in an age in which such men thrived;

the ghost whom Eddie contacted could not have fitted Howard's description more accurately.

The Grenadier, Wilton Row, Hyde Park Corner

Our final port of call was The Grenadier, tucked away in the corner of a private mews behind Hyde Park Corner. In the summer months, hanging baskets of flowers cascade over the entrance and a vine forms a natural canopy that provides welcome shade.

Eddie and I climbed the worn stone steps to the main bar of this wonderful old pub. We were greeted by Peter Martin, a thirty-two-year-old New Zealander who had managed the pub for the last six-and-a-half years. He had gleaned most of his information about the pub's ghost from Thomas Westward, who was publican there for thirty-seven years, from 1937 until 1974. When Eddie was out of earshot, Martin told me about the haunting.

'There are supposed to be two ghosts here – a young army officer who was caught cheating at cards, brought upstairs and flogged to death, and an ex-publican,' he said. 'Most of the disturbances seem to take place in September – the month when the young officer died. They are general things – strange knocks, lights being switched on during the night, things being moved and odd shadows on the walls, even during the day. One woman said that she had seen the shadowy figure of a man walking up the stairs who vanished before he got to the top.

'I'm sceptical myself, but one strange thing did happen to me in 1990. Some workmen were rewiring the kitchen and they had to go down to the cellar. I went to fetch the keys – I always kept them under the mattress – but when I looked they weren't there. I looked all over for them – even took the mattress off the bed, but I still couldn't find them. Ten minutes later I went back and they were exactly where they should have been. But when I tried to open the door they wouldn't work, so I asked one of the locals to have a go and they worked first time for him.'

Martin said that there were two areas where disturbances had occurred; the cellar, which was the original level of the bar, and the bathroom, which used to be an office. Eddie and I headed first for

174

the bathroom on the top floor. Martin rented his spare rooms to young Australians and New Zealanders who worked as waitresses in the pub's restaurant. The bathroom itself looked as if it had not been modernized in half a century, with a cracked old porcelain sink and stained bathtub. Underwear was hanging from a washing line strung across the room, and bottles of cheap shampoo and talcum powder littered the floor. As soon as we entered the room, Eddie closed his eyes and began to speak.

I sense a person who's feeling very restless and wants to turn everybody out. The person grabbed my arm as I walked across the bathroom and tried to escort me out of the house. I think this person regards this part of the house as their territory and resents the intrusion of anyone else. 'I want them all out,' the person says. I don't know whether this is a feminine man or a masculine woman – it's not at all clear-cut. There's a strange sexual aspect to this, a secret of some sort. The person is pleading with me now: 'Please, please take them all away.'

I must impress upon this person that it would be better if they went away instead. There's no future in staying here. But this person does not want to go away. I think it's a man. He didn't live here, but he spent a lot of time here and clearly regarded it as his territory. He's using very effeminate language: 'Come on, dearie, please take them all away. I can't stand all these women around – they don't agree with me.'

It's rather sad, really. He was homosexual and was conditioned to feel very guilty about that; he's hiding here and thinks there's nowhere else for him to go. He thinks he'll be judged harshly if he goes elsewhere. I must make him understand that this won't happen. I feel shooting pains in my hands – I've never felt such pain before. It's gone now. I think the man committed suicide in this room. He electrocuted himself with an electric cord. It was very quick. He did it to avoid call-up to the army; it was 1940 or 1941. The suicide would have been enough in itself to trap him, but his homosexuality is adding a great burden of guilt.

We must encourage him to leave, although he may not be

able to. He is bound to stay unless he had fulfilled his natural lifespan. I must ask for some help for him. His period of isolation, I understand, is nearly at an end. Something will be done to help him. The picture looks very dark for him, but if he's willing, his journey can start now. We must make him understand that he won't be judged at all. The gateway will be opened to him, but he must make the decision for himself. 'You won't force me to leave, will you?' he asks. 'If I decide to go now, will you help me?'

The best way to release him is to find a companion for him. Here it comes; a cat that was once his pet has come for him. He has a collar and a light lead. I think the journey will be rough for him at first, but it will get better. He will move towards the light.

Eddie stopped speaking. It seemed that he had contacted the spirit of a guilt-ridden homosexual who had killed himself in the bathroom, probably in the early years of the Second World War. The communication had been vivid and moving yet, interestingly, the spirit had never revealed itself before.

Now Eddie and I returned to Martin, who showed us down to the cellar, an icy cold, whitewashed room. Eddie walked around for a few minutes, but soon admitted that he could not sense anything. Martin led us to another room at the back where he stored whisky, brandy and rum. According to Martin, there was a secret passage leading from this room to Apsley House, the Duke of Wellington's residence on the other side of Hyde Park Corner. Here Eddie made contact with someone.

I can see a man in a red and black uniform with gold buttons. He's quite young. He's being very cautious; he's circling round us without coming in closer. I'm trying to encourage him, but he says: 'Too much curiosity about me and not enough help.' I tell him he can trust me. He says: 'My life is very circumscribed. I try to get away and make a little progress, but then I am pulled back again. Those cruel idiots that caused my death could not have known how they were imprisoning me in this purgatory.'

I asked Eddie if the man had been cheating at cards.

'Cheating was not my way – I was much the worse for drink.
It was not my malicious intent at all. But the code of conduct
among us was very strict indeed. I suffered considerably
before I died – but, to give them their due, my death alarmed
them greatly. I find it very hard to forgive them their
foolishness. They had all done things just as bad when they
were in their cups, but those things were not matters of
honour. It was a waste of my life. I would rather have died
on the battlefield. I cannot forgive them.'
I can see a fence around him now and I ask him if he will
come with me to the gate. He says: 'I would do much to get
away.' He goes through the gate and I sense a feeling of
happiness. He is stretching out his arms and taking deep
breaths of air. He is on a path and the landscape around him
is stony, with a few scrubby trees. He will make good
progress and will eventually be able to forgive the people who
killed him. I must leave him now to his learning.

With that, Eddie released The Grenadier's famous September
ghost. Thankfully, Martin had not understood the process of the
release and was unaware that the ghost would not appear again.
The public and the press had flocked there over the years, hoping
to see the ghost; but, thanks to Eddie, the cellar was now just a cold
room full of rather good whiskies, rums and brandies. But I thought
it best not to mention that to Martin.

Chapter 11

Ghosts in Greasepaint

If this were played upon a stage now,
I could condemn it as an improbable fiction

William Shakespeare, *Twelfth Night*

We do on the stage the things that are supposed to
happen off. Which is a kind of integrity, if you look on
every exit being an entrance somewhere else.

Tom Stoppard, *Rosencrantz and Guildernstern Are Dead*

There are few places where feelings run so high as in the theatre.
Theatres and opera houses tend to attract a particular kind of
person – sensitive, romantic and escapist – and that applies just as
much to the audience as the actors. In a few hours on stage, the
performers can explore the full range of emotions – anger, fear,
love, hate, sadness – distilled into their purest form through the
words of the playwright or the music of the composer. This
cathartic experience charges the theatre's atmosphere and leaves
behind a powerful feeling.

In the last few minutes before they face the audience, actors
rehearse their lines, change into their costumes and apply their
greasepaint. Tension mounts, too, among the supporting cast who
make it all happen – the costume supervisors, lighting technicians

178

and stage-hands. A few hours later, judgement has been passed: a rousing ovation with several curtain calls or a dutiful bout of clapping as the audience rushes to the nearest exit. Left behind either a sense of triumph or humiliating failure. Over the years these emotions build up in a theatre like layers of wallpaper.

Actors are extremely superstitious people and the profession is riddled with quaint observations, which must be strictly followed to ensure success on stage. 'Break a leg,' they are told as they make their entrance; this is, for some reason, considered safer than saying 'Good luck.' Actors never quote from Shakespeare's *Macbeth* offstage – particularly from the witches' scene – as this is thought to have the power to raise evil spirits and doom the production.

Since theatres are the crucibles for such intense emotions it is hardly surprising that they have such a long tradition of ghosts. These are generally welcomed by actors, who feel comforted by the presence of a benign spirit. In 1935 the entire cast of *The Dancing Years* saw the ghost of the Man in Grey in the upper circle at the Theatre Royal, Drury Lane, and Sir Alec Guinness claimed to have seen the figure of Shakespeare looking up from the stalls while he was playing Hamlet at the Old Vic. Daniel Day Lewis, now a Hollywood star, broke down during the ghost scene in *Hamlet* at the National Theatre after seeing the face of his deceased father in front of him.

Eddie Burks could easily have devoted his whole working life to theatre ghosts. So, I decided that we should concentrate on three great London venues: the Theatres Royal of Drury Lane and the Haymarket, the oldest and second oldest theatres, respectively, in London, and the Adelphi, the most popular music hall of the eighteenth century. As always, Eddie had no inkling of the stories in advance. Sometimes he confirmed the legend; sometimes he came up with an entirely different story. However, in all three cases, he proved that theatres are, indeed, a welcome haven for many ghosts.

Theatre Royal, Drury Lane

In 1662 King Charles II, a keen theatre-goer, granted Thomas Gilligrew a Royal Charter to establish a company of actors and build a theatre in Covent Garden. The Theatre Royal in Drury

Lane, which cost £2,400 to build, opened its doors on 7 May 1663 with *The Humorous Lieutenant*. It was constructed on the site of a burial ground for a nearby convent, hence the name for this area of London – Covent Garden. The early Drury Lane was dogged by ill-fortune. It survived the Great Fire of London but was then burnt down a year later. The second theatre was designed by Sir Christopher Wren and was even more impressive. King George II was in the theatre in April 1746 when he heard that his army had defeated the Jacobite rebellion led by Bonnie Prince Charlie at the Battle of Culloden, near Inverness. The third theatre opened in 1794 and was supposed to be fireproof; but that, too, burnt down. The fourth building, dating from 10 October 1812, survives today.

Drury Lane's 332-year history is inextricably linked with England's leading actors and playwrights, including David Garrick, Mrs Siddons, Sheridan, Lord Byron, Sir John Gielgud, Ivor Novello and Rodgers and Hammerstein. Today, Drury Lane is the third largest theatre in the West End, with a capacity of 2,188. Recent productions have included *42nd Street*, *A Chorus Line*, *Carousel*, *My Fair Lady* and the musical *Miss Saigon*, which was taking bookings for a year ahead in summer 1994.

According to Nina Smirnoff, who runs daily public tours of the theatre, Drury Lane boasts 500 ghosts, the most famous of which is the 'Man in Grey'. This ghost is thought to be a theatre patron who was murdered 200 years ago by one of the theatre managers and then bricked up behind the wall of the upper circle. In 1921, when the wall was knocked down to create some new entrances behind the upper circle, a fully clothed skeleton was discovered there with a dagger still between the ribs.

Although little is known of his identity, the Man in Grey is held in great affection at Drury Lane; usually he appears at rehearsals, walking slowly from one end of the balcony to the other before disappearing into the wall. 'If he's seen in Row D1 of the upper circle during rehearsals, it's supposed to be an omen that the show will go on to success,' Nina said.

In 1948 the American actress Betty Jo Jones saw him during rehearsals for *Oklahoma*. When the show opened, she said, her performance was not going well – until she felt an invisible hand gently push her into a different position and guide her around the stage on two successive nights. A few days later, when her performance had improved, she felt a ghostly pat on the back. More recently, in the mid-1980s, the entire cast of *42nd Street* saw the ghost in the Duke of Bedford's box. Needless to say, the show was one of the West End's biggest ever hits.

Nina was eager to offer Eddie and myself a private tour of the theatre on 6 June 1994. 'Ghosts are an important part of my tour,' she said. 'We usually mention the main ones – the Man in Grey; Dan Leno, the Victorian pantomime dame; Edmund Kean, the nineteenth-century actor . . . obviously, we cannot include all 500.'

Eddie was waiting outside Drury Lane at 10.30 a.m. on 6 June. He had travelled down to London from Lincoln that morning and was looking rather tired. I hoped he had had breakfast on the train as I had no chocolate in reserve; then I spotted three coffee shops nearby, so I knew that I could easily dash out for supplies if Eddie started to flag. Inside the plush red Victorian foyer I admired the crystal chandeliers while we waited for Nina to arrive. Five minutes later she appeared: a tall, chunky woman in her late twenties, dressed in white shirt and black trousers.

'Welcome to Drury Lane. You must realize I'm the world's greatest sceptic,' she announced as she escorted us up the grand central staircase to the upper circle reception. 'But I promise to keep an open mind.' She led us to the upper circle bar, where the skeleton had been found. After a few minutes, Eddie walked over to the bar and said:

I have an old man with me – a psychic imprint – and this is the way he stood, leaning here on his elbow at the bar. I can hardly stand up. I reckoned he died here. He just dropped down.

He asks: 'Why can't I get away from this place?' Even in his lifetime he was trapped by the atmosphere in this theatre, which he found fascinating. But he also had a tendency towards alcoholism – that made a pretty miserable mixture. 'I need to go now,' he says.

I'm puzzled because I'm aware of him walking down and

out of this place, but where's he going to? His home, perhaps? He's climbing some stairs. I think he lived in an attic nearby. He says: 'I want to say goodbye to this place.' He means his home, not the theatre.

He was standing at the bar when he died. His legs gave way under him. I think it may have been a stroke. It all happened quite suddenly. He's with me again. He says: 'I'm ready to go.' An old friend from the theatre is taking him away. He's starting a journey before he goes to the spirit world.

Nina watched as Eddie came round; he rubbed his hands, stretched his legs and opened his eyes. 'Good, well, he's gone now,' he said. 'Where next?' Nina asked us where we would like to go; there had been sightings under the stage, in the dressing rooms and in the reception by the upper circle bar. I looked at Eddie expectantly. 'I'll let the spirits guide us,' he said. 'Wait a moment.' As we emerged into the reception from the upper circle bar, I could see that Eddie was on to something already. 'I have someone with me,' he said. 'It's a woman and she wants us to go below stage. She's in her forties or fifties and is a rather exuberant personality – she seems to be bubbling with energy, but she's quite purposeful, nonetheless. She's adamant that we go below stage.'

Nina led us behind the stage, past the flickering computer screens that monitor the theatre's state-of-the-art lighting system, through the maze of corridors and dressing rooms, deep into the bowels of the theatre. Underneath the stage we were escorted along a steel walkway and down a spiral staircase. There, encased in strong steel cages, were Drury Lane's famous Victorian hydraulic lifts, each capable of lifting three tons, which are still used to change scenery and create outstanding stage effects – such as the sinking of an ocean liner in one of the theatre's recent productions.

'Why did she want me to come down here?' Eddie asked aloud. 'I need to walk around a bit – I think I may have come down too far. I think I need to go back up the spiral staircase.' He climbed back up to the upper level, paused for a moment and said:

I'm picking up a man now; he's very restless. The woman [entity] who brought us down here was very concerned that

182

we help him; I can feel her offstage – pardon the pun – now, watching and helping us. I get the feeling that he was injured here. The memories of his death are very unpleasant. The lower rib on the right-hand side of the back was broken. I shall pick up some more detail in a moment, but I must first get him past the recollection of this terrible pain.

He's stunned, unable to understand what's going on. [Eddie pauses for a few minutes.] Now he seems to be relieved and is hauling himself upright. I ask what happened to him. He says: 'I worked in the flys. I thought I knew my job pretty well, but we all make mistakes.' Yes, I think he fell here to his death. He's in his late twenties, early thirties – a lithe, muscular man who's quite tall, around five feet ten. The date is 1930. I think he enjoyed his job and took great pride in it. He says: 'I didn't take unnecessary risks, but you can become too familiar with these things and sometimes the unexpected catches you out.' He's wearing a navy blue bib-and-braces overall which he carries his tools in.

I think he was interested in boats during his lifetime. He's going to be taken away in a boat, I think, as I can see him moving towards a scene by a river, where there's a jetty and a small boat rowed by a friend of his. He's stepping into the boat and sailing off, so I expect he's free now. The woman who encouraged us to come here is very relieved. She says: 'Thank you. I knew you could help.'

I noticed that Nina had been watching Eddie very carefully during the communication; she had said nothing, but I could tell that she had been very interested in what he was saying. 'What do you think, Nina?' I asked.

'Very interesting,' she said. 'We do know of an accident here, but it's a rather sensitive issue at the theatre.' I could not press her further, but a week later I found out what she had been alluding to. I was researching the history of the theatre at the Theatre Museum in Covent Garden when I found a small newspaper cutting tucked among the first-night reviews and old programmes. It was from *The Times* of 9 November 1991:

THEATRE FINED

Negligence by the owners of the Theatre Royal in Drury Lane, London, led to an electrician falling head first through a trapdoor from a 27ft gantry onto the stage during a performance of *Miss Saigon*, breaking an arm and a wrist and suffering severe concussion, a jury at Southwark Crown Court decided. Stoll Moss Theatres was fined £5,000 and asked to pay £5,000 costs.

The electrician, fortunately, had escaped with his life, unlike the unfortunate man Eddie had contacted. But there was clearly a connection, as the accidents were eerily similar, despite the sixty-year gap. There are many instances where a terrible accident or murder leaves a psychic imprint on a place, and if this is not cleared, it will tend to build up an energy which can attract repeats of the original accident. It is possible that the man who fell from the gantry in 1991 was influenced by the man who was clearly haunting the theatre below stage. Thankfully, there is less likelihood of this happening now that the original accident has been recognized and dealt with.

★

From below stage, we walked up to the Green Room, a quick costume-change area for the cast right next to the stage. Every theatre has a Green Room; green is an unlucky colour in the theatre, so – perversely – actors gave it this name to avert bad luck. This one was small, with wooden benches and a dress rail stacked with costumes from *Miss Saigon*. Then we crossed the corridor, into the offices. Nina said that there had been a number of disturbances here too, including a powerful lavender smell. Eddie sat down in the corner and closed his eyes:

There's someone with a heavy jaw here with me. A man in his forties, I think late Victorian. He held himself very upright. He may have had a managerial job here. I'm picking up a psychic imprint rather than a haunting, but he may appear sometimes; I don't think he's stuck.

184

Nina seemed impressed. She said that Eddie must have picked up the spirit of Dan Leno, Victorian England's best-loved comedian, who died in 1904 aged forty-four. She said: 'The offices were Dan Leno's dressing room. He suffered from incontinence and needed to have a dressing room near the WC. He always used lavender water to cover up the smell of urine. For years we thought the scent of lavender was the ghost of a flower lady from Covent Garden, but then we realized it was Leno. He was a small man, with twinkling, dark brown eyes. You can see his bust in the royal retiring room upstairs, which is used for private parties.'

Dan Leno, born George Galvin to poor, working-class Irish parents in King's Cross, London, danced through his childhood in working-men's clubs and music halls and became a champion clog dancer at the age of twenty. Leno, who took his stage name from his stepfather, was also an acrobat, singer and sketch-writer. His big break came in London in 1885 when he found that it was his mimicry and comedy, rather than his musical skills, which audiences loved. From then on he concentrated on comedy, and for the next three years he was in great demand in music halls around the country. In 1888 he was invited to perform at the annual pantomime at Drury Lane, which was then the Mecca of music hall. For the next fifteen years he was adored as a pantomime dame, immortalizing roles such as Widow Twankey and Mother Goose. But overwork caused several nervous breakdowns and led many people to believe he was mad. Even so, his death was regarded as a national tragedy.

Nina was now almost enthusiastic about our tour. 'Let me take you to another place where there has been a sighting. A couple of years ago, the entire cast of the musical *42nd Street* claimed they saw a figure sitting in the Duke of Bedford's box during a performance,' she said. Eddie and I followed her through the twisting corridors into the private box. Four plush red velvet seats overlooked the left-hand side of the vast stage; behind were a banquette, chaise-longue, standard lamp and side table. Eddie interrupted as I was imagining elegant theatre-goers sipping perfectly chilled champagne here. As he began to speak I switched my tape-recorder on.

I have a strange sensation in my fingers and arms. I'm getting the feeling of an old gentleman. It's as though he just wants to go to sleep. This man had a good, long life. He found coming here on this occasion difficult and tiring. I think he just sat down and died here. The sensation in my hands and arms was a precursor to his death. It's as though the body was dying from the fingertips upwards. Again, I think this is an imprint rather than a haunting, though he may well appear from time to time. I think it's a strong imprint because a lot of people were affected by his death. I think he came here to see a performance and collapsed and died in the middle of it or shortly afterwards. It doesn't feel like a stroke, just a gentle passing away.

I think he was Edwardian. He wielded some power and influence at the theatre. He was a grandfather when he died and his last visit here was a family occasion. He's a revenant; he had such happy memories of this place that he keeps coming back.

I asked Nina if she had any ideas about the identity of Eddie's Edwardian spirit. 'It's definitely Arthur Collins, who was theatre manager here from 1897 until 1921,' she said. 'He was known as Druriolanus because he had so much influence at the theatre. He often used this box, as it's the best in the house.'

As we prepared to leave Nina told me that dozens of psychics had visited Drury Lane; most of them had 'picked up' something, as she put it, but none had been as detailed or uncannily accurate as Eddie. 'I must say that I am impressed,' she said generously. 'I may have to rethink our tours after this. I don't think there's enough emphasis on our ghosts.' I did not have the heart to tell her that Eddie did not just communicate with spirits; he helped them depart.

I felt her eyes follow us down the street; I wished that we had been able to make a more dramatic exit – stepping into a long black limousine or even disappearing into a puff of smoke. Then I realized that I had lost Eddie. As I scanned the street I saw him go into a nearby café; he obviously had more worldly things on his mind.

Adelphi Theatre

On 17 December 1897 the *Daily Telegraph* reported the dramatic news of the murder of William Terriss, aged fifty, one of the great Victorian theatre idols. The headlines read: 'Murder of Mr William Terriss at the Adelphi last night; Stabbed to the heart; Assassin arrested; Supposed act of revenge'. The newspaper reported:

> All London was ringing last night with the news of a terrible tragedy. There is no actor more generally popular in the Metropolis than Mr William Terriss, and when it was known that he had been the victim of a sudden and dastardly attack . . . the horror and indignation of those to whom Terriss was a familiar and household name, cannot be described. Everywhere, in all the clubs, in the green rooms of theatres, and on the pavements where late editions of the newspapers were greedily bought, there was a universal feeling of sorrow and astonishment and dismay.
>
> An eye-witness to the tragic event said: 'I was standing near the front of the Adelphi Theatre, shortly before half-past seven this evening, and I observed a man who is very familiar to frequenters of that part. He wore a soft felt hat and a sort of ulster with a cape to it . . . Mr Terriss came along and went to the private door of the theatre. He stopped in front of the door for an instant, doubtless to take out his keys from his pocket. The man I have described, who I noticed had a sort of wild look in his eyes . . . walked up to Terriss and quickly stabbed him with a knife. Terriss was heard to cry out: 'You have stabbed me! Arrest him!' but before the assailant could be seized he had aimed another determined blow at Mr Terriss – a blow which appeared to have completed his dreadful work. The actor staggered and reeled, and a few minutes afterwards he was heard groaning in the agony of death. Two Commissionaires rushed up and seized the murderer, and very soon the police took him in charge and put him in safe-keeping at Bow Street.

At the time of his death, William Terriss was one of the most popular actors on the English stage. After an adventurous youth – he joined the navy when he was fourteen, worked on a tea plantation and studied medicine briefly – he made his acting début in Birmingham in 1857. He first appeared at Drury Lane in 1871, as Robin Hood in Andrew Halliday's drama *Rebecca*, and soon established himself as a leading man in Shakespearian productions at the Lyceum under Henry Irving. He was good-looking and dreamy, perfect for roles in *Romeo and Juliet* (1852) and *Much Ado about Nothing* (1853), and he soon became London's leading matinée idol. By the late 1880s, he had found his niche in the then fashionable genre of patriotic melodrama, of which the Adelphi was the leading exponent. It was there that he starred in most of his hit plays, including *In the Days of the Duke* and *Secret Service* in 1897, the year he died.

Terriss was also popular with his fellow actors – except for one. Richard Archer Prince, who once appeared in a minor part with Terriss at the Adelphi, developed an undying hatred of him. Terriss had once lent him money, but Prince was nonetheless convinced that he was preventing him finding work. In October 1897, when he was fired from a touring company in Newcastle, Prince said that he now had two enemies in the world: the manager there and 'one at the Adelphi, Terriss, the dirty dog!' Later that month he returned to London and shadowed Terriss for six weeks. On 17 December 1897 he bought a butcher's knife for ninepence.

Early that evening Prince went to the Adelphi, where Terriss was playing in *Secret Service*. He hung round the stage door until Terriss arrived in a cab with a friend. Prince attacked, stabbing him twice in the chest. Terriss died within the hour. Prince made no attempt to escape and pleaded 'guilty with provocation' at his trial in January the following year. He was pronounced 'guilty, but insane' and sentenced to life imprisonment in Broadmoor, where he died in 1937 at the age of seventy-one.

Soon after the murder, actors at the Adelphi were disturbed by strange noises in Terriss's dressing room. Over the years they reported footsteps, odd noises, lights going on and off, and a presence in the theatre which watched them constantly. Visitors to the theatre also reported seeing a tall, handsome figure dressed in old-fashioned clothes disappearing through the door where Terriss was struck down.

★

Tommy Baxter and Callum Cunningham, assistant house managers at the Adelphi Theatre, were clearly excited when they met Eddie and me at the stage door on Wednesday 25 May 1994. Tommy, who had previously worked as a tour guide at Glamis Castle in Scotland, had always been interested in the paranormal. He hurried us to the upper circle bar, where, only two weeks previously, he had seen the reflection of a figure in the mirror that disappeared when he turned his head. Tommy said he had a shrewd idea of the ghost's identity but said nothing more. As Eddie paced around the room, Tommy gave me a potted history of the theatre.

It was built in 1814, became the Royal Adelphi in the 1820s, and became one of the great music halls of the nineteenth century. In 1843 changes in the law meant that Drury Lane and Covent Garden became the only legitimate theatres in London, forcing other theatres to become music halls. In the mid-nineteenth century the Adelphi had become famous for melodrama, especially works by Dion Boucicault, which drew the rich and influential, including Queen Victoria. The Adelphi saw its apogée in the 1880s when it was sponsored by the Gatti Brothers, rich Swiss–Italian immigrants to London, whose sponsorship attracted leading actors such as Charles James Lewin and William Terriss. In 1930 the theatre was redecorated in the Art Deco style that visitors see today. The multi-millionaire composer Sir Andrew Lloyd Webber bought the Adelphi in January 1993 and refurbished it for the production of *Sunset Boulevard*.

I looked over to Eddie, who was sitting by a side wall, underneath a set of old framed photographs. I moved over to inspect them more closely when he said that someone was approaching him.

I'm getting an impression of sadness and sorrow. Distress
over a loss, perhaps. An actor – he's quoting lines from a play
– perhaps Shakespeare – which are appropriate to his

189

suffering. This person is slim, almost feminine. He is saying:
'Why should I suffer thus?' I think he's quoting Shakespeare
again; he seems to deal with his life's problems this way.
'Death is what I'm seeking . . .' he says. 'We die, but die but
once/what of the manner of the passing/it is of no great
import./The darkness is the darkness, whichever door we go
through.'

This man has no belief in an afterlife, which has a lot to
do with why he's stuck. He's hiding behind his power of
quotation, not showing himself. Like some actors, his
personality was overtaken by the part he played, and when
he hadn't got a part, he didn't really know who he was. He
doesn't seem to regard his death as being very important –
he still hasn't shown me how he died. Again, he's quoting,
saying: 'I did cause offence and that this should come about
was out of all proportion to the offence. Is it not shameful
that people should be so sensitive to injury, even if it be
slight, that they would go to such lengths to mend their
honour?

'What thinkest thou?' he asks. I think he's nineteenth-
century, but it's difficult to pin him down because he keeps
playing parts. He was murdered. As he sees it, the offence
was trivial. He could be very astringent and would deliver a
barbed comment and then cover it up with a quotation, as if
he weren't really responsible for what he was saying. He was
the sort of man people loved to hate. He could be very
offensive, but this was probably a cover for his own
inadequacies. He'd been asking for this trouble for a long
time.

For him, death was like walking into darkness. But we
must try to release him. He says: 'Release me into what?'
He's showing himself in Elizabethan costume – but again,
that's one of his parts. I think he was homosexual and this
troubled him a lot. He used his acting ability to make sexual
advances and if they were rejected he would withdraw very
quickly into another role, pretending he had just been
play-acting. But he did it to a man who took deep offence.
This is where the honour comes in – the other man, the

murderer, was very angry. Now he says that he's looking at himself more analytically. He says: 'I must confess, I did ensnare myself.' It comes hard to say this, but 'tis true.'

I see him now wearing a rather rich cloak, red and black. It's the costume of a part he played. I think it's the robes of an Elizabethan judge, a character in a play by Marlowe, perhaps. He's put them on to show he's judging himself. He says: 'And this poor wretch, what think ye of him?' He's referring to himself, of course.

He can't see where he's going. We must make clear to him that there is a place for him to go that will make all this look like a bad dream. A fellow actor, a man, is coming for him. He says to our man: 'Come, sweet friend. It's time we were away from this place.' I see them going along a forest track to a green wood. I'll let him go now.

Tommy and Callum were staring at Eddie. 'Look at the photograph on the wall behind you,' Tommy said. 'The man sitting there is William Terriss. I think he was the man you contacted and the one I saw here two weeks ago. I came in through the bar door and looked into the mirror opposite; someone was staring at me – I thought it was a maintenance man. My first reaction was to turn to my left to look at him more closely, but he'd gone.

'Terriss apparently offended a fellow actor in some way. You were right about another thing – Terriss was a homosexual, but very few people know that, as he was married with a daughter. He performed a lot of Shakespeare – excerpts, rather than whole plays, – but very badly. He was a reasonable actor, but was never in the same league as the great Shakespearian actors such as Beerbohm Tree, who played at the Haymarket, or Irving at the Lyceum. I think his major claim to fame is haunting the Ad

'Well, he won't come back now,' said Ed gone.'

Tommy's face fell. This was the last thi say. Before we had met Tommy and C Eddie that it would not be diplomatic released ghosts as well as communicate any theatre, the Adelphi was proud not want them banished. Now I tried to smooth the water: 'What Eddie means is that the ghost will not appear as often – of course he will still be here,' I said rather weakly.

'No, he won't,' said Eddie, oblivious to my attempts at diplomacy. 'He's gone to a much better place.' Tommy looked resigned; he would have to tell the management that the Adelphi's famous ghost had vanished.

We followed Tommy to another area where staff had noticed paranormal disturbances. 'I don't know why, but I have a major problem with this staircase,' said Tommy as we went down to our next stop, the Vivian Ellis Bar. 'I always feel as if there's someone walking beside me.' The Vivian Ellis Bar was next to the stage where the cast were rehearsing for that evening's performance of *Sunset Boulevard*. As soon as Eddie walked into the bar, his expression changed. He usually looks rather severe, and when he is concentrating his face has a blank appearance. But this was an expression I have seen only twice; he looked cheerful, open and positively joyous. Tommy, Callum and I watched as he hugged himself and danced around the room.

There's a great feeling of happiness and gaiety here. I walked straight into it. It's a woman, someone who has lovely memories of this place. She was a well-known actress, I think. I'm sure she's a revenant as she can't leave the place alone. The music attracts her; she wants to dance. I can feel her feet moving mine. But I can't dance – not the way she could anyway.

This woman played many gay roles in her time – and I mean that in the old-fashioned sense of the word! She says: 'I'm happy to be here, and I'm always happy when the show is good.' I think she gets an inkling of whether the show is going to be good or not. [I asked her what she felt about *Sunset Boulevard*.] She says: 'I wish I were in it.' [I asked Eddie: Did she dance or sing?] She danced. She says: 'I did my best to sing; not everybody thought I had a good voice, but I did my best! You know, you have to do what the part mands, and you just do your best. If it's the best you can ʼhat's all right.'

She comes from the age of the music halls. I think she was around during the war years. It's very difficult to place her with any exactness, because she keeps coming back into the memory of the theatre. I think that she took the opportunity to come to us when she saw that we were here.

[I asked Eddie: What does she look like?] She's amused by the question, but not very forthcoming. 'Some say I went on too long,' she says. I've got to be careful here, because I think she was a brunette naturally. She says: 'I had more success as a blonde!' She's a very nice lady – very truthful about herself. She knows she's got to let go of this place, but she can't help herself coming back.

[I asked: Does she watch over the production or help the actors?] She laughs when you ask that. 'Have you ever tried helping a producer?' she says. 'But, to be serious, yes I do help in very subtle ways. Oh! How I wish I could teach them to dance sometimes. But there are some excellent young people coming on and it's good to see them. This theatre has a good future – a great future.' I think what she means is that she can see the future of this production. She says: 'It will have its rough moments – it's going through a few now – but if they persist with it, it will do very well.'

When Eddie had finished Callum said: 'I'm sure you had Jessie Matthews with you – she had a strong association with the Adelphi. I'm surprised she's here; everyone thought that William Terriss was the Adelphi's only ghost. It's nice to know that someone's here for happy reasons.'

Eddie replied: 'As soon as you mentioned her name, I got a strong sense of recognition. I'm sure it was her, too, although I had no idea that she performed here.'

Callum then said: 'Come with me, I'm going to show you something very interesting.' We followed him into the small, dimly lit back-stalls bar, whose walls were covered with posters of productions from the 1930s. 'This is the Jessie Matthews Bar,' he said. 'She was once tipped to be Fred Astaire's dancing partner. Sir Andrew Lloyd Webber is a great fan of hers and insisted we dedicated a bar to her memory.'

193

Jessie Matthews was born in Soho, London, in 1907, the seventh child of a market-stall fruiterer. As a child, Jessie was so full of energy that her mother took her to a doctor, fearing she was suffering from the nervous disorder, St Vitus' Dance. She made her West End début at the age of sixteen in Irving Berlin's *Music Box Revue*, where she was noticed by the great producer Charles B. Cochrane. The following year she went to Broadway, and by the time she was twenty-one she was a star earning the (then) huge amount of £200 a week. The show that made her a household name was *Evergreen*, first performed at the Adelphi in 1930. She made many songs her own, including Noel Coward's 'Room with a View', Cole Porter's 'Let's Do It' and, most famously, Harry Woods's 'Over My Shoulder'. The film of *Evergreen* launched a glittering film career in Britain and America, with credits including *The Beloved Vagabond*, *It's Love Again* and *This England*.

But her private life was sad. Her three marriages ended in divorce and she lost two children at birth. Her affair with, and subsequent marriage to, matinée idol Sonnie Hale, created a national scandal, after Hale left his first wife, the other great 1930s star Evelyn Laye, for Jessie. After the war her career declined. 'Suddenly it stopped,' she said in her autobiography, *Over My Shoulder* (1974). 'I'd been right at the top, then smack down at the bottom.' She toured in repertory theatre and then, towards the end of her life, won a new generation of fans in the 1960s as Mrs Dale, wife of a country doctor in a long-running radio series, *Mrs Dale's Diary*. She died of cancer on 21 August 1981. Dame Anna Neagle paid this tribute: 'She was a lovely, light-hearted person, elfin-like with huge eyes and lovely legs, and she danced divinely.'

Sir Andrew Lloyd Webber has long adored Jessie. His ex-wife, Sarah Brightman, who bears a strong resemblance to Jessie, starred in a BBC documentary on her life entitled *Catch a Falling Star*. Sir Andrew has also bought the film rights to her autobiography and plans one day to make a full-length feature film about his heroine.

★

Tommy and Callum were obviously impressed by Eddie, even though the Adelphi had probably lost one of its star ghosts through him. They seemed convinced that he had a genuine gift; he had known nothing about the Adelphi, yet had given astonishingly accurate information about the ghosts there.

Two weeks later I called Eddie and mentioned that I had found an old programme from Jessie Matthews' 1930s show *Evergreen* at Covent Garden's Theatre Museum. Suddenly I realized that he had become distant. 'Have you been listening to me, Eddie?' I asked, and he replied that Jessie Matthews had come to him again.

'She's very interested in the film you mentioned, the one Sir Andrew Lloyd Webber is planning to make,' said Eddie.

'Why, is she still interested in what people say about her?' I asked.

Eddie replied: 'Yes, very much so. She's telling me that if he doesn't get a move on, it will be too late and everyone will have forgotten her. She's asking us to help her. We are a direct line of contact for her to Sir Andrew. She saw her chance and has made the most of it! I think that was characteristic of Jessie Matthews – she never let an opportunity pass her by.'

The Theatre Royal, Haymarket

The Theatre Royal, Haymarket is haunted by several ghosts, including an unknown elderly man who walks noiselessly about the passages of the theatre and backstage; John Baldwin Buckstone, an actor–manager who presided over the Haymarket in its golden era, from 1853 until 1879; and David Edward Morris, who managed the theatre in the early 1800s.

Until the late eighteenth century, the Theatre Royal, Drury Lane was the only theatre in London with a royal licence, but the Haymarket defied the law and continued to operate as a playhouse until it, too, was eventually granted a licence, secured by David Edward Morris, who managed the theatre until 1837.

'Many psychics have visited the Haymarket in the hope of catching a glimpse of one of its ghosts,' said Mark Stradling, the manager, when I called him in May 1994 to arrange a tour of the theatre. 'You're welcome to look, but I won't be able to help you as I don't believe any of it.' It was left to Robert Ross, the stage-doorman, to show us around the Haymarket when we arrived on 6 June. Mr Ross, who had worked at the theatre for six years, led Eddie and me across the stage and into the front rows of the stalls, and said he would come back after half an hour.

As Eddie settled down I wandered around the deserted auditorium and gazed at the striking scenery for that evening's show, *Arcadia* by Tom Stoppard. The stage was empty save for a few chairs and a huge wooden table where a globe, a basket, several photographs and a hat were scattered. But it was the backdrop that caught my eye: four huge Palladian windows looking out on to an almost cloudless blue sky, a tree casting its leaves and branches across one corner. It was simple yet uplifting. Then Eddie waved me to come back. He said:

I've got someone with me. He says: 'What are you here for? What are you doing? I don't remember asking you.' Our arrival here is a threat to him, so I'm trying to reassure him and encourage him to tell me where he comes from. My first impression is that he spans the First World War and into the 1920s. He says: 'My life here continues.' He's giving the impression that he was an actor.

He says: 'I still know my parts and could quote them at you. It still gives me great pleasure when they come here in their hundreds. The odd one sees me and recognizes me, but mostly, I'm just a shade that they pass by. But I would not wish to alarm anyone.' He uses Shakespearian language a lot – I think he played some Shakespearian parts. He sniggers when I say that. He says: 'How could you be in the theatre and not be acquainted with Shakespeare?'

I want to know how he died. He says: 'But 'twas a small thing.' There's something odd about his death that he won't reveal. He says, rather haughtily: 'It was not what you would call an honourable death.' I think there was a sexual aspect to his death. He says: 'If you press me, I would admit that I over-indulged. Taxed myself once too often. It gives me no pleasure to recollect, so I would be pleased to leave the matter at that.'

[I asked Eddie when the man died.] He says: 'It all seems much of a muchness to me. I was here one evening and then again the next evening. It made no difference.' I've got to try and release him. One of the reasons he won't consider going on is because he feels guilty about how he died. He's getting disturbed now; he knows he's got to face up to it. I get the impression that he had a heart attack which was very painful. He says: 'I would have cried for help had the circumstances been different. Oh God, I was glad when it was all finished.'

He says: 'In my latter years, they would call on me for the fill-in parts. I didn't enjoy these much, but they kept me in the theatre. This was my real life so I would do any menial part if it brought me back in here.'

We must let him go now. I tell him that there's a very large part for him to play, that he must make his exit here and pass on to a larger stage. That idea appeals to him. Someone has come to him now dressed as a jester and is bowing. 'If it would please my Lord, I will lead the way,' he says. I can see them moving on to another stage; the scenery and backcloth are extraordinary – it just goes on and on into the distance for ever. He's finding it exciting and the jester is somersaulting in front of him, amusing him. He says: ''Tis a fancy scene thou dost present and fetches me on.' He's on his way now.

Mr Ross had joined us for the last few minutes. 'I think that must be the elderly gentleman who haunts the boxes and auditorium as well as backstage,' he said. Mr Ross led us backstage to dressing room number one, by the stage door, which was once used by John Buckstone himself, the legendary and much-loved actor–manager. On the door was the name of Roger Allam, the leading man in *Arcadia*. Inside, the room was decorated in soothing blues and yellows; deep blue carpet, yellow walls, striped chintz curtains and a single bed. A dark oak chest of drawers and a writing desk stood against one wall and a small wash-basin surrounded by a large mirror faced the bed.

In 1963 the late Margaret Rutherford, the brilliant character

actress, spent the night in the dressing room with her husband
Stringer Davis while she was appearing in *School for Scandal*, as it
had been too foggy to drive home. During the night both had heard
creaking noises from the cupboard. That cupboard, they later
discovered, hides a bricked-up doorway which once led to the
stage. The following evening Miss Rutherford and her dresser
glimpsed a figure disappearing into the cupboard and decided that
it was the ghost of Buckstone. Other performers, including Susan
Hampshire, Fiona Fullerton and Donald Sinden, have also said that
they have felt his presence.

I sat down opposite Eddie on a velvet chair and he began to
speak:

Someone is gesticulating at me. He's remembering a part he
played. His arm is pointing upwards in a victory salute. I
think this gesture was a very important part of his role – his
moment of triumph, perhaps. He is dressed in Georgian
clothing, although it could be a costume. He's wearing what
looks like a frock coat with tails – it's very colourful and
decorative, but I can only see it from the back. He's wearing
white breeches, with white stockings and buckled shoes, but
no wig. He's very proud of himself, very proud.

He says: 'But I died in poverty – that was the nadir. I was
neglected and, for the most part, forgotten. So I come here
and stay here, for this is the memory of my triumph. I cannot
let it go.' I now see him wearing a heavy brown coat with
quite large lapels. He's also wearing spats and a rather fancy
wide-brimmed trilby hat with an affected flop on one side of
the brim. And black shoes. But I'm not sure about that – he
objects to the mention of black. 'Brown shoes,' he corrects
me. They're rather nice shoes with decorative stitches on
their uppers. He's holding a splendid cane with a brass knob
at the top.

I think he died of pneumonia. He appears as he would have
looked during his moment of triumph – in his fifties – but he
was much older when he died. He says: 'In my real life, I
played the part, you know.' There's a lot of affectation, but I
think that was expected in those days. I think he died during

the First World War. I like him – he has a nice feeling about him. He was well liked and I get the feeling he was very generous to his fellow actors.

But no-one remembered him during his declining years. I think that's what upset him at the end. He says: 'There were one or two who helped me, but most forgot. They were too busy with their own triumphs.' He's open and frank and is not hiding anything. I think he would be quite pleased to leave. 'But not without regret, you understand. For it was a good life, except in the end,' he says.

I think we're ready to help him go. He says: 'Yes, it is time for me to drop the curtain on this present scene. I'm ready.' There's such an exciting feeling building up. Several people are coming for him out of the light. It's quite a special departure; this befits the man, as he is a good soul. Three friends from the theatre are coming for him; I cannot make out their faces or see very much of them as the light they bring is blinding. He sees them and goes up to them; he shakes hands first and embraces them. 'We must be correct in all things, you know,' he says. 'And thank you, thank you.' We can leave him now, because they're taking him away. Wish him Godspeed, he's a good man.

John Baldwin Buckstone managed the Haymarket from 1853 to 1879. As well as being a manager, Buckstone was an accomplished playwright, comedian and actor. He was a particular favourite of Queen Victoria, who *was* amused by his flagrant disrespect of the classics. Before he moved into theatre management, Buckstone teamed up with Benjamin Webster (who took over as manager from David Morris in 1837), who helped Buckstone stage farces at the Adelphi.

When Webster retired, Buckstone ran the Haymarket and soon established a reputation for mounting marathon programmes of farce. His policy was to give value for money; his shows began early and lasted until one o'clock in the morning. Unlike his predecessor, Benjamin Webster, who had private means, Buckstone relied on box office takings, which were not enough to fund the extravagant programmes and the generous wages he paid to actors and staff.

By 1861 the theatre was in trouble. Then Buckstone produced a new play, *Our American Cousin*, written by the Haymarket's chief dramatist, Tom Taylor, and hoped that it would turn his fortunes around. He invited E.A. Sothern, an English actor who had made the play a hit across the Atlantic, to the Haymarket. At first the play was not a success, but Buckstone persevered and Sothern built up the main character, Lord Dundreary – a caricature of an English gentleman with a ridiculous frock coat, eyeglass, huge whiskers and a stutter – until he became the most fashionable and talked-about actor in London.

Buckstone's gamble had paid off; the crowds grew and takings mounted. But he was a hopeless businessman and let most of the money slip through his hands. He was also going deaf; he could not hear his cue and would lip-read actors until it was time for him to say his lines. Meanwhile, Sothern, his huge success behind him, was starting to take control at the Haymarket. As Sothern's star rose, Buckstone's declined. By 1878 he was stone deaf and playing fill-in parts; but he did not mind. He had saved the Haymarket, which was all that mattered to him. He was old, frail and in debt, but remained cheerful to the end. In August 1879 the Haymarket's new manager, J.S. Clarke, organized a farewell benefit for Buckstone. He was to play The Old Member in the play *Money*, but he suffered severe paralysis just before the show opened and died on 31 October 1879.

Part III

The Power of the Past

Chapter 12

Haunted Ramparts

Had I but served God as diligently as I have served the King, he would not have given me over in my grey hairs.

Cardinal Wolsey

Most visitors to England's stately homes and castles are impressed with the overwhelming sense of history that these magnificent buildings exude. Blenheim Palace, Leeds Castle and Castle Howard – to name just a few – are outstanding examples of what might be called living history: although open to the public, most are still inhabited by the descendants of England's most illustrious families. However, for a psychic as sensitive as Eddie a stately home imbued with the history of generations can be a difficult place to negotiate. He might be overwhelmed – not only by the sheer weight of history, but by the countless psychic imprints, revenants and trapped spirits within their walls. It was for this reason that Eddie had always avoided England's castles and houses; he feared that they would be too much of a drain on his powers.

I had found that more and more major historical figures had come forward during the research. Some of these appeared by chance – an unprepossessing pub in Croydon turned out to be haunted by Lord Howard of Effingham, who commanded the campaign against the Spanish Armada – while Charles I contacted Eddie after our visits to the Civil War battle sites of Naseby and

Edgehill. In July 1994 I decided Eddie was ready to visit a few castles and stately homes. He agreed; our quest to discover ghosts around the country had sharpened his psychic skills, he said, and he felt ready to tackle a larger subject. I suggested three locations: Hampton Court Palace, Chatsworth in Derbyshire and Warwick Castle. We were excited and moved by the results; a cast of colourful characters approached him and confessed their sins, recounted injustices against them and wistfully recalled their earthly lives. Their conversations with Eddie also shed fascinating new light on characters whose exploits are recorded in countless history books.

Hampton Court Palace

On the banks of the Thames, opposite Kingston, Surrey, stands Hampton Court, perhaps England's finest royal palace. Last used by George III, who eventually abandoned it in favour of Windsor Castle, Hampton Court was built in the early sixteenth century by Thomas Wolsey, then Archbishop of York, who later became Cardinal and the second most powerful man in the country after Henry VIII. Wolsey had leased the site for £50 a year from the Knights Hospitallers of St John in 1514 because he wanted a home which would be convenient for London. Here he built himself a grand house around two courtyards at a cost of 200,000 gold crowns; there were reputed to be 1,000 rooms, including apartments for 280 guests. The Venetian ambassador reported that he had to cross eight rooms before reaching the Cardinal's audience chamber.

As soon as Eddie walked through the Great Gatehouse, he sensed a spirit approaching him. It was a man who was bringing with him a great deal of sadness and strong feelings of remorse. He was not earthbound, but he had not advanced very far in the next world. 'It was clear that his eminence in his earth life had hampered him in his journey,' said Eddie later. 'His comments were moving and profound and although I was not sure who he was, I had a reasonable idea.' Eddie was being laudably cautious here; from what the spirit told him it seemed certain that we had been contacted by the ghost of Cardinal Wolsey himself:

'How doth ambition for power betray a man! I forgot who my true master was and when at last I saw the path from which I had long strayed and sought my way back, the price was indeed a heavy one. I had to give up everything, even my life. It seems a long way off now, yet when I come back to the recollection, all the feelings, the fears, the sense of self-importance and – I dare to say it, the greed – are with me again. I am reminded that even now my soul is not sufficiently cleansed.

'Those who exercise power of state do little understand the mighty trap that can ensnare them and call themselves great for this is what the world doth see, the pomp and the majesty, often borrowed. But the one who is so raised is still a man, a puny thing set against the majesty of our Lord. Should he forget this, or push the thought aside, the trap doth receive him and once within, the one who thinks himself great puffs up his own importance yet further. It is a sad progress and one that invites the great fall that is sure to follow. So it was with me.

'To lead others is a task that is a privilege, but yet a great responsibility. Our Lord will strengthen the arm of one who takes this on himself in true humility. Yet how very few are those who can resist the temptation to imagine that their new-found power is their right and possession. Such poor stuff we are made of.

'These are my thoughts that I share with you. Think of me in return and pray that I may make better progress towards the source of love and light to which I strain. Farewell.'

Under Henry VIII Wolsey held unprecedented power. He became Chancellor in 1515 and Cardinal the same year; he controlled every area of government, shaping domestic policies in finance, the law and towards the Church; and, abroad, he was single-handedly responsible for giving shape to Henry's many, often contradictory, ambitions. But his ostentatious lifestyle, epitomized by lavish parties at Hampton Court, fed the jealousy of his enemies at Court, who moved against him when he failed to persuade the Pope to grant Henry's divorce from Catherine of Aragon in 1529. Wolsey was impeached and arrested on a charge of high treason. He died in 1530 at Leicester Abbey on his way to the Tower of London.

Henry took over all his property, including Hampton Court, and ordered a lavish programme of rebuilding and expansion. The palace's kitchens were deemed too small for royal entertaining, so Henry added a second kitchen. Food had always been close to Henry's heart and his prodigious appetite has been the subject of many books. It was no surprise to Eddie, then, when a spirit approached him in the great kitchen.

This man was involved in the rebuilding of the great kitchen. His father was a stonemason, who had apprenticed him as a boy to another stonemason working at the palace. He says:

'Carts drawn by teams of six horses brought the blocks of stone from the south. They had to strengthen the approach road to the palace and to do this they sometimes used the waste stone. Although they had a simple form of block and tackle; handling the large blocks of uncut stone could be dangerous.

'In order to reduce the stone to useable blocks, they would roughly face up the stone to give four parallel faces. Then a groove was cut, running round all four faces. This was done with a chisel to start with and made a little deeper with a crude form of saw. Next, the block was held in a large clamp with the groove close to the edge of the support. A massive weight in vertical lines was dropped on to the portion of overhanging stone. This usually caused the overhang to break off at the groove, leaving a new face that was then trimmed.

'Offcuts were used for carved figures, but there was a lot of wastage. Some stone was rejected as too treacherous to work. We would say the devil was in it.

'I worked at Hampton Court for a number of years, although I was sometimes sent off to other sites to help and instruct. I died at Exeter Cathedral when an overloaded part of the wooden scaffold collapsed while I was inspecting repairs.'

Hampton Court is probably most famous as the scene of Henry VIII's marital dramas. Before his divorce from Catherine of

Aragon, Henry built Anne Boleyn private lodgings there; Jane Seymour delivered a frail son in the palace who died there less than two weeks later; and Catherine Howard, Henry's fifth wife, was cross-examined there by Thomas Cranmer, Archbishop of Canterbury, about her infidelity.

Today, Hampton Court's guidebook relates the story of how Catherine Howard's ghost is supposed to run screaming along the gallery between the Great Watching Chamber and the Chapel in Henry VIII's State Apartments. Eddie knew this story, but as he walked the length of the gallery, he failed to pick up any trace of the unfortunate Queen. However, four days later, in his home in Lincoln, she unexpectedly approached him:

She says: 'I pleaded in vain; he was a man to be greatly feared. I found his appetites repelled me – I could not bring myself to his bed without feelings of apprehension and revulsion. I could not find it in me to serve him. The case made against me was in large measure false; Henry wanted rid of me and his hints to his courtiers were enough. Opportunities were made for me to be alone with those poor young men who offered me some solace. Neither they nor I realized the fatal peril. No deed took place between me and them that was other than restored my dignity; I truly had them keep a distance. When I found out what had been done to them to extract a confession my heart was rent.

'Faced with threats to violate my person, I too yielded to the demands to confess my guilt where none there was. But I could not save those two young men, nor myself – my pleas for mercy went unheeded. I know I forfeited my life with ill grace, but I was filled with terror and could find little courage. No wonder my shade still bears witness to that same terror.

' "Where am I now?" you ask. I linger still within earshot, but not bound to earth as some are. My heart is burdened with remorse that I allowed those young men to comfort me and thus led them to their doom. I fear for their safety even now, for I have a sense that heaven has not yet received them. If I could be assured that God has taken them and they

207

have forgiven my thoughtless actions, the weight that holds
me down would be lifted from me. Thus I come to ask what
help you can afford me in my search for peace for my sorely
troubled soul.'

Catherine Howard, the young grand-daughter of the second Duke
of Norfolk, became Queen in July 1540, the month when Henry
divorced Anne of Cleves. Catherine began to appoint her own
allies to the royal household, including, in August 1541, Francis
Dereham, to whom she had once been betrothed. It was a foolish
and fatal error, since Henry had long been feared for his jealousies
and suspicions; the presence of Dereham at court would inevitably
be used by Catherine's enemies.

As Henry's fifth wife, it was incumbent upon Catherine to
produce an heir. But during the early days of their marriage,
Henry, by now a middle-aged man, suffered from repeated bouts of
bad health. After a jousting accident in 1524 he had suffered from
varicose veins, ulcers and fevers and, anxious not to let his young
wife see him in such a state, Henry rarely slept with her. It was
during one of these bouts of ill-health that Catherine renewed her
friendship with Thomas Culpeper, a handsome young courtier
whom she had met the previous year in the King's Privy Chamber.
Catherine's reason for pursuing an affair may have been to provide
her husband with an heir – or perhaps she simply sought an exciting
diversion in her cloistered life.

It was John Lascelles, a courtier and the brother of one of
Catherine's former chamberwomen, who ended the Queen's
ill-advised dalliances. Lascelles told Thomas Cranmer, the Archbishop of Canterbury, that the Queen's life before her marriage
had been far from spotless and that she had been pre-contracted
to Frances Dereham, thereby annulling her marriage with
Henry. Cranmer confronted the King with the news at Hampton
Court on 2 November 1540. At first Henry refused to believe the
charges; but then Dereham confessed under torture and implicated Culpeper. Catherine was charged with treason and
beheaded in 1542.

Shortly after Eddie's contact with Catherine, he was approached
by Culpeper himself, who said:

'I am received of God. The torment inflicted on me purged my soul and when I died I found myself in the presence of God's angels, surrounded by their love and light. They healed the wounds which my mind still held, since when my soul has been nurtured by the glories of heaven. I hold no bitterness over my earthly end and would hasten to assure my beloved Queen that there is nothing I need to forgive. I have sought her spirit since coming here; I was told that she was bonded and would be released in God's time. I pray that this is now the time.'

Eddie then asked whether Culpeper knew what had happened to Dereham. As he asked the question, he felt another contact beginning, with Dereham. This time, Eddie sensed great pain and anguish:

'Your light doth reach me in my wretchedness. Look upon me if you can. Am I not a sorry sight? Not content with trying to tear me apart, they quartered my poor racked body. It caused me further torment to feel my parts being severed, even though my spirit had just quit the body. What cruelty and degradation to heap upon one scarcely into manhood. I cannot forgive them, though they were only doing their master's bidding. My Lady, the Queen, saw me racked, and screamed; then I could find it in me to forgive her.
   'Now it seems they still have power over me, for am I not still imprisoned in this dark place? Where is my Saviour, my Lord? I have tried to pray as I was taught, but always great bitterness invades my mind. Do you bring some relief for my misery? I pray you do not leave me.'

Eddie told Dereham that he would pray for him to find the strength to let go of his bitterness. That same evening, the spirit of Culpeper returned and told Eddie that a bright being had come to him – perhaps an angel – to ask him (Culpeper) if he would help a poor soul out of darkness. 'He agreed to do this and was taken down to a strange region,' said Eddie.

209

As they descended, said Culpeper, it grew darker until the only light was that which they themselves cast around them. There they met Dereham, at first without recognizing him. He said: 'Have you come to take me from this place?' to which Culpeper replied: 'For no other purpose, I understand.' Then the angelic being told them to make ready for another journey. They linked hands and moved up to a brighter place where their Queen, Catherine, was waiting for them. She was overcome by their sudden appearance and at first could not grasp its significance. The angelic being told her to take their hands, 'For they hold only their love for you,' it said. All three of them then moved towards the light of heaven.

Eddie now thought hard about his encounter with Catherine Howard. 'I think she gave a rather more innocent account of herself than was strictly true,' he said. 'But then, she had made little progress into the spirit world when I encountered her and was essentially the same person that she had been on earth. When we pass into the next life, we are not suddenly made pure; the improvements have to take place gradually and sometimes – as in Dereham's case – painfully.'

Chatsworth

Although not the largest or most magnificent stately home in England, Chatsworth, seat of the Duke of Devonshire, is one of its most famous. Every year, hundreds of thousands of visitors pass through its doors, attracted by its unique and quintessentially English atmosphere. Eddie had suggested it simply because he had so enjoyed his last visit there, over twenty years previously. Neither of us knew much about the house, except for the fact that Elizabeth I had confined Mary Queen of Scots, the Catholic claimant to the English throne, to Chatsworth for fifteen years after Mary had fled to England in May 1568.

The house had been built in 1549 by the Earl of Shrewsbury on a levelled terrace above the River Derwent in Derbyshire. The fourth Earl, later the first Duke of Devonshire, inherited the house in 1684; the existing house is the result of his twenty-year rebuilding programme.

Eddie walked through the main entrance hall into a suite of rooms now called the Scots Rooms. Although nothing remains of the Elizabethan house, Eddie was aware that Mary Queen of Scots would have left a strong imprint in the area. When he reached the Green Satin Bedroom, he became aware of a spirit presence. But he was sure it was not Mary; this was an elderly woman with a rather autocratic manner. Puzzled, Eddie asked a guard whether the room was known to be haunted. The guard said that there was indeed a ghost, Evelyn, Duchess of Devonshire, who was born in 1870 and lived at Chatsworth until she died at the age of ninety. By now, the spirit had become insistent, so Eddie moved to a quiet corner of the room and took out his pen and paper:

'I know that the condition I am in is most unsatisfactory. I am neither in this world nor the next. I am aware that you think it is because I am attached to my possessions. That is all very well, but you know that this place and all it contains is a great responsibility which I have taken very seriously. It is a family and a national treasure.

'I do get so nervous about the people that come through the house – the children especially. Many of them are not well behaved and try to handle things here – not that I try to do anything about it any more. It is most frustrating at times.'

She seems exhausted after saying this; she sits down on one of her favourite sofas and sighs; she looks old and tired, but she still holds her back very straight. I can see a light playing on her from above and a transformation is beginning to take place. Her years are starting to fall away; she is standing up now, looking bright and alert. She asks: 'What has happened? I feel different. What have you done?'

I tell her I haven't done anything – she's done it herself, she's let go. She asks: 'May I go now? And to where?' I tell her to wait a short while as someone is coming to escort her away. It is her husband; he is going to her, dressed very formally in the way she remembers him. He holds out his hand and she takes it. They walk away to a beautiful garden. They are gone.

211

Eddie sensed no other presence at Chatsworth that day and made his way home. The following day, at home in Lincoln, he wondered whether Mary Queen of Scots had moved on to the next world; she had endured such injustice, Eddie reasoned, that she might well have been trapped. Then Eddie sensed a spirit; it was a woman and she was clearly distressed.

'I am weary and can go no further,' she says. It is Mary, dragging a large, iron-bound, barrel-topped chest behind her. It contains her royal regalia as Queen of Scotland and items that supported her claims as heir to the throne of England. The scene is rather distressing; her own state of mind is confused as she is still trapped by her earthly ambition.

She is on a rough, stony path, and it is going to be very difficult to help her. I don't have the energy at the moment. Then she says: 'Why did you bring me hope and then forsake me?' She sounds very petulant. 'I thought you would help me pull this load I have to take forward.' I ask her where she is taking it and she says: 'Wheresoever I am going. I cannot leave it. It has to come with me – it is mine own. How can I prove myself, except by those things I bring with me?'

I ask her where she thinks the upward path she is taking will lead her. Impatiently, she says: 'I know not. Will you help me with my possessions?' I decide to be more direct: 'Can't you see that heaven awaits you, but you can't take that treasure chest with you?' I say. 'Where am I then? Am I in purgatory?' she asks. 'Yes, you are,' I say, 'and you are holding yourself there.' She replies: 'Must I then forsake my possessions?' 'Yes, my Lady,' I tell her.

At this point, Eddie's contact with Mary faded and he watched her sit down on a large stone at the side of the path. He had been surprised by Mary's behaviour; accounts of the calm and courage she showed at her execution were at odds with the petulant, demanding and insecure young woman he had contacted. Mary's own sense of royalty, it seemed, was holding her back in the next world.

In Catholic eyes, Mary, the only daughter of James V of Scotland and his second wife, Mary of Guise, had been the legitimate heir to the English throne. But her efforts to establish a base in Scotland ended in 1568, after the Scottish nobles had rebelled against her; she fled to England, where she spent the rest of her life confined to castles, under the protection of the Queen. Mary became the focus for several opposition groups to Elizabeth I, supported by many Protestant noblemen, who were concerned that Elizabeth had not produced an heir, and by English Catholics. In 1586 Mary was tricked into providing evidence of her involvement in a plot to destroy Elizabeth. She was tried, found guilty of treason and beheaded on 8 February 1587 at Fotheringay Castle, in Northamptonshire. According to eye-witnesses, she met her end with dignity and courage.

The day after his first contact with Mary, Eddie received confirmation that he had indeed been in touch with her. As he sat down with a cup of tea in his living room, he had the impression of heavenly rejoicing. 'The joy and happiness that came through to me left me in no doubt that Mary had been released,' he said. 'At that point, I was content to accept all that had happened.'

Warwick Castle

Behind the Gothic façade of this picture-book castle on the banks of the River Avon, the Earls of Warwick have enjoyed their position of privilege since the early days of the Norman Conquest. Little survives today of the earliest stonework, an octagonal Norman keep that was destroyed by the Barons' Revolt in 1264; most of the outer features of the present castle date from the fourteenth century, when it passed to the Beauchamp family. Its two main defences are Caesar's Tower, a magnificent six-storey edifice crowned with an unusual double parapet, and Guy's Tower. The former was built by Thomas Beauchamp, one of Edward III's most distinguished generals; Guy's Tower was built by his son, again Thomas, in 1394.

As Eddie walked through the main bailey into the courtyard, he sensed the presence of a spirit who wanted to converse with him. He quickly made his way to a nearby bench where the spirit began to speak:

213

'Grant me an audience, I pray thee. I went into battle with my Lord Warwick. It was a duty which sometimes befell us; if my Lord fell in battle, I would be at hand to give him the last rites and comfort his soul's leaving. Though my Lord did fall, I was already fallen. I did my best to stay with him after my death, but there came to me my brothers [fellow priests] who prevailed on me to go with them, so I departed into a land of light where my soul did find its rest 'til the pains of mortal life passed from my mind. Now I serve a greater Lord, the Lord of love and his sweet mother, Our Lady.

'As to my Lord Warwick, whom I had near forgot 'til you awakened my faded memories, he had a hard journey after his death in battle. The fire in his heart for Henry and England took much time to quench. He kept his armour – his sword and his lance – with him, but they became exceeding heavy as he journeyed upwards until he had to let them go. Then the goodness of his nature shone forth and he was taken up into this heaven where I met him and stayed with him awhile. Our paths have long separated and I have had no more call from him, though I believe he has been well received. Thank you for your interest – I ask God's blessing on your work.'

My research suggested that this was the spirit of a chaplain to Richard Neville, whose dazzling political and military manoeuvres in the Wars of the Roses, together with his vast wealth, had earned him the title 'Warwick the Kingmaker'. The Wars of the Roses were really a series of seventeen battles, which began in 1455 and lasted until 1487; during this time the crown changed hands five times as the protagonists, the two rival branches of the House of Plantagenet, the Yorkists and the Lancastrians – the White and Red Roses of popular history – struggled for supremacy.

Richard Neville was created Earl of Warwick in 1450 and championed the Yorkist cause. In 1460 he defeated and captured Henry VI at Northampton, had his cousin, Edward of York, proclaimed King Edward IV in 1461 and then destroyed the Lancastrian army at Towton. When Edward tried to assert his independence, Warwick joined the Lancastrians, forced the King to flee to Holland and restored Henry VI to the throne in 1470. He

214

Dr Faustina Raciti and her elder daughter, Rosaria

Dr Raciti's eighteenth-century house in Sicily. The malign influence of the house almost destroyed her health and her medical practice

Dick Turpin was a regular lodger at the Spaniard's Inn on the edge of Hampstead Heath in London. Could he have been the evasive highwayman that Eddie contacted there? (*Mary Evans Picture Library*)

The Grenadier pub is said to be haunted during September by the ghost of an officer who was flogged to death after he was found cheating at cards

Dan Leno in one of his best-loved roles of pantomime dame (*Hulton Deutsch Collection Limited*)

Dan Leno. His psychic imprint manifests itself as a strong smell of lavender in the Green Room of the Theatre Royal, Drury Lane (*Hulton Deutsch Collection Limited*)

William Terriss, one of the great Victorian theatre idols (*Hulton Deutsch Collection Limited*)

Jessie Matthews. Her spirit carries a great sense of happiness and gaiety to the Adelphi Theatre in London (*Hulton Deutsch Collection Limited*)

Catherine Howard. Eddie felt that during his communication with her 'she gave a rather more innocent account of herself than was strictly true' (*Mary Evans Picture Library*)

Cardinal Wolsey. He spoke of the corrupting effect of power (*Peter Newark's Historical Pictures*)

Mary Queen of Scots. The petulant, demanding young woman who made contact seemed at odds with the image of calm courage which she is reported to have displayed at her execution (*Mary Evans Picture Library*)

An artist's impression of the execution of King Charles I in Whitehall in 1649 (*Peter Newark's Historical Pictures*)

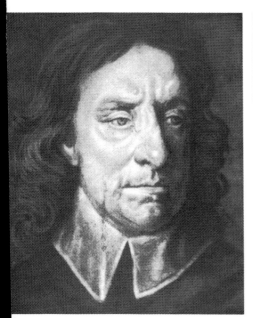

Pastel drawing of Oliver Cromwell, attributed to Samuel Cooper (*Peter Newark's Historical Pictures*)

John Wellens shows the deep gash that inexplicably appeared on his head. His injury was identical to that suffered by a Roundhead, who had been haunting his house (*Gillian Cribbs*)

Anne Boleyn. She made contact on the exact anniversary of her death 458 years earlier (*Mary Evans Picture Library*)

Robert Devereux, second Earl of Essex. He said: 'If it could be said of a man that he died of ambition, that man is me' (*Peter Newark's Historical Pictures*)

Eddie and Gillian at the Tower of London (*Christopher Johns*)

Christopher Panton. His brothers, Fred
and Harold, created the Lincolnshire
Aviation Heritage Centre as a tribute
to him

Tommy Pinkham

Gillian Cribbs with Donald
Macer-Wright, the current owner of
Littledean Hall (*Christopher Johns*)

Eddie outside Littledean Hall, one of
the most haunted houses in England
(*Gillian Cribbs*)

The *Marchioness* is lifted from the Thames on 21 August 1989. Only eighty-seven passengers survived; twenty-five bodies were recovered, but at least thirty-eight were never found (*Syndication International*)

An example of the appalling devastation wrought by the Armenian earthquake in December 1988 (*Associated Press*)

was eventually defeated and killed by Edward IV at the Battle of Barnet in 1471.

In 1994 Warwick Castle was managed by the National Trust. One of its most striking features was an exhibition of waxwork models from Madame Tussaud's in London which portrays some of the illustrious scenes in the castle's long history. As Eddie was admiring the display, he became aware that he was being drawn deep into the psychic imprint of the castle's past. He said:

Quite suddenly I saw a number of figures in medieval dress standing beside the waxworks. To my surprise, one of them, a man in his early thirties, stepped forward and bowed, with a flourish of his hat. He was wearing woollen hose and a jacket with puffed sleeves that was belted at the waist. He said:

'I step forward at your bidding and would be of service to you. In the times you probe, life was very hazardous, especially for those of my station who knew not whether a quick or slow death awaited them. We had a very strong sense of station and quickly took offence if someone of lesser standing presumed to push us aside or take precedence. We had to keep our wits about us; the only ones who could be excused badly judged actions or lack of deference were the simple ones, the fools. Some took advantage of this and feigned foolishness; a few dressed for the part for the entertainment of their fellows and masters.

'As for me, I tried to walk the best path I could judge, hiding my sharp mind where it was prudent to do so, but using it to further my interests. But in the end, fate took a hand and I was pressed to take up arms on behalf of my Lord, an occupation that did not suit me. I lost my life painfully, dying in my thirty-seventh year. My only comfort was that I shared my fate with many of my fellows.'

Then the man repeated his initial gesture, bowing and stepping back among the rest of the figures. It was one of the strangest encounters I have ever had. But the simple message was that although the lives of great men dominate our history books, the unknown and forgotten people also played an important part.

Chapter 13

His Divine Right

He nothing common did, or mean,
Upon that memorable scene.
But with his keener eye
The axe's edge did try:

Nor call'd the Gods with vulgar spite
To vindicate his helpless Right
But bow'd his comely head
Down, as upon a bed.

Andrew Marvell, 'An Horatian Ode on
Cromwell's Return from Ireland'

The right divine of kings to govern wrong.

Alexander Pope

In April 1994 John Wellens, a retired schoolteacher, asked Eddie if he could help rid his picturesque sixteenth-century cottage at Naseby, Leicestershire, of the bumps and crashes which had interrupted his sleep for many years. A bluff Yorkshireman, Wellens had always ignored the odd, irritating noises at night. Recently, however, he had heard voices and had seen shadowy figures disappearing into the wall of the bedroom.

Naseby was the site of Oliver Cromwell's famous victory over Charles I during the English Civil War. On 14 June 1645, Cromwell routed the Royalist troops and ended the King's chances of defeating the Parliamentarian army. Locals had always claimed that a ghostly conflict was re-enacted in the sky on the anniversary of the battle – 'the Naseby Phenomenon' – when troops of ghostly soldiers could be seen wandering across the fields amid the cries of battle and the tortured groans of the wounded.

The memorial at Naseby is an unimpressive fenced-off pillar in a field outside the village. A small plaque is the only clue to the dramatic conflict that took place there, and which turned the tide of English history. Charles had been caught in the Midlands, unable to decide whether to push northwards and join up with his Scottish allies, or move towards the south-west where there were still areas under Royalist control. He divided his forces, taking some north and sending some south-west. This was a grave mistake, as it allowed the Parliamentarians to strike. The New Model Army, commanded by Lord Fairfax and Oliver Cromwell, scattered the King's cavalry and destroyed most of his infantry and munitions. It proved a fatal blow to Charles.

Sun House, John Wellens's cottage, which he bought in 1964, is a delightful, rambling, stone-built house on the main road out of Naseby. At the turn of the century it had been a public house – hence its name – until it was bought from the brewery by a private owner. Over tea in the pretty garden one afternoon in late April, John and his companion, Clare Cleary, explained to Eddie and me how the disturbances had begun.

The problem, John said, had started four years ago. 'Guests who stayed in the bedroom we called the haunted room always said that they had had nightmares. The doors and windows also rattle terribly in the house. Clare once heard a scratching on the door; the next minute, a man in a cassock came into the room. Another time, four young men stood at the foot of my bed looking down at the floor.'

Then Eddie interrupted. 'There's someone listening to our conversation,' he said. 'He's very restless. I'd like to go into the house now, if I may.'

We walked through the kitchen and oak-beamed dining room into a small store room at the back of the house which John had once used as a study. In one corner, by the tiny leaded window, was a pile of dusty old books; a huge desk littered with yellowing papers crowded the small room, while a tangle of old furniture threatened to collapse into the only free space beside the desk. Coughing and spluttering, I pulled a chair up to the desk and sat beside Eddie. John and Clare stood nervously by the door as he began to speak.

This man has been trapped here for a very long time; I'm going back to the seventeenth century. He's very restless, searching. I'm getting a pain in the middle of the forehead, going back across the skull. This man is very suspicious. He's quite young, I think. He's showing some interest in your tape-recorder – let's hope he doesn't interfere with it.

He's wearing shoulder armour – it's almost certainly Civil War. I feel the constriction of it; it's a mixture of leather and plate. I think he's a Roundhead. He was killed by a musket ball that hit his skull. He died shortly afterwards in considerable pain.

I want to know why he's earthbound. What is he searching for? I think he came in here looking for something. He came to the house on a horse, which he tied up outside. He was looking for something in this room. Whatever it was, he continued to look for it even after his death. It still dominates his thoughts.

I think he was sent here to find something, rather than somebody. Wait a moment, it's a bit of both. He'd been told that a King's Messenger was staying here, carrying an important document. I think he came here with a troop of soldiers, left them outside, instructing them to arrest or detain anyone seen leaving the house. He came in here and was shot. Then mayhem erupted. He shouted: 'Don't let him get away' just before he died. He was so anxious that this man should not get away that his anxiety trapped him here. He tried to follow the man, but couldn't.

I think these events occurred during the run-up to the Battle of Naseby. The man they were after was carrying some information on the disposition of the Royalist forces, so it was vitally important that they captured him.

It's terribly painful; I've got to release him. He says: 'Can I let all this go now?' He's beginning to understand he's been here a long time. He's asking where he's going from here. I've got to keep him steady as someone comes for him. His wife is approaching. They turn and walk away together.

John had blanched when Eddie described how the man was killed. 'It cuts right across my logic,' he said to me when Eddie had finished, 'but there is another thing that really disturbs me. Come over here, I want you to look at my head.' He parted his thick white hair to reveal a deep gash, about seven inches long, that ran from the top of his forehead to the back of his head. Nine stitches bound the wound together. 'This happened five days ago,' he said.

Clare took up the story. 'John was staying at my flat in Kensington last Sunday evening. We had had a dinner party and I was showing the guests out. I was only out of the room for a few minutes, but when I returned I saw John sitting on the sofa, his head covered in blood. Blood was everywhere. I thought that someone had broken in and attacked him.'

John was taken to hospital, where he had three X-rays and was given nine stitches. He said: 'I felt nothing at the time, but then I saw blood dripping on to my face and hands. It just happened – and no, I had not been drinking. But I felt no pain until the nurse put in the stitches.'

Eddie looked utterly bemused. Could it be, I asked him, that the man who was haunting John's house was so desperate for help that he projected his own injuries on to John? There was just the suggestion of irritation in Eddie, perhaps because I had made a useful connection before him. 'Yes,' Eddie told John, 'I think the man projected his injuries on to you. By sharing the pain of his death you have helped him to leave. All that was left for me was to lift his feelings of despair and depression.' Eddie admitted that he had never come across anything like this before. People can experience the psychological or emotional trauma of a trapped spirit, but physical injuries are extremely rare.

Clare ushered us into the garden for tea. 'I feel very relieved,' said John. 'A great weight has been lifted from me. It's not the sort

219

of thing you can discuss with your friends. No-one would have believed me.'

John had always prided himself on being thoroughly down-to-earth; he did not relish the fact that what had happened to him made no sense. I wondered whether he had been chosen to experience this precisely because he was so irredeemably rational. He was, indeed, the classic sceptic, the sort of earthy character who always laughs off the idea that the world may be far more complex and mysterious than most people like to believe.

As we left I asked John whether this experience had changed the way he felt about the paranormal, more out of curiosity than any evangelical zeal. 'It has made me think about death – I spent two hours this morning rewriting my will,' he said. 'I suppose I have to believe now that there's another world. This has made me wonder what lies beyond this life.'

★

On Saturday 6 May, a week after we saw John Wellens at Naseby, I telephoned Eddie to arrange a visit to a haunting in London the following week. It was a busy press day on the *Independent on Sunday*, where I was working, and so I wanted to be brief. 'Just a quick call – can you meet at Covent Garden tube on Wednesday . . .?' I asked Eddie. But he was already talking over me.

'I think King Charles I is with me. I have been reading a book on the Civil War this morning and have sensed his presence building up around me. He's coming through very strongly – can you write this down for me?' he asked.

I glanced up to see whether anyone in the office was listening and told him to go ahead. 'But be quick,' I said. I should have known that Eddie could not operate at speed when he was being contacted by a trapped spirit. Normally, this does not matter, but his communication that Saturday seemed almost preternaturally slow. But Eddie plodded on – and delivered a remarkable communication from a man who had changed the course of English history, King Charles I, who now appeared to be telling Eddie and me that he was prepared to guide our search for more trapped souls from the Civil War.

'Your acquaintance with the incident at Naseby is important
to me. I did indeed know the man who was hiding in the
house. My messenger died defending the intelligence I had
entrusted to him. He hid it well and it was not found, so that
did not influence the outcome of the battle. I should have
heeded the warnings I received. Had I done so, the course of
history would have been changed.

'I will try to help you uncover more. For a long time I had
difficulty in detaching myself from my earth life. I have been
through experiences of great intensity and have found this
hard to accept. I thought that God had forsaken my cause,
but I am lately come to a greater understanding and no longer
hold myself above God's other children. I am not the only
monarch who has had to face this difficulty. Think of me with
Christian love and I will try to repay your interest. Farewell.'

I told Eddie that he now had an obligation to learn about the Civil
War; perhaps then Charles would see fit to give us further
guidance. The Civil War is so complicated that it is one of the
dreaded black holes of undergraduate history courses. Eddie could
recall only the barest details, such as Charles I's defeats at Naseby
and his execution at Whitehall. But, though I was as ill-informed as
Eddie about the war, we both knew that it had bequeathed a huge
legacy of ghosts, who continued to haunt locations close to the
major battle sites. One of the reasons for this was that the Civil War
had divided communities, families and friends and had left what
might be described as a great psychic stench, with the victims
trapped by grief and desire for revenge.

Eddie had never been contacted by such an influential figure
before. 'My interest was raised from the historical to a very
personal and immediate level,' said Eddie. 'I had a strong impulse
to help him, if I could.' So we read voraciously on the war and the
main characters who might contact Eddie. Our hard work paid off;
on 10 June 1994, as he settled down to read Charles Hibbert's
biography of Charles I, the King was with him again:

'I wish to share certain reflections on my earth life with you,
particularly as they have affected my present life. As I

221

indicated previously, my attitudes, heavily ingrained in me in my earth life, have proved a great hindrance. I have a longing to move into the distant scene. It attracts me and yet I can only move towards it slowly in fits and starts.

'Read of my struggles in the war and you will feel moved to visit certain scenes. I will accompany you and bring you my understanding of the events – my fears and hopes. Thus you will help free me from the weight of my earth memories.'

Charles seemed to be sensitive, kind and strong-willed, if verging on the obstinate. He also appeared to be trapped somehow by the demands of office. Through June and July 1994, Eddie and I visited the places we thought would have the strongest associations for Charles – the battle sites at Naseby; Marple Hall, the ancestral home of John Bradshaw who presided over the council that condemned Charles to death; and Banqueting House, Whitehall, where he was beheaded in January 1649.

There were times when I, too, sensed Charles's presence. One morning, during the early stages of my research, I picked up a book on the Civil War and accidentally dropped it. As I bent down to pick it up, I noticed that the page had fallen open at an account of a ghostly encounter between Charles and one of his former advisers two nights before the Battle of Naseby. Charles was billeted in the Wheatsheaf Hotel in Daventry, Northamptonshire, with his nephew and commander, Prince Rupert. According to the book, the ghost of the Earl of Strafford, who had been executed in the Tower in May 1641, appeared to the King and urged him to continue his march northwards. Charles resolved to take Strafford's advice, especially after the ghost appeared for the second time on the night of 13 June. However, he was persuaded by Prince Rupert that he should instead attack; he lost the battle and from that moment on was doomed.

We had discovered that the Wheatsheaf Hotel had been turned into a nursing home in 1991. Eddie decided that he should just turn up – and hope that we would be welcomed. So, one fine June afternoon, he found himself explaining to the matron, Anne Broadbent, a charming woman in her fifties, that he was interested in ghosts and needed her help. To her credit, she did not throw him

out as a crank; instead, she listened patiently, as if Eddie were
selling health insurance rather than discussing the paranormal, and
said that she would be pleased to help. 'We know all about Charles
and Strafford,' she said. 'There have been reports of a tall man in
black wearing a wide-brimmed hat in some of the bedrooms. We're
sure we're haunted.' She led Eddie to the rooms where they had
had most trouble; in one of them an old lady had been tipped out of
an armchair by an invisible force while she was sleeping.

Eddie told me later that he had been contacted at the nursing
home by the spirit of a long-dead Cavalier. It had been a long,
draining communication from a wandering, confused soul, but it
had not been the Earl of Strafford, as he had hoped. We had no
right to be dissatisfied – spirits cannot be graded according to their
value, in terms of either their worldly past or their usefulness to an
author. I was also grateful because, under the pressure of research,
I had begun to treat Eddie as a psychic antenna, someone who
could always pick up material providing that he had been plugged
in at the right spot. So the Wheatsheaf was a useful exercise in
humility for both of us.

★

The English Civil War was actually a series of complex power
struggles, beginning in 1642 and lasting beyond the execution of
Charles in 1649, during which one failing system of government –
the 'divine right' of kings, championed by the Cavaliers – was
challenged by another – constitutional rule, represented by the
Roundheads. Loyalties were mainly geographical, although they
changed throughout the war: the poorer and pastoral shires in the
north, north-west, south-west and Wales were mostly Royalist,
whereas the prosperous counties of the south and London – where
there were more merchants – supported Parliament. This was not a
class war: families from all strata of society were frequently split
between one side or the other; father fought against son, brother
against brother. Some of Oliver Cromwell's relatives fought as
Royalists, while the first Roundhead army contained many peers.

The first Civil War, which Parliament won, ran from 1642 to
1646. The King lost in spite of the loyalty of most of the nobility and

gentry and their dependants. The second phase began after the Army quarrelled with Parliament and divided into two factions, moderate and radical. But Charles effectively condemned himself by his refusal to compromise over the monarchy's divine right to rule. On 20 January 1649, Charles was brought to trial on the charge of high treason. He was impeached as a 'Tyrant, Traitor and Murderer, and a public and implacable enemy to the Commonwealth of England'. Charles defended himself with dignity and courage, but it was hopeless; he was beheaded outside Banqueting House on 30 January 1649.

The history, I realized as I struggled in libraries with fat, learned books, was hard to grasp. But for both Eddie and me the facts, the constantly shifting alliances, the betrayals and the dispositions of troops were less important than the characters of the main players. First, and most important, there was Charles I.

Born in 1600, the second son of King James VI of Scotland and I of England and Queen Anne of Denmark, he had been overshadowed as a boy by his glamorous elder brother Henry, Prince of Wales. A shy, delicate child, Charles became heir to the throne in 1612 when his brother died of fever. Charles was crowned King in 1625, a young man with bold ideas but little self-confidence.

In May 1625 Charles was married by proxy at Notre Dame Cathedral, Paris, to Princess Henrietta Maria, the fourteen-year-old sister of King Louis XIII of France, as part of a policy to unite with France against Spain. The terms of the marriage agreement included a promise by Charles to make major concessions to English Catholics, a policy that was deeply unpopular at home.

Charles was a devoted husband and father, but he was also solemn and reserved. Worse, he was extremely tactless. Individuals could shrug this off, but it was fatal in his dealings with Parliament. He also believed that he ruled by divine right. From 1629 to 1640 Charles attempted to introduce an absolute monarchy. Assisted by the Earl of Strafford and William Laud, Archbishop of Canterbury, his period of 'Personal Rule' lasted for eleven years. Then Parliament united behind John Pym, a West Country gentleman, and forced the King to accept limitations on his power. But MPs were divided – over Church reform and the extent of the Crown's subordination to Parliament – and grouped into Royalists, faithful to the King, and Parliamentarians. Charles negotiated help from City financiers, while Pym canvassed rich aldermen and preachers in the City of London. On 4 January 1642, Charles invaded Parliament with 400 supporters. His opponents, sensibly, had decamped to the City. From 1640 onwards Charles remained blind to the need for compromise.

Eddie and I were equipped now to understand Charles; but we also had to be prepared to encounter his wife, Henrietta. When they married, Henrietta Maria was still a child; the first time she met Charles she is said to have burst into tears. Although they were married first by proxy in France, another marriage ceremony took place at Canterbury on 12 June 1625. They seemed ill-matched at first, but slowly the relationship grew into one of real, deep love. In May 1630 Henrietta bore a boy, who was to become Charles II, and they had a further seven children: five daughters and two sons. Charles relied on her throughout his life and they remained devoted to one another until his death. In his letters from the Civil War, Charles said that it was her love that gave him the strength to continue. Henrietta survived Charles by seventeen years, dying in 1666.

Then there was Thomas Wentworth, Earl of Strafford. An efficient and authoritarian minister, he was described by his enemies as 'arrogant, ruthless and awe-inspiring' in his promotion of the King's and his own interests. He was impeached and imprisoned in the Tower of London in November 1640, and beheaded in May 1641.

Our attempts to make sense of such a difficult period in English history were rewarded a few days after Eddie's trip to the Wheatsheaf Hotel and his communication with the mysterious Cavalier. Over lunch with a friend in Lincoln the following week, he received the following message from the Earl of Strafford:

'I am not one of your ghostly spirits, yet I am not entirely free. I have been on a long journey and still have the last part to travel. I know I have to forgive my Prince, but I find this the most difficult step of all, for I served him well.

'I counted him as my friend, as much as one could so regard a King. I can feel that our two paths do converge to a fateful meeting point. I find the prospect daunting, for I do not know whether I will find the courage to bring myself to an acceptance of his presence without bitterness. I beg you to lend me your support and prayers for the moment and the meeting which now lies not far ahead.'

I could see him then wearing a Cavalier costume of silver-grey, embellished with silver ornaments. He was wearing a broad-brimmed hat decorated with a single large white feather. He carried within him still a great sadness and heaviness of spirit.

We had waited for several weeks for a further communication from Charles, but nothing had come. In an effort to retrace the King's steps, we visited the most famous battle sites of the Civil War, Edgehill and Naseby. At neither site did Eddie make contact with Charles. He had not expected any message, he told me, because by now that he had realized that it was important simply to visit a site and soak up its atmosphere; the communication would then follow.

Back in Lincoln, Eddie re-read the transcripts of the first two communications from Charles. 'For a long time I had difficulty in detaching myself from my earth life . . .' it read. It made sense. Charles, it seemed, had wanted us to understand the events of his life on earth and was waiting for us to get to grips with that before he would tell us more. 'I have been through experiences of great intensity . . .' Eddie was puzzled by this; he was keener than ever to make contact again.

A couple of days later Eddie had again been thinking about the fate of Charles, when the phrase 'Praise be to the Lord for all his kindness' came into his head. Recognizing that a spirit was near, he sat down in his living room and noted what was coming through:

The man who is with me is a clergyman, I think. He says he was the religious tutor to the young Prince Charles. He tells me: 'I have been trying to help him in his present predicament. He cannot let go of his [earth] memories with their many shades. He has asked for your help and I have

come to ask for this. We can work together to help His
Majesty, though I know he wishes to put this title aside. I
must confess that I find it difficult to think of him as my
brother in God, so perhaps I also need help.

'I could have moved on, but when I saw his plight I offered
myself to him as his humble servant. I have observed the
changes in him and marvelled at them, but there are
stumbling blocks which somehow we must help him to deal
with.

'Others have also held back, but their attentions and their
flattery do not help him, for he has come to understand the
shallowness this represents. If you could help me make them
see the light too, they would hopefully move on and cease to
cling to His Majesty's coat-tails.'

When the clergyman had departed, Eddie realized what it meant:
Charles was being prepared for release and Eddie's help was
needed. Two days later, while he was holding his Tuesday evening
development group at home, Charles returned. Eddie asked one of
his students to record the encounter.

King Charles knows these attentions are shallow, but he still
enjoys the flattery. He has to play his part in letting these
people go; he must let them know that he doesn't want them
to carry on this way.

I am getting a strange and unusual impression. He is
making an effort not to wear his crown, but people are still
fussing around him. I am seeing something akin to a
backdrop to a stage play – a court scene with ornately
decorated walls which keeps disappearing and then coming
back into view. There is a half-conscious attempt by the
courtiers to recreate this court scene.

Charles is in a terrible dilemma. It's as though he keeps
changing his mind about what he wants to do. [A few minutes
later.] Now he is making some attempt to shake all this off.
He is getting up and walking out into the open air, telling the
others to leave him. The cleric is standing by to help, but he
knows that Charles has to make a free choice to get rid of his

flatterers and trappings at Court.

Charles has gone halfway in what he has to do: he has accepted that he is no more important than other men, though this thought is still in his mind, if not in his heart. Having got this far, he is still unwilling to relinquish the trappings of royalty. 'What am I if I have no last vestige of kingship?' he asks. He has to make a mental leap and trust that he will find his true self if he lets everything go.

The others have now sensed that they are being cut adrift . . . now somebody has come to them who says: 'Come, gentlemen, you need to follow me.' They are rather bewildered, but they follow him, talking among themselves and asking where they are going. I think they are beginning their journey on an upward path; this would not have been possible if Charles had not let them go, so that's a step forward for him.

The cleric is close by and says to Charles: 'I know that soon I shall have to relinquish this duty to another, one more fit than I to conduct Your Majesty to his rightful place in heaven.' A spirit voice is telling me that a period of adjustment and preparation now awaits Charles.

Later, Eddie described the extraordinary encounter to me. 'He was too attached to the glamour of his earthly life to let it go,' Eddie explained. 'He had attracted some of his courtiers who themselves had made little progress in the next life and still had some yearnings for the life they had once led. Together, they tried to reconstruct the court Charles had on earth but this was impossible.

'I sense that in life he loathed the sycophantic attentions of his courtiers, but accepted that it was part of his duty to tolerate them. He longed for true and equal friendship but felt that because of his position, which placed him above others, he could never achieve this. I feel a lot of sadness for him in his isolation. I think Charles must learn one or two things about himself before he can move on to the spirit world.'

We heard nothing more from Charles and his courtiers until two weeks later, when Eddie felt a spirit presence. He had been sitting with his development group for about twenty minutes when he became aware of a man weeping beside him. One of his students said she also sensed a woman in the room.

'I see a woman wearing a long skirt,' she said. 'She is quite buxom and is carrying a fan. I think she is a noblewoman. I am getting a terrible pain in my chest.' Eddie asked her if the woman was Queen Henrietta. 'She answers "yes" very emphatically. She tells me she was French and that she tried hard to make her husband see sense.' Eddie then contacted the Queen himself.

> She says she was unable to contact her husband, Charles, while he was trapped in the recreated court because she had moved beyond that level and didn't want to be part of it. When he put that behind him, she saw that he hadn't made much progress in the spirit life, so she came to accompany him along the path he now has to take in order to reach heaven. I can see a wonderful reunion between the two of them; they are weeping for joy – and sadness, too, over the way his earthly life ended. As they move away together, I can hear Henrietta softly singing a song in French to Charles.

Of all the cases Eddie and I investigated, the Civil War gripped him most; he became so absorbed that he seemed reluctant to let it go. He developed a strong empathy with Charles, who had set off events that changed the face of English history. After the Restoration of his son, Charles II, in 1660, England settled into a legal and constitutional framework which enabled centuries of peaceful evolution. The tragedy of Charles I was that he paid the ultimate price for helping give birth to democracy.

But one thing puzzled me: why had Eddie's contacts, apart from the Roundhead encountered in John Wellens's house, been exclusively Royalist? After all, the Parliamentarians had prevented the rise of an absolute monarchy. Did they have nothing to say? I became fascinated by the colossus of the Roundhead cause, Oliver Cromwell, the outstanding general of the Parliamentary army and leader of the republican government from 1649 until his death. He was born on 25 April 1599 and became an MP in 1640; he was an eloquent defender of the little man, of the rights of the common people against landlords, of religious independents against Anglican prosecution and of toleration in all things. As well as being a Puritan idealist, Cromwell was a traditionalist and a natural military leader.

In 1648 the Army voted to try the King, 'that man of blood – for the blood he has shed'. Cromwell hesitated but, eventually, realized that Charles would have to die. But Cromwell, too, ultimately failed. He died of pneumonia on 3 September 1658 and his brave new republican England crumbled soon afterwards. But he left an indelible mark. He had led the country through a violent but formative period, in which both absolute monarchy and democracy had been rejected, but which, paradoxically, ensured centuries of peaceful evolution towards a modern society of religious toleration, intellectual freedom and social mobility.

I had been meaning to ask Eddie about his lack of contact with Charles's opponents for some time when, on the morning of 22 August 1994, I received a fax from him. Unlike most people of his age, Eddie was always enthusiastic about new technology and would use his fax whenever he could, whether or not he had anything to say. He admitted himself that he found the process of sending letters down the telephone very satisfying. I was about to throw one such message away when I suddenly noticed the name Cromwell at the bottom of the page.

'Dear Gillian,' Eddie had written, 'This morning I have been reading about some of the more obscure battles of the Civil War. After an hour or so, I put the book down and decided to do some long-overdue washing-up. But into my everyday musings came a strong spirit presence. I sensed it was Cromwell, but what would you think if someone like that came into your living room? Doubt your sanity or wonder if you were dreaming? I've not become so blasé about this sort of thing not to wonder if I've got it right. But it was definitely him, and this is what he said to me:'

'You read and try to gain an oversight of all these events, but for me it was my life's work. The power of the King had to be broken. I was driven and I had to convince others of my conviction that men had the right to more control over their lives than the sovereign would allow.

'I understand now that I was impelled forward in order to lead men into a new idea that had to find its place. In the end, the idea, like men themselves, became corrupted. I, too, was misled by my own vanity.

'It is an irony of life that when a great idea is fought for and succeeds, the fruits of that success can prove hard to pluck and too soon sour upon the branch. But what fruits were plucked you now enjoy, and much more besides, so I comfort myself that my life played its part.

'But what of me, you may ask. Have I found my place in heaven? I could say much in reply that would not be understood, but I say this, that my soul has moved a long way and has learnt much. I had first to forgive and seek forgiveness and then, when freed of this necessity, I began my true journey towards a better understanding of God's love. This is an endless journey, it seems, but full of joy and wonder.

'After a while, I cannot say how long, my great concern for your world, the world that once held me so close, dropped away. This is not to say I no longer cared; rather that my view of its meaning and place in things changed by degrees as my eyes were further opened to God's purpose. So it is with all of us in this great realm of light.

'You ask what made me come to you. Your quest, undertaken in honesty of purpose, is like a silent call to souls who would respond, and I am one of these. And now I beg leave to depart. Farewell, in the love of God.'

★

In late August 1994 Eddie came to London to visit a friend. I met him in the morning at Westminster Abbey and suggested we walk along Whitehall to Banqueting House, the site of Charles I's execution and now the only surviving part of the Palace of Westminster, razed to the ground by fire in 1698.

As we walked down the broad avenue, I thought about Charles's final indignity as he was brought before Bradshaw's court. On

231

30 January 1649, Charles stepped on to the scaffold erected outside the first floor of the house. Surrounded by massed ranks of soldiers, he whispered a few words to the people around him. An eye-witness recorded that when the executioner struck the fatal blow, 'there was a grone by the thousands then present, as I had never heard before and desire I may never hear again'. Troops of horses dispersed the crowds and Charles's body was embalmed and taken for burial at St George's Chapel, Windsor.

As we stood in the great hall on the first floor, Eddie turned and spoke to me. 'I feel Charles's presence,' he said. 'I feel his overwhelming sadness and a great sense of regret. I think he knew we were coming here today. He wants to tell us something:

'This was my stepping-off place into eternity. I believed in eternal life, but I little knew what was ahead of me on that fateful day, the beginning of an unlearning. There was so much to be understood. Why did I get it so wrong? Why did I not understand?'

This was the final place Charles wanted us to visit, the last piece in the jigsaw of his life. By seeing his departure point to the next world, we could judge how far Charles had progressed during his spiritual journey. Released by Eddie from the tyranny of his elevated earthly role, he had found a new determination to relinquish his mistaken ideas about his divine right to rule and his superiority over his fellow men.

Charles's ability to see his life in a historical context was confirmed in a communication a few days after our visit to Whitehall, marking the end of our extraordinary association with the tragic King. It seemed to me that he wanted to seal the relationship before his transition to the next world. After everything that historians have written about him – condemned as either a helpless puppet of revolutionary social forces or a narrow-minded bigot whose thoughtless absolutism provoked the Civil War – he surely deserves to have the last word.

'Write of me in kindly terms. I was cast in the role that was necessary for England, but it demanded much from me. I had to fail, else the part I played would not be complete. I had to die to put a seal on the royal past.

'At last I am becoming free from the memories and constraints of life. No longer do I hold to the fantasy of divine royal prerogative nor to the false glamour of courtly life. These illusions are fading fast and in their place grows a sense of the true divinity within, the same as every man shares.

'I feel free in spirit as never before and for this liberation I give thanks to God.'

Chapter 14

Prisoners in the Tower

Surely there is no sadder spot on the earth than this.

Thomas Babington Macaulay

Of all the haunted places in the world, the Tower of London is surely the most infamous. A prison for more than a thousand years, it had been the scene for some of the most gruesome acts of torture, imprisonment and execution in England's history. Today's visitors say that they can still sense the fear that once enveloped the Tower.

Ghost stories from the Tower are legion: St Thomas à Becket, who was murdered in 1170, was spotted in 1241; Anne Boleyn's ghost has been seen gliding towards Tower Green; Sir Walter Raleigh's ghost haunts the path between the Queen's House and the Bloody Tower, where he was imprisoned in a small cell for thirteen years; and inexplicable groans have been heard in the Council Chamber of the Queen's House, where Guy Fawkes and his accomplices were tortured in 1605.

The two execution sites are particularly poignant: Tower Hill, outside the castle walls, and Tower Green, within its ramparts, where the memorial lists 125 people who were beheaded, including such legendary figures as Sir Thomas More, killed in 1535, and Robert Devereux, second Earl of Essex, executed on the orders of Elizabeth I in 1601. Many of these unfortunates were buried in unmarked graves by the tiny Chapel of St Peter ad Vincula.

Given the endless opportunities for a ghosthunter, I was surprised to discover that Eddie had last visited the Tower as a ten-year-old on an outing with his father. I was about to suggest a visit when Eddie told me that he had received an invitation to the Tower from the (then) Governor, Major-General Christopher Tyler. The Governor asked Eddie if he would investigate the noises which had been heard in the Queen's House; in return, he offered Eddie breakfast followed by a private tour of the new £10 million Jewel House, which had just been displayed to the world's media.

Eddie had never met Major-General Tyler, but the father of one of his friends, Sarah MacGinty, an interior designer, had known the Governor and his wife for some years. Sarah had mentioned Eddie's work to her father who had, in turn, told the Tylers. On 18 May 1994 I met Eddie at Sarah's home in Battersea, south London, to discuss his appointment at the Tower the next morning. He immediately sensed a communication coming through. This is what he said:

> There are people living out false lives at the Tower. It will need more than one visit. We will lead you into this step by step. Don't be anxious and don't rush the process. We will arrange it so that what needs to be done will be done. This is very important work.

It was clear now that Eddie's invitation to the Tower was not an accident. I sensed that there was something urgent for him to do there – someone, perhaps, who desperately needed his help.

Early next morning, 19 May 1994, Eddie and Sarah parked outside the Tower, its white stone shining in the morning sun, and introduced themselves to the guard on duty. Five minutes later a Beefeater, resplendent in his red and gold livery, appeared and escorted them to the Governor's residence. It was too early for tourists; for an hour they would be able to enjoy the rare experience of having this historic site entirely to themselves.

But there was another, fascinating dimension to the visit. Eddie and Sarah did not know – and neither did I then – that they were beginning their tour exactly 458 years after a young Queen, now immortalized in countless books and films, rose from her bed for the last time and walked wearily to Tower Green. Eddie, I

235

discovered weeks later, was attempting to communicate with the unhappy spirits of the Tower on the anniversary of the death of Anne Boleyn – second wife of Henry VIII and mother of the mighty Queen Elizabeth I – who was unjustly executed in 1536 for treasonable adultery.

The Queen's House, a picturesque, timber-framed Tudor building by the Bell Tower, is the official residence of the Governor and is not open to the public. Built by Henry VIII in 1530 to house the Lieutenant of the castle (hence its original name, the Lieutenant's House), it was later used as a prison for the nobility, who were lodged under the supervision of the Lieutenant. Anne Boleyn spent the last four days of her life there before her execution.

Major-General Tyler, a tall, handsome man in his late fifties, and his wife, Sue, welcomed Eddie and Sarah into the house. Upstairs, their private dining room had been set for breakfast. The Major-General sat at the head of the table and, as the meal was served on silver salvers, the Tylers told Eddie about recent disturbances in the Council Chamber and the Lennox Room.

After breakfast, Sue Tyler escorted Eddie to the Council Chamber. Eddie walked slowly around the long, narrow room. A long oak table dominated it, the walls were painted cream and a heavy brass candelabrum hung from the wooden-beamed ceiling. Eddie paused by the window and looked out over the Inner Ward; then he walked to the opposite wall and sat on a stone bench below a shallow bay window. He closed his eyes as he sensed the spirit approaching:

I am aware of a presence in the south-west corner of the
room. I am getting the sensation of my shoulder being
dragged down. This is a man . . . in his sixties. The pain in
his right shoulder has been caused by torture or an accident. I
sense that he held his right forearm against his body to relieve
the pain. The base of the neck, on the right side, is the origin
of this pain. He is doubled up; I think he underwent torture
which left him crippled.

He says: 'I was put on the rack to extract information. I
was a servant and evidence was sought against my master, but
I was not privy to much of my master's doings, so I did not

have very much to say. I was not believed and I was tortured until I was glad to die. But the memories of the agonies I suffered hold me here still and I wish to leave this place . . .'

A lady is coming for him out of the light. She is dressed in Tudor costume. I think she's his wife. He says: ''Tis my good lady.' Now they are going off into the light, so we have helped him away.

I want to find out more about him. I think his master had a foreign connection and was thought to have been plotting espionage. This man was brought here for interrogation; he was then tortured and died of shock and heart failure.

Men sat in judgment here as interrogators. This room has a nasty feeling – of men with power, but little humanity. Perhaps it would be fairer to say that their sense of Realm was much greater than their humanity, so they felt justified in their behaviour. The room needs a psychic cleansing to diminish this atmosphere.

When Eddie had finished Sue led him to the north wall, where there was an ornate wooden plaque commemorating the discovery of the Gunpowder Plot in 1605. She told him that Guy Fawkes himself had twice been brought there for interrogation.

But Eddie said that she was mistaken if she thought that he had just been contacted by Guy Fawkes. He said: 'It was an older man, who was a servant of someone involved in the Gunpowder Plot. But he was definitely tortured.' Later, Eddie went further; he believed that he had been contacted by Guy Fawkes's own servant.

Guy Fawkes was born in 1570, the son of a Yorkshire advocate who died soon after Fawkes was born. Little is known for certain about his early life, except that he converted to Catholicism when he was very young and became a soldier in Holland and, later, a spy in Spain. In 1604 a former schoolfriend, John Wright, asked him to join a group of conspirators who were plotting to blow up the Palace of Westminster on the opening day of Parliament and launch a Catholic uprising in the Midlands.

The conspirators were meticulous in their preparations but forgot that the essential element of a conspiracy is secrecy. There was a disastrous leak about their plans and on 4 November 1605, the day before the opening of Parliament, the King sent two search parties into the cellars. Fawkes, the only conspirator present, was arrested when the gunpowder was discovered. The other conspirators died when they resisted arrest or, like Guy Fawkes, were imprisoned in the Tower, tortured and executed.

As well as being the scene of Guy Fawkes's interrogation in 1605, the Council Chamber witnessed the imprisonment of William Penn, the founder of the American State of Pennsylvania, in 1668 and, in 1941, the incarceration of Rudolf Hess, the Nazi leader who flew to Scotland during the Second World War in a bizarre attempt to negotiate a rapprochement between Britain and Germany.

The Tylers had also experienced disturbances in the Lennox Room, at the far end of the north wing. A small room, no more than twelve feet square, it has dark oak panelling and a small leaded window on one wall, looking out on to Tower Green and the Chapel of St Peter ad Vincula. The room had once been occupied by Countess Lennox, the mother-in-law of Mary Queen of Scots, who had been imprisoned there by Elizabeth I in 1565 until her death the following year. Next door was an identical room where Anne Boleyn had spent her final night before her execution.

After a few moments, Eddie was aware of a strong presence in the Lennox Room:

I'm getting the impression of an old lady. I'm ill and feel as though I've got a deep bronchial complaint. It's affecting my spine, too. She says: 'I died sitting at this window. Not much of an outlook, is it? But it's a lighter room than some in this place.

'I put my illness down to lack of proper nourishment, but then I was not here to be nourished.' I sense that she is very bitter about her treatment as a prisoner. 'I have some freedom to move about here, but I cannot go outside this place. I cannot fathom the reason for this. Oh Lord! set me free, for I do not deserve this fate.'

She felt a bitterness that she seldom expressed. A noblewoman, she is distressed that she no longer has any control over her affairs. She says: 'They affected to be caring, but it was in appearance only.' I think there was some malicious envy in the accusations made against her. She says:

238

'The world sees little of what it does not want to see. Such
was my fate. People soon forgot, or so it seemed.'

I am going to try to get her away from here. She had a
maid of whom she was very fond; this woman seems to be
coming forward for her. The old lady senses this and is
becoming quite excited. The maid is here and is preparing her
for a journey, as she would have done many times during
their earthly lives. She says: 'Are you ready for your journey,
my lady?' They step on to a gravel path where a coach is
waiting. The maid helps her into the coach and they depart.

Like so many of the men and women who perished in the Tower,
Lady Lennox had been a victim of the intrigues and paranoias of
the small, perpetually feuding circle who had ruled England for
centuries. Elizabeth I had sent Lady Lennox to the Tower in 1565
in a fit of pique after her son, Lord Darnley, had grown too close to
Mary Queen of Scots, who believed that she was the true successor
to the English throne. Elizabeth had schemed hard to try to prevent
Mary marrying Lord Darnley, since she feared that the two would
form a threatening alliance. But she failed and they married in July
1565, the day after he was proclaimed King of Scotland. Their
marriage proved a failure; but by then it was too late to save Lady
Lennox.

When Eddie stepped into the next room, he picked up a strong
impression of a spirit: there was no doubt who it was this time.
Eddie did not know, but this section of the Queen's House had
been built by Henry VIII as a token of love to Anne Boleyn before
their marriage. As usual, Eddie had not done any research before
visiting the Tower, and that morning he simply knew that Anne had
been one of Henry VIII's famous six wives. He said:

I feel the shade of Anne Boleyn. She is very strongly
impressed on this room, but I don't think she's haunting it.
She's beside me now and says: 'Thank God I am free.' I think
she wants to talk to us. She says: 'I do not relish the memory

of my time in this place being raised, but I would wish to help you in what you are doing for the sake of others who are fixed here. It is a place which demands much work, so do not make light of the task.

'I have long been interested in the fate of others who followed in my footsteps here and I have done all I can to help them in parting from it. I can tell you that it is in the anticipation of the cruel end that the worst of the suffering lies. It is a cruel place with a very cruel history. Some would make light of it and seek to find in it what they would call romance. It is not the word we would use to describe the blackness of incarceration here.

'If you try to do more here, I would offer you whatever support I could. May the blessings of the Lord be with you.'

The grief which Eddie had picked up was understandable and palpable but there seemed, remarkably, to be no trace of bitterness or anger, despite her appalling treatment by Henry VIII and his closest advisers. She had given her love – and her life – to a man who had rewarded her with an undeserved death. And yet, after death, there was no righteous earthly rage.

Born in 1504, Anne was the daughter of Lady Elizabeth Howard and Sir Thomas Boleyn, England's ambassador to France. She spent her youth abroad and by her twenty-first birthday was an accomplished and attractive young woman. She was a talented linguist and, while not considered beautiful – her olive skin and dark eyes were at odds with the contemporary ideal of fair skin and blue eyes – she was graceful and slim. She also possessed a sexual magnetism that captivated men, including Henry VIII.

She first appeared at his court as maid of honour to Catherine of Aragon, Henry's first wife, on 1 March 1522. By the spring of 1526 the King was passionately in love with Anne. He was thirty-five years old and had been king for seventeen years. He was also still married, to Catherine of Aragon, but was determined that nothing would prevent him making Anne his wife. He had become ruthless and arrogant; now he wanted Anne. In May 1527 Henry sought a divorce from Queen Catherine, who resisted strongly.

In January 1533 they were secretly married; Anne was already pregnant and Henry was not yet divorced. However, on 23 May the Archbishop of Canterbury, Thomas Cranmer, pronounced Henry's marriage to Catherine null and ruled that Anne was the King's lawful wife. On 1 June 1533 Anne, then six months pregnant, was crowned Queen of England.

But the birth in September 1533 of a healthy baby girl, Elizabeth, the future Elizabeth I, did not cement the marriage; on the contrary, Henry was furious that his new wife had failed to provide a male heir. There were other, tragic and doomed attempts to produce the son craved by Henry who would, so his advisers insisted, ensure a smooth succession. One baby, it is believed, was still-born; and then there was a miscarriage.

By now Henry was tiring of Anne; he complained that she had grown argumentative and that her beauty had faded. So he turned his attentions to the young Lady Jane Seymour, sister of the Earl of Seymour. Henry's courtiers, always prepared to support the King, wasted no time in plotting Anne's downfall. Henry appointed a group of judges and noblemen, including Anne's father and her uncle, the third Duke of Norfolk, to investigate her activities. They arrested Mark Smeaton, a musician and dancer of humble birth who, under torture, claimed Anne was guilty of adultery, incest and conspiracy to murder the king. On Tuesday, 2 May 1536 Anne was arrested and sent to the Tower. After a travesty of a trial, she was executed two weeks later on Tower Green.

When Eddie had finished speaking, he glanced at his watch; it was 11.30 a.m. A private viewing of the Crown Jewels was now impossible because the Tower was packed with sightseers. But there was more that had to be done; he knew that he would have to return soon.

★

A month after Eddie's visit to the Queen's House, we met outside Tower Hill underground station. In the intervening weeks, I had been troubled by the fact that there were many more trapped souls in the Tower. The words of Anne Boleyn had kept echoing in my mind: 'It is a place which demands much work . . . If you try to do more here, I would offer you whatever support I could.' Another visit was vital. By now I had a broad outline of the history of the Tower, though I realized that to become really expert in the violent, sinister and yet gripping events which had taken place there would take years of study.

It was during Henry VIII's reign, from 1509 until 1547, that the Tower, previously a royal residence-cum-fortress, became a prison for the usually hapless victims of court rivalries, dynastic disputes and religious animosities. Yet it also became clear, as I read histories of the Tower, that, despite its fearsome reputation, only a small number of prisoners were tortured there.

The tower was pressed into service again as the fortress of royalty when the Duke of Wellington was appointed Constable in 1826. Believing that Britain was on the brink of a revolution, he restored the Tower's military functions and stripped it of fripperies, such as its menagerie. But the threat was exaggerated and Queen Victoria turned the Tower into a national monument after Wellington's death in 1852. By the end of Victoria's reign in 1901, half a million people were visiting the Tower each year. Today there are two million visitors annually, three-quarters of them from overseas.

On this early summer's day in 1994 business was brisk at the Tower as Eddie and I strolled along the perimeter wall. Eddie stopped by the Bowyer Tower. 'Let's sit down on that bench,' he said, 'I think I have someone here.'

It's someone here in distress, a man – he's bewildered. He says his situation does not make any sense. He finds the crowds distressing; he's frustrated because he cannot take part. He's wearing a black cloak and has a cap on his head. He says his master's name is on the Tower Hill memorial.

I need to find out how he died. He says he was hanged, drawn and quartered, during the reign of Henry VIII. His body was not given a proper burial. He's feeling disorientated – I think that is because of the way they disposed of his body.

The man says: 'I was not of noble birth, but I played an important role, assisting one who was. I was his servant, his clerk, judged to be implicated in his treasonable actions, though I only wrote what he told me. But of course I knew too much.'

242

He's remembering some of his life. I'm seeing, through his
memory, a rural scene – sheep, fields, I think the foothills of
the North Downs. He was a scholarly man – he went to a
school attached to a church and then to Oxford, where he
studied Latin and Greek. His life was successful, up to the
point of his master's betrayal and arrest. His own arrest
followed shortly after. He was imprisoned in the Tower.

He says: 'I saw my master's death through the arrow slit in
my cell. I followed him not long after.' He says his master
was attached to Henry's court. Sometimes his master dealt
with taxation, sometimes with matters of diplomacy. It was in
the field of diplomacy that his master got involved in a plot
which was connected with Henry's cause against the Catholic
church.

He says: 'We were watched closely, suspicion was
everywhere. Henry VIII knew that he had many enemies
among the Catholics and some in Court. There were very few
he trusted. If he distrusted them he was apt to put them to
the torture.' I keep seeing the man who was one of Henry
VIII's chief ministers. (His name begins with the letter C.)
He was executed in the end.

The man is much more composed now. It's helped him a
lot to recall these things. I think he will soon shed his etheric
body. His master is coming to take him away and tell him that
he is sorry for drawing him into this tragic end. He will ask
for his forgiveness. His master says: 'Come with me, I wish to
make amends and in the process seek your forgiveness.'

They are leaving and they have a short journey to make in
which much will be explained and forgiven. That's it, he's
gone.

It was impossible to be certain, of course, but my researches in the
following days suggested that the clerk who had communicated
with Eddie had worked for Baron Thomas Cromwell, later Earl of
Essex. Cromwell had become Henry VIII's secretary in 1530. The
son of a wealthy citizen, Cromwell, then aged forty-five, had
earned his living as a lawyer, merchant and moneylender. He
masterminded the subordination of the Church to the King, to

Henry's huge profit, and also supervised extensions and repairs to the Tower.

Cromwell had been instrumental in introducing Anne Boleyn to the King, but by the spring of 1536 she was already falling out of favour and Henry was pursuing Lady Jane Seymour, a liaison which Cromwell encouraged and which ended in marriage on 30 May 1536. Henry's long-hoped-for son, later Edward VI, was born on 12 October 1537; but twelve days later Jane died of fever.

After Lady Jane's death Cromwell busied himself to find Henry a new wife. He recommended marriage, for diplomatic reasons, to an unlikely partner, a rather plain young woman called Anne, daughter of the Duke of Cleves, a small dukedom on the border of France and the Netherlands. Reluctantly, Henry agreed and the marriage took place on 6 January 1540, when Henry was forty-eight and his bride just twenty-four. But it was a disaster and was never consummated.

Despite his role in this débâcle Cromwell was made Earl of Essex and, after ten years of loyal service, was believed to be the second most powerful man in the kingdom. But Henry was fickle and was always ready to see conspiracies against him. Cromwell's many enemies moved in for the kill and convinced Henry that the Earl was guilty of a lack of orthodoxy – or the heinous crime of sacramentarian heresy. Cromwell was taken to the Tower and sentenced to death by an Act of Attainder: there was to be no trial. Henry divorced Anne and married Catherine Howard on 28 July 1540, the day Cromwell was executed at the Tower. By spring 1541, however, Henry was muttering that the execution of Cromwell – 'the most faithful servant I ever had' – had been engineered by the 'false accusations' of his ministers.

Eddie and I strolled down to the entrance, through the imposing bailey and the Byward Tower, the second line of defence. Walking parallel to the river, along Water Lane, the original foreshore of the River Thames, we stopped by the infamous Traitor's Gate. A wooden gate below St Thomas's Tower, this was the main point of entry for prisoners during Henry VIII's reign. Ahead was the huge

Lanthorn Tower, where Edward III had resided during his reign. Eddie complained of a pain in his head and asked if we could sit down.

> This feels darker than anything I've picked up so far. I have
> a man with me who helped torture prisoners in the Tower.
> He's at the bottom of a pit and he's trying to find his way out.
> He cries: 'Don't leave me.' He's in a dungeon. He's been
> suffering some of the misery he inflicted on others. He's very
> remorseful now, but he's been in darkness for some time. He
> says: 'Can you raise me out of here?'
>   I see three people standing at the top of the dungeon. They
> were victims of his torture. They are throwing him a rope and
> between them they are helping him out. He can't climb out
> on his own – the walls are too smooth. They are telling him
> they have forgiven him and wish to help him on his way. The
> man himself looks crippled. The three helpers are telling him
> that they will take him to a place where he will be healed. All
> four are going upwards and out of my sight now.
>   I think he was a torturer during the reign of Queen
> Elizabeth, but he spanned the era of Henry VIII, Bloody
> Mary and the beginning of Queen Elizabeth's reign.

I could see that this communication had drained Eddie. Often he would experience the physical pain of his contacts, and this could leave him in a state of near-exhaustion, but he looked so tired now I was concerned that he would not be able to walk out of the Tower. So I walked to the small gift shop at the end of Water Lane and bought him a king-sized bar of English Heritage chocolate.

The chocolate restored Eddie and we moved off, through the gate into the Inner Ward. There, looming in front of us, was the White Tower, an impressive grey stone edifice flanked by four tall towers. A wooden staircase led into the tower, which today houses an impressive display of historic arms and armour. I walked towards the tower, sure that Eddie would want to go inside; after all, it had been used as a prison for some of the Tower's best-known captives. But he was looking in the opposite direction, towards the steps leading up to Tower Green. 'Where is your nose leading you?' I asked.

'To the execution block,' he said.

We walked past Tower Green to the small, chained-off enclosure that marked the spot where the executioner's axe had crashed down so many times. Today, huge, black-eyed ravens suspiciously eye the crowds of tourists who make the pilgrimage to the sad little spot. I waited for Eddie to speak, but he said nothing. Surely, I reasoned, he would be inundated with distressed souls trapped at this unholy place. But he looked blank. 'There's nothing here,' he said.

I wandered off, disappointed that he had not made contact with any spirits, to survey the ravens. These sinister birds have occupied the Tower from its early days, originally coming to scavenge off its heaps of rubbish. They soon became part of the castle's lore, the legend being that when the ravens leave the Tower the Kingdom will fall. The six birds in residence that day had had their wings clipped, just to be on the safe side.

Eddie joined me after a few moments. 'Shall we be off, then?' he asked cheerily.

I could not believe it. Here we were, in the most haunted place in the world, and Eddie had had enough for the day. 'Are you sure there's no-one else here?' I asked. But Eddie was adamant. I was baffled, perhaps uncharitably, by him. We had visited far less promising places than the Tower – very ordinary pubs, cottages, even shops – and he had been able to sense the past. But today, at the Tower, where the weight of history was so immense that even the worst-informed tourist gaped at the thought of what had happened here, he seemed lacklustre and uninterested.

Just as we were about to leave, I heard a Beefeater announce a tour of the Chapel of St Peter ad Vincula, which stood behind us. I ignored Eddie's protests that he could not think clearly among a group of chattering tourists and we joined them as they trooped into the tiny Tudor church. The last resting place of the executed, it was incorporated into the Tower by Henry III and rebuilt by Henry VIII. As the crowd settled down to listen to the Beefeater's potted history, delivered in a theatrical voice intended to delight the tourists, I looked around the chapel. Above our heads was an ancient tie-beam roof of Spanish chestnut; on the walls were plaques commemorating the lives of the warders. More than 1,500 bodies were found beneath the flagstones when Queen Victoria renovated the chapel in 1876, I heard the yeoman say, but only thirty-three were identified. The Queen herself insisted that all should be given a Christian burial.

After five minutes, Eddie nudged me: 'I have Anne Boleyn with me again,' he said. 'She's very glad we came here. I think she is bringing someone forward for me. Let's go outside, where it's quieter.' We pushed through the row of people next to us and made our way outside. Eddie led me to the foot of the Flint Tower and stopped. He was breathing heavily and swaying. Then he began to speak rapidly and, as he did so, I realized that he had contacted a man who had lived half a century after Anne but who, like her, had also been executed at the Tower.

His name was Robert Devereux, second Earl of Essex, beheaded at the Tower in February 1601, sixty-five years after Anne had died. But, unlike her, he had not been an innocent victim of the intrigues of power; Devereux had once been a favourite of Queen Elizabeth and had died because he had played – and lost – the game of high politics. I listened carefully as Eddie spoke:

> I think I'm picking up Essex . . . he says: 'If it could be said of a man that he died of ambition, that man is me. I like it not, I like it not . . . And yet I am not [ambitious]. Where are all those who were my friends? They have deserted me. I see none of them. It is a sad, dark place. Sir, you offer me a light. Can you offer me a way out? I have been here long enough. My Queen – what has become of her? I served her well, but she forsook me.'
>
> I get the impression of a very proud man who is not willing to acknowledge his mistakes. [I asked if Eddie was sure it was Essex.] Yes, I am sure it is he. He's wearing stockings, and a doublet and hose made of fine silver thread; on his feet are soft shoes with pointed toes, also embroidered in silver thread. I'm looking at the back of his head; his hair is long and falls below a small ruff. I think he has a beard. He is tall and carries himself proudly. He has a sword encrusted with jewels with a very ornate scabbard and he seems to be

247

flourishing a handkerchief in his right hand.

'I beseech you to take me from this place. I am ready to go. There is nothing I want from here and the place cares not for me,' he says. I get a great sense of earthly power and pride from him, but it seems to have been dented by his long wait as a trapped soul. He has felt the pain of his incarceration much more than some. He has a lot of work to do on himself when he leaves here – that's quite clear.

I see no-one coming for him, but there's a gate through which he can leave. No doubt he will be helped on his journey. He says: 'I do not need much bidding to leave, though where this path goes I know not. But it does offer me hope.'

The path I see is a rocky one. There are no plants, just a rocky path in a rocky landscape – but it is an upward path and it will eventually take him to the spirit world. Someone will help him; they are invisible to him now, but they will appear later. He gives a bow with a sweep of his right arm as he turns and departs. He's a very courageous man; I don't think he will be daunted by the journey, but he has many lessons to learn along the way.

Everything that Eddie had said made sense. Historians acknowledge Devereux's courage but they also describe him as vain, over-ambitious and politically naïve; certainly not a bad man, but one who was ruled by emotion. From what Eddie had said it seemed that, even in death, Devereux had struggled to attain true self-knowledge.

Robert Devereux, born in 1566, was the eldest son of Walter, first Earl of Essex, and Lettice Knollys, whose mother was Mary, Anne Boleyn's sister, which meant that he was the Queen's cousin. After his father's death his mother had remarried Lord Leicester, one of Queen Elizabeth's favourite courtiers, which helped Devereux establish his place at court. Elizabeth, thirty-four years his senior, was immediately drawn to this charming young man with his shock of auburn hair and flashing dark eyes. He entranced women and impressed men; but easy success made him impossibly self-centred.

In 1590, as the ageing Elizabeth grew dangerously fond of him, Devereux secretly married. When, later that year, his wife Frances became pregnant, he was forced to confess his marriage to Elizabeth. She took it as a personal affront and Devereux, desperate to regain favour with his patron, begged the Queen to let him go to France to help the French king, Henri IV, in the siege of Rouen. When he returned in 1594 Essex was able to re-establish his power base. He was, once again, Elizabeth's favourite and he began to exploit that influence to enhance his own failing financial fortunes. The great politician, essayist and philosopher of science, Francis Bacon, saw the dangers facing Essex and likened him to Icarus, the classical Greek hero who had put on wings made of feathers and wax and had flown too close to the sun.

But Essex would not, perhaps could not, reform. He tried to monopolize Elizabeth and seemed unable to grasp that, as a result, he was making powerful enemies. In 1599 Elizabeth despatched him to Ireland to subjugate the Earl of Tyrone. But Essex disobeyed the Queen's instructions and, instead of attacking Tyrone, made a truce with him. Then he returned to England, despite express orders forbidding this, and rode non-stop from Chester to Elizabeth, who was residing at Nonsuch Palace, Surrey. He strode upstairs to her private apartments, pushing aside sentries, and burst into Elizabeth's bedchamber. The Queen, who had only just risen and was not wearing her wig, rouge or robes, was not impressed by his excuses about Ireland. He was imprisoned at York House.

Elizabeth freed him three months later, but by now Essex's main worry was not his reputation but his enormous debts. With bankruptcy fast approaching, he decided to take a final gamble. Urged on by a ragged group of adventurers who were as desperate for money and power as him, Devereux decided to overthrow Elizabeth and stage a *coup d'état*.

On Sunday, 8 February 1601, he was summoned to court. When he refused to go, the Queen sent her men to his house; instead of persuading him to submit, they were themselves imprisoned. Essex's followers urged him to attack Whitehall, where Elizabeth was residing, but he rode towards the City, intending to make it his stronghold. A herald rode ahead, declaring him a traitor, and the

City remained loyal to the Queen. The coup against her had always been doomed and was clearly the act of a desperate man, but it was nonetheless treason and Elizabeth could not afford to be merciful. She signed Devereux's death warrant on Shrove Tuesday, 1601, but did not immediately send it to the Tower, perhaps hoping, in her heart, that she could find a way to spare him. The next day, he was executed on Tower Green. He was the one of the few people Elizabeth had genuinely cared for, but ambition and pride had led him inexorably to disgrace and death.

★

My badgering of Eddie had clearly paid off; he was obviously surprised by the clarity of Essex's message. Nor did Anne Boleyn break her word, for three days later Eddie received his final, and most poignant, communication through her. It was from the young princes, Edward and his younger brother, the sons of Edward IV, who had been lodged in the Tower following their father's death in 1483, under the protection of their uncle, Richard, Duke of Gloucester. Although preparations were made to crown Edward, his uncle eventually succeeded to the throne as Richard III. The two boys were imprisoned for some time and then disappeared. History has drawn its own grim conclusions about their fate, but even today it remains something of a mystery. Eddie was sure that this was the final secret the Tower had to release. His work there was now complete.

'They did foully murder us, buried our bodies in the Tower,' they said. 'They brought a man to us who purported to be a physician. He asked after our health and we were each asked to drink a vial of physic which he told us would help guard against the miasma in the Tower. After that, we could not – and did not – struggle.

'Our uncle, Richard, had already died in battle, so 'twas not he that ordered this. We later met our uncle and he was much distressed that his name had been besmirched in history for the deed he did not commit. But it suited the King who followed Richard [Henry VII] to lay the blame on him. It

250

seems that history is sometimes what a powerful king would make of it.

'Mercifully, our suffering was not great and at this late time our simple wish is to tell the truth of the event; otherwise, we are well beyond earth's cares and find much happiness. This is all we have come to say.'

Postscript

It was several weeks after Eddie's first visit to the Tower that I realized the significance of the date of his invitation. I had been flicking through Antonia Fraser's book, *The Six Wives of Henry VIII*, when the pages fell open and my eye was drawn to a paragraph on Anne Boleyn. I could not believe what I read: Anne Boleyn was executed on Tower Green on 19 May 1536 – Eddie's visit in May 1994 had coincided with the anniversary of her death. I realized then that Anne had played an important role in bringing these poor unfortunate souls forward to Eddie. She herself was not trapped, but she had wanted to help other, less fortunate spirits. The date of Eddie's visit to the Tower had not seemed important at the time; now I could see that it was actually the most significant thing about the whole episode.

Chapter 15

Aces in the Sky

From the position of the dying moon I knew we were heading back to the Norfolk coast, and for the first time I could see him well. To my surprise, my shepherd was a de Havilland Mosquito, a fighter bomber of Second World War vintage.

Frederick Forsyth, *The Shepherd*

Corpus non animum muto

(The body changes, not the spirit)

Motto of 57 Squadron, RAF East Kirkby

On the morning of 27 August 1943, after yet another nerve-snapping night raid over Germany, Lancaster bombers from 57 Squadron touched down at RAF Scampton in Lincoln for the last time. But there was no rest for the exhausted crews and no time for the usual fried breakfast and precious sleep. The aircraft were pumped with fuel for the short hop to their new station at East Kirkby, twenty-nine miles away, to be followed by the squadron's 900 back-up personnel. Number 5 Bomber Group operated almost exclusively out of Lincolnshire, and the strategists at Bomber Command had decided to upgrade East Kirkby, originally a decoy airfield, to accommodate two squadrons, 57 and 630. On the evening of 30 August, fourteen Lancasters took off for East Kirkby's first war operation, an attack on München-Gladbach. All returned safely the following morning.

Breathless with excitement, Fred Panton and his younger brother, Harold, had cycled down the country lanes from their home in Old Bolinbroke to a hilltop overlooking East Kirkby: like every schoolboy in England, they were desperate to catch a glimpse of the legendary bombers. Fred and Harold gasped at the scene below. There were Lancasters slowly turning into the hangars like great primeval birds; trollies scootered across the airfield carrying the 4,000 lb 'Cookie' high-capacity bombs and ground crew ran around like ants, fuelling and checking the aircraft.

At fourteen, Fred dreamt about flying a Lancaster on a secret night mission to Germany, after hearing his eighteen-year-old brother Christopher, a flight engineer with a Pathfinder crew, describe night sorties over enemy territory. But little Harold, aged ten, had always been left out, deemed too young to understand. He had asked Fred to explain what Christopher was talking about, but his older brother did not have the time or patience to explain.

Christopher, the eldest of the Panton brothers, had joined 405 Squadron, based at RAF Skipton-on-Swale in Yorkshire. Tall, flaxen-haired and the brightest of his class, he had joined the crew at seventeen, a rare achievement as most young recruits had to complete a full tour of duty with another squadron before being assigned to a Pathfinder. The PFF (Pathfinder Force) had been introduced in August 1942 and played a vital role in Bomber Command's raids on Germany, dropping aerial route markers to guide the bombers across Germany, then marking the targets by flares or radar.

Bomber Command's offensive against Germany was one of the most remarkable campaigns of the Second World War. Winston Churchill had decided in 1940 that air power – especially the ability to launch devastating bombing raids against Germany – would prove crucial in the coming years. From Lincolnshire, known as Bomber Country because of its fifty airfields, the RAF planes flew every night to pulverize Berlin, Stuttgart, Mannheim, Nuremberg and the industrial Ruhr region. The cost of the bombing campaign was high: a third of a million sorties were mounted against the

253

enemy at a cost of 9,000 aircraft and 55,000 men. A further 10,000 were shot down and taken prisoner. Bomber Command's casualties amounted to almost one-seventh of all British deaths in action by land, sea and air. At the end of the war, Air Marshal Sir Arthur 'Bomber' Harris, leader of Bomber Command, said: 'There are no words with which I can do justice to the air crews who fought under my command. There is no parallel in warfare to such courage and determination in the face of so prolonged a period of danger which, at times, was so great that scarcely one man in three could expect to survive his tour of thirty operations.'

In the weeks that followed the arrival of the bombers at East Kirkby, Fred and Harold would often rush into the street outside their home, their supper half-eaten, to watch the planes head off towards Germany, huge winged creatures that blotted out the evening sun, until the sky was clear and the silence deafening. Often, in the early hours, the boys would be woken by the roar of engines as the bombers returned, and would fling open their bedroom window. The Lancasters were always so low that the boys could clearly see the pilots in their cockpits as they prepared to land.

On 30 March 1944 the Panton family received a letter from Christopher saying that he had just been promoted to Pilot Officer on the eve of his thirtieth sortie with 433 Squadron. He was obviously excited and proud, but he also said he was looking forward to taking some leave as soon as possible.

That night, Fred's mother did not sleep; she prayed, with all her might, for her eldest son, somewhere over enemy territory. But fate did not spare Christopher that night. His aircraft, a Halifax bomber, was hit over Nüremberg and, despite the desperate efforts of the pilot, it crashed and exploded, killing all seven crew. There were many such losses. The RAF sustained more casualties on 30–31 March than during any other night of the war; of the 800 Lancasters and Halifaxes that left bases in Yorkshire and Lincolnshire, ninety-four did not return.

Fred and his family never recovered from Christopher's death. 'He was the one in the family who had everything going for him – the looks, the brains and the personality,' Fred recalled more than fifty years later. After the war, Fred and his brothers worked hard to turn their father's poultry farm into a prosperous business. Then, in 1971, Fred decided it was time to visit Christopher's final resting place at the Durnbach Military Cemetery, thirty miles outside Munich. When he saw his brother's grave for the first time, Fred was engulfed by a powerful feeling of love that had been given no expression for over a quarter of a century. 'I was overwhelmed by the experience,' he said. 'All those memories of my childhood, which I had supressed in my grief, came flooding back. I decided there and then that I had to do something to commemorate Christopher's death.'

Fred's chance to do something came exactly ten years later, when he saw that the Ministry of Defence was selling East Kirkby airfield. By then Fred and Harold were secure financially; as the airfield adjoined their land, it seemed a sensible proposition that they should buy it. But Fred also had a dream, which had nothing to do with sensible business plans: the airfield that had meant so much in his childhood would become a shrine to Christopher. In late 1981 Fred and Harold restored the old control tower, a squat black building in the middle of the site which had been the nerve centre of the base. Then they positioned models dressed in RAF uniforms on the spots which they would have occupied when the tower was a night-time 'ops' room. The windows were blacked out, the clock was set at 10.20 and the maps on the wall showed the flight routes of the aircraft; the tower now was frozen in time.

A year later Fred and Harold converted a NAAFI shop on the airfield into a café and covered the walls with cuttings from Second World War newspapers and photographs of Christopher. In 1983 they built a hangar outside the museum to house an exhibition of wartime memorabilia, civilian and support vehicles from the 1940s and the burnt-out wreckage of a Spitfire fighter plane with a photograph of the young pilot who died in the crash. Pride of place, however, belonged to a well-preserved Lancaster NX 611 from the war.

In July 1989 Sir Michael Beetham, Marshal of the Royal Air Force, who had himself been a pilot there in 1945, opened the Lincolnshire Aviation Heritage Centre, East Kirkby. In 1994 the centre received around 30,000 visitors a year from the UK and all over the world.

★

In April 1994 Eddie asked me if I would like to accompany him to a disused airfield outside Lincoln. Eddie said that the owner had invited him there because of a series of inexplicable events; as usual, Eddie had insisted that he should not be told any details of the possible hauntings.

As we drove down the twisting lanes of the Lincolnshire Wolds towards the village of Stickney on 26 April, the bright morning sunlight blinded me. After a few minutes a small sign appeared, pointing leftwards to our destination: Lincolnshire Aviation Heritage Centre. At the base we found the NAAFI shop and asked for Mr Panton.

Eddie took a cup of tea and a Kit-Kat and sat down at one of the tables in the café. The walls were plastered with hundreds of newspaper articles about Bomber Command and 57 and 630 Squadrons, which had flown from the base between 1943 and 1945. A small glass cabinet containing a beret, three medals and various letters stood against one wall; above it was a picture of a handsome young man in uniform, squinting into the sun. The plaque below read: Christopher Panton, 1925–1944. As a Vera Lynn record crackled in the background, I looked at the young man's open, honest face. He looked too full of hope and courage to have died so young; his picture embodied the heartbreaking years of war, when the young lived on the edge of experience and departures were more poignant because they could well be final.

The pilots of Bomber Command were – and remain – the unacknowledged heroes of the war. Their chances of survival were much lower than other air crew and their sinister night sorties on slow, lumbering aircraft loaded with thousands of bombs made them a sitting target. Worse, they were not even sure if their missions – to bomb industrial and civilian targets – were useful or even morally right. For many years after the war the bomber crews were virtual pariahs as historians argued about the rights and wrongs of Bomber Command's campaign; only recently have the crews been paid the tributes which they are, surely, owed.

The slam of a door broke my daydream. A small man in his early sixties, wearing a heavy tweed coat and muffled against the cold, strode across the room and introduced himself. 'Fred Panton,' he said and held out his hand. As we finished our tea and picked up our coats, Eddie asked us to wait a moment. A spirit of a young man was drawing close.

He says: 'I don't mind coming back one little bit – it's a wonderful opportunity.' He's so full of joy. I'm quite sure that this is how he was in life. He says: 'My death does not worry me at all now. I came to terms with that a long time ago, so don't be fearful of my remembering. When I died I was very quickly taken over and I soon met the people I had loved on earth. I had a wonderful time and it has got more wonderful ever since. I shall meet you when you come over.

'What you have done at the Heritage Centre is a tribute I hardly deserve. I have tried to give you guidance all the way and when things have felt difficult I've come along and given you a nudge and said "Get on with it, you're going to get there, you're going to win through."

'The important thing about the centre is that it brings joy to many people – and brings back memories to older people. In a way, these experiences can never die. I send my love to you and the rest of the family. I tune into you all at different times and I feel your thoughts for me. One day we shall all be together again and I'm very much looking forward to that. I will leave you now. God bless and goodbye.'

At one point Fred's eyes had flooded with tears, and he was unable to speak for a few minutes after Eddie finished. Then he said that Eddie had just been in touch with his brother, Christopher. After Fred had composed himself we followed him out of the café, across the airfield, past the hangar to the control tower, a two-storey rectangular building with an iron stairway leading to the roof lookout. As we climbed the cold stone steps, I sensed the fear and anticipation that once had hung heavy in the air. At the top of the steps was a communications room, the radio and Morse code machines manned by dummies in WRAF uniforms. On the left was an officers' rest room, complete with original 1940s-style easy chairs, lamps and newspapers.

At the end of the corridor was the *tour de force*: ten models manned the main operations room, at the flight control desk and by the blackboard, which showed the battle orders of Silksheen (the wartime codename for East Kirkby) for a raid on Berlin in early 1944. I asked Eddie whether he sensed anything in the control tower.

'I'm aware of the presence – half-seeing and half-feeling – of several people around me,' he said. 'They are very curious about us. I think they are RAF officers. They seem to belong to this place. I'll see if I can get any closer to them to find out what this is about.' Eddie sat down on a chair by the flight control desk and closed his eyes.

A man in an RAF uniform is asking: 'What are you doing here? You don't belong here.' I think there's more than one entity here; I'd like to find out how many there are. 'Oh, there are quite a few of us,' he responds. 'We come and go, you know, but we don't allow civilians in here.' He thinks I'm a civilian intruder, so I tell him to carry on, as I won't be long and I won't interfere.

He says: 'Sometimes people come in here and then go and we never see them again. But I'm here all the time – I organize the place and although it is fully manned most of the time, I stand in if we haven't got the numbers we need. I'm sorry if I was a little rude to you to start with, but you're quite welcome – I can see that you're not causing any problems. In fact, you bring a little light into the place. It's a little gloomy, you know. I get a bit fed up with the gloom sometimes, but wartime restrictions and all that – got to keep the light down.

'I must say that it's not as busy as it was – I miss the activity. I said to one of the others here the other day: "I wouldn't mind a posting, I've been here long enough." Even the best posting gets boring after a time. I think I've done my bit here and someone else can take over, so I don't know

258

what influence you've got. If you can arrange for me to be posted somewhere else, I'd be glad.'

I asked him how he got posted here in the first place. He says: 'I have a job to remember, to be honest. It seems a long time ago. I think there was a raid and a bomb dropped quite close to me. It knocked me out for a time. When I came to, I felt rather strange. I started wandering around the airfield, not being able to make much sense of things, and eventually ended up in the watch tower. It seemed they needed someone to take charge – the place was half-empty. I'd done this sort of work before, so I came in here and I've been here ever since. Do you think you could get me away?'

I tell him I shall try, if he can stand still for a little while. An officer has now come into the control tower; I think he may be a squadron leader. He's announced that a plane is waiting for anyone who wants to go. Our friend says he'd like to go and so does one other; there's no response from the rest of them – I don't know how many there are altogether. It looks like only these two want to leave. They are walking off with the squadron leader out of the picture.

Fred said that visitors had experienced strange happenings in the tower. He added that he had also been troubled there. 'One weekend last winter I had to repaint the steps of the control room and was applying the second coat late in the Sunday afternoon. As it fell dark, I began to sense a strange silence in the stairwell. Then a voice in my head told me I should get out – NOW. But I refused – I shouted aloud that no-one was going to force me out of the tower until I'd done the job I came to do. The last few steps were impossibly hard to finish – I just could not get it right. As I lowered the cushion to the final step, a shiver went down my spine. The step was already wet; someone had painted it. I picked up my paint brushes and ran.'

I could see that Eddie was growing tired, but Fred insisted that we went to one more place before we left. As we walked into the sunlight towards the hangar, Fred told us that his son, David, had seen a figure walking from the hangar to the control tower. David, who lives in a house by the airfield and works as its caretaker, had called his father to inform him that someone was trespassing on the site. But there was no trace of the intruder when they searched the area. Fred had also seen the same figure, at around 9.15 one summer's evening as the sun was setting.

Fred drew back the doors of the enormous hangar and revealed his most prized possession, a Lancaster bomber. On the side of the aircraft was a painting of a bikini-clad woman astride a huge bomb, with the caption 'Just Jane'. In front of the plane stood a simple wooden table bearing a vase of flowers and a plaque to commemorate the thousands of men who never returned to East Kirkby.

I left Eddie to his own thoughts as Fred showed me the hundreds of photographs and press cuttings that visitors to the centre had sent him. Then Eddie interrupted. 'I'm getting the impression of a group of women and children; it's a psychic imprint,' he said.

They are distressed and the women are protesting about something. They are saying: 'We should not have been left in this situation. We can't look after ourselves like this.' One of the women is wearing a WAAF uniform. I think there had been some sort of disturbance; the women are protesting because the airfield was attracting enemy fire and the women and children of the village suffered because of it.

Fred looked excited by Eddie's words. 'Like many airfields around here, East Kirkby was originally set up as a dummy operational station to draw enemy action away from the other RAF bases,' he said. 'Parts of the village were close up to the boundary, and I remember a bomb was once dropped here that killed several people.'

On the way back to the café, Fred's son introduced himself to us and talked about other extraordinary incidents which he had seen, such as the night when three balls of lights had danced on the path leading into the hangar. Eddie did not pretend that he could explain any of this but I knew that he had, at least, helped Fred make contact with his long-departed brother Christopher. As we prepared to leave he thanked Eddie again. 'It's a thousand pities that Christopher died,' he said. 'But at least I know now that he's happy where he is.'

As Eddie collected the car from the car park, I walked towards the memorial I had seen on the way into the airfield. It was a tribute to 57 and 630 Squadrons, and to the 112 Lancasters and over 1,000 men who had been lost to enemy action. In front of the simple headstone bearing the crests of the two squadrons was a scale model of a Lancaster. Two plaques flanked the memorial, erected in 1979; one was inscribed with a poem by Walter Scott, an air gunner with 630 Squadron, entitled 'Old Airfield'.

> Laughter, sorrow, hope and pain;
> I shall never know these things again.
> Emotions that I came to know
> Of strange young men so long ago.
>
> Who knows as evening shadows meet
> Are they with me still, a phantom fleet?
> And do my ghosts still stride unseen
> Across my face, so wide and green?

★

The Second World War was the most destructive conflict in human history. Tens of millions of people died: between five and six million Jews in Hitler's concentration camps, twenty million Russians, five million Germans and 700,000 British and American troops. It was a time when emotions reached an intensity unknown before or since, when unbreakable friendships were sealed and loved ones lost. But the war also saw a new style of scientific carnage. This was the conflict of night sights, pilotless rocket planes, the first computers and, finally, atomic bombs. The only arena where the remains of the old chivalry survived, at least in the popular imagination, was in the air. Like white knights from another era, the young Allied pilots jousted with the enemy high in Britain's skies, ironically in some of the most sophisticated killing machines ever invented.

Of all the campaigns of the war, the Battle of Britain is the one that is closest to the nation's heart. If it had been lost, Hitler would have invaded and the course of world history changed irrevocably.

261

Between 10 July and 31 October 1940, the Allied fighting force of British, Canadian, Polish and Free French pilots drove back the Luftwaffe's 1,350 bombers and 1,200 fighter planes who had launched a series of attacks against British shipping and airfields. The Germans had secured France and now planned to invade England. The Allied air defence consisted largely of Hurricane and Spitfire fighters, which were, on average, outnumbered three to one by the attackers. On 15 September 1940, the climax of the battle, fifty-six enemy planes were destroyed and Hitler was forced to postpone, for ever, his invasion.

Half a century later, these Battle of Britain pilots seem to embody the timeless ideal of the warrior knight, a deeply rooted idea which extends back into Arthurian legend. Quintessentially English, they have become part of the national mythology and have bequeathed a series of unforgettable images: the insouciant young man driving down country lanes in an open-top sports car; the dedicated pilot dashing across the airfield as the siren calls while his tearful fiancée waves goodbye; and the frightened young man whose life flashes before him as he spirals downwards in the burning wreck of his aircraft.

Eddie believes the Second World War has left such a tragic legacy of ghosts because, perhaps more than even during the First World War, so many victims were young men bursting with a passion for life which was savagely denied. 'They were simply not ready to die. Many of the ghosts I have released had carried their earthly energy across to the other side. They felt cheated and angry that their life had been cut off in their prime,' he said.

In June 1991, Eddie was asked to help a young man who was sure that he was haunted by a ghost from the Second World War. At one stage, the man thought he was losing his mind – he had even asked his doctor to arrange a brain scan. The doctor had also referred him to the College of Psychic Studies in London, whose staff had recommended Eddie. On 16 June Joseph Wright (this is an alias since the man still fears ridicule over his experiences) left his house in Kingsbury, north London and drove fifty miles to Grayshott, east Hampshire, where Eddie was then living. Joseph explained what had happened and asked Eddie if he could help. Eddie was non-commital but agreed to try.

Joseph, a self-employed builder in his late thirties, explained that in 1990 he had stumbled across the derelict grave of a Battle of Britain pilot called Tommy Pinkham; after clearing the weeds and repairing the headstone, he had somehow become obsessed with the RAF. He said that his life had become a nightmare, but he remained rational and sceptical; obviously he was desperate for help, but he also wanted to see if Eddie really possessed the rare psychic abilities described by the College of Psychic Studies. So he told Eddie few details.

Joseph and Eddie drove to St Andrew's Church, a mile from his home in Kingsbury. He led Eddie to a small, neat plot surrounded by a low wall; at the head of the grave was a fifteen-inch granite plinth which supported two pillars topped by a small arch. The centre of the arch was engraved with the RAF insignia and motto, *per ardua at astra* (through hardships to the stars). The plinth below was engraved with the words:

To the memory of
Squadron Leader P. Campbell Pinkham
(Tommy)
Killed in air combat, 5 September 1940
aged 25 years

Eddie sensed a strong psychic power around him, but that contact would be made later in the day. He suggested that they should go back to Joseph's house, where he thought that they might be able to pick up more.

At Joseph's house Eddie did, indeed, feel a strong force. He said that he sensed Joseph's father, who had played a role as a spiritual intermediary, drawing together the souls of the Second World War air crew and Joseph. Then Eddie continued:

This is interesting; I'm with four people, but they are not earthbound. I can hear someone using the word intruders and laughing. I will have to reach up beyond the earth level.

I'm on an airfield; there's a single runway, several hangars and other buildings, but I can't see any aircraft. I'm standing next to a group of airmen who are laughing and chatting. They seem to have created their own sub-heaven; it's as though they have recreated a place where they can carry on just as they were, reliving the excitement of the war, but sensing that they can no longer be killed. They are quite happy.

Tommy Pinkham is here; he's saying: 'They've got to be woken up, they've got to be helped. I can't do it, they think I'm part of the scene.' He wants us to give him our support.

Tommy says: 'I'm going to be the pilot of that aircraft. They'll come then. I'm going to shepherd them all in; I don't want any to be left behind.' I think the aircraft is approaching now; it's coming in on the far end of the runway. I can't see what sort it is yet. It's a prop jet, I think. It's small and quite colourful – not camouflaged anyway.

Tommy has climbed out of the aircraft and he steps down, shouting to them to come. 'Come and have a look at this,' he says. I get the impression that there are twenty or thirty of them waiting to go. They are coming forward from different parts of the airfield, walking along with their hands in their pockets. Tommy asks if there are any more to come. There's a lot of bantering going on and they are asking Tommy questions, but he won't reply. 'I'll tell you when you're aboard,' he says.

They're sauntering along, now, but not hurrying and getting into the plane. They're having a good look around, especially at the cockpit – it's got features they haven't seen before. 'Come on, help me,' shouts Tommy as they wind up the ladder. They close the door and crowd up at the front of the aircraft. 'Come on, we don't want it to get front-heavy,' he jokes. 'You can come up in turn later.'

He starts the propellors and the engine whines loudly – a sound they have never heard before. Tommy turns the aircraft round and taxis back along the runway. They are asking 'Don't you have to turn into the wind?' as he revs up for take-off. He says: 'Don't worry, there's more than enough power.' He's up well clear of the runway now and climbing through the clouds into a bright light. They haven't seen light as bright as this for a long time.

Tommy gets out of the pilot seat and walks back to them. He says: 'Don't worry, it's on auto-pilot. There are a few things I want to say to you, then we'll make a landing. None of you have been to this airfield before. It may seem a little strange, but I'm sure you're all going to like it. Anyway, there's a big crowd waiting to greet you when you get there.' The pilots are still asking him questions, but he is reluctant to answer them. He says: 'There's enough time, you'll see.'

Tommy is making his approach to a runway set in the open countryside. The runway is in the middle of trees and meadows. They are puzzled because there is no control tower, only a runway. He reassures them: 'This is a private runway,' he says. 'It's only used for special purposes.' They taxi along towards the end of it, where crowds are standing on both sides, waiting for them. The lads are looking out of the windows and crying in surprise: 'That's my mum and dad – how did they get there?' asks one. 'There's my wife!' cries another.

The plane comes to a halt. Tommy drops the ladder down the side of the aircraft and they all get out. I have to leave them – it's too overwhelming now. The joy and excitement are tremendous.

Then Joseph told Eddie the full story. It began, he said, when his son, Brian, was born in 1988. One night, when Brian was about three months old, Joseph and his wife Diana saw a man walk from their son's cot through the door of the bedroom. Joseph thought it must have been his father, who had died nine months before the baby was born. But he decided that it would be best to forget the whole incident.

In spring 1989, Joseph said, he had begun to play football regularly. He had also bought a Porsche. This might not have been strange in your averagely prosperous lad, but Joseph had always hated football and smart cars. Then, in April, the Porsche broke down and Joseph decided to walk home, taking a short cut through the graveyard at St Andrew's Church.

'Something stopped me in my tracks as I passed one of the graves. I looked down at this overgrown grave with a broken headstone and fell to my knees. I felt incredibly upset. I cleared the weeds and saw a name on the headstone: P. Campbell Pinkham (Tommy) who had died in action on 5 September 1940.'

Joseph wrote to the local newspaper, complaining about the state of the graves. His letter drew a large response and in a few weeks a group of volunteers had gathered to clear the cemetery. Six months later, Tommy Pinkham's sister wrote to him and he went to see her. She gave him a letter that a colleague of Tommy had written to their father in 1940, explaining the circumstances of his death. He read the letter and resolved to put the whole affair behind him.

Joseph had taken a year off work to help bring up his young son. At two years old, Brian had grown into an endearing little boy, with auburn hair and flashing brown eyes. One day in December 1989, as Joseph was pushing Brian in his buggy through Hendon, they had come across the RAF Museum. It was a wet and miserable day, so they went inside.

'Brian was terribly excited by it all, especially the pictures of the Spitfires and Hurricanes,' said Joseph. On the way out, they stopped at the gift shop attached to the museum. Brian picked up a book from a pile that had been reduced for a quick sale. 'Brian couldn't talk properly, but he kept saying "picture, picture". I realized that he was upset, so I bought him a copy of the book to keep him quiet. On the way home he kept pointing to the picture on the cover – the RAF roundel used on Allied aircraft.'

When they got home, Joseph looked through the book, *Spitfire Squadron, No. 19: Squadron at War, 1939–1941* by Dilip Sarkar. Joseph realized that it was the history of Tommy Pinkham's own squadron, but he saw nothing significant in that. He simply flicked through it absent-mindedly, pausing over a photograph of a group of young 19 Squadron pilots who had just returned from an air battle. Without thinking why, Joseph tore the picture out of the book and pinned it on the kitchen wall.

A few weeks later, Brian woke up one evening at nine o'clock, screaming and crying. 'He seemed to be having a nightmare,' said Joseph. 'He kept screaming aloud that a tree had fallen and smashed their faces. My wife said that we should dress him and take him wherever he wanted to go.' They set off in the car and drove to St Andrew's, as Brian had been shouting 'church' to them. When they opened the car doors, he ran off. He led Joseph to Tommy Pinkham's grave and sat down beside it. Joseph gasped; a huge oak tree had fallen and smashed the headstone.

A couple of days later Joseph stopped to look at the picture he had pinned on the kitchen wall. A shiver ran over him as he read the names below the tired faces of the young men: one of them was Brian Lane, the man who had written the letter to Tommy's father which Tommy's sister had passed to Joseph. Lane had taken over command of 19 Squadron after Tommy's death in 1940.

During the following year, Joseph became obsessed with the wartime RAF, so much so that his sitting room came to resemble a shrine to these years of aerial battle. He also began to take flying lessons in a light aircraft and sent Brian on regular, and expensive, helicopter flights. They visited Tommy's grave every few weeks, tidying away the weeds and taking flowers. 'I was convinced that I was losing my mind,' he said. 'I thought I had a brain tumour or an incurable disease that was slowly driving me insane.' But as well as arranging for him to have a temporal lobe epilepsy scan, Joseph's doctor also gave him the telephone number of the College of Psychic Studies. 'He never once said I was imagining all this, and I'm grateful to him for that,' said Joseph.

Before they parted, Joseph handed Eddie a copy of *Spitfire Squadron* so he could read about Tommy Pinkham himself. Tommy, christened Phillip Campbell Pinkham, had been born in Wembley, north London, in 1915. He was a great-nephew of Sir Charles Pinkham, former Deputy Lieutenant of the County of Middlesex. Tommy had been educated at Kilburn Grammar School, after which he had joined the London Yeomanry. He joined the RAF in 1935 and by early 1936 was a top instructor. He was so highly regarded that he was awarded the Air Force Cross in the King's Birthday Honours for 1939.

In June 1940, Tommy Pinkham officially took over as 19 Squadron Leader, based at Duxford, near Cambridge. In the build-up to the decisive battle for air supremacy over Britain, he tested the new cannon-equipped Spitfires and devised new tactical formations in an effort to outmanoeuvre the Luftwaffe's formidable Messerschmitt Bf109E aircraft.

On Thursday, 5 September 1940 seventy German aircraft crossed the English coast at Dungeness and headed inland to attack Fighter Command airfields in No. 11 Group. Tommy's squadron scrambled to intercept and spotted an enemy formation of forty Dornier bombers and an escort of forty Messerschmitts approaching from the west and heading down the Thames estuary. Pinkham ordered 'A' Flight, led by Brian Lane, to attack the fighters and 'B' Flight the bombers. It was Tommy's last action; his Spitfire was caught in the combined cross-fire of three enemy aircraft. Later, his plane was discovered in the Kent countryside near the small village of Birling. He had attempted to bale out of the aircraft, but wounds to his head, chest and hips had slowed him down; he had baled out too close to the ground and his parachute had failed to open in time.

Just twenty-five years old, Pinkham's body was handed over to his family for burial; the service took place the following Tuesday, 10 September, at St Andrew's Church, Kingsbury, London. His log book was stamped 'Killed in action'.

In February the following year, Eddie called Joseph to see if things had improved. 'I'm not obsessed with Spitfires any more, and I haven't sensed Tommy around me. But I can feel my father's presence very strongly in the house,' he said. Eddie also had a message for Joseph. On 26 February 1992 Tommy Pinkham had come through to Eddie during one of his psychic development groups. The communication read:

> Tommy Pinkham's here and he's laughing at all the confusion
> he caused you. He appreciates what you did, but he's very
> amused at the way you reacted. He jokes: 'We had you on
> the run there, didn't we?'

Chapter 16

The Littledean Saga

All houses wherein men have lived and died
Are haunted houses. Through the open doors
The harmless phantoms on their errands glide,
With feet that make no sound upon the floors.

Henry Wadsworth Longfellow, 'Haunted Houses'

It is generally acknowledged that Britain is the most haunted country in the world and that the Tower of London is the most haunted place in the country. But there is no similar consensus on the most haunted city, house or castle in the UK. Competition for the 'most haunted' cachet is fierce: London, York and Edinburgh all declare themselves Britain's most haunted city, while Glamis, Ludlow and Belvoir Castles claim the most ghosts in residence. The same is true for haunted houses. Every Hallowe'en is marked by a rash of newspaper articles on 'Britain's most haunted house' – but every year a different house is selected. Borley Rectory in Essex held the title for nearly twenty years, largely because of the work of Harry Price, a renowned psychic investigator; after his death in 1948, his research was discredited and Borley Rectory lost its place at the top of the league table.

The publication in 1977 of a sensational book, *The Amityville Horror*, about an American poltergeist case, rekindled the public's interest in haunted houses, and in the same year a British Amityville was miraculously 'discovered'. Peggy Harper and her four children, aged seven to thirteen, had noticed disturbances in their suburban house in Enfield, north London, which ranged from beds jolting to strange knocks, and objects flying through the air. Journalists from the *Daily Mirror* witnessed some of these phenomena and several books were written about the case, but the story 'died' when the two Harper girls were caught bending spoons and jumping up and down on their beds.

However, in autumn 1993, in the depths of the property recession, the 'most haunted' cachet was used in a very novel way. Estate agent John D. Wood, perhaps in an attempt to draw rich American buyers, advertised the ghost of Boys Hall, a Jacobean manor house in Kent, as one of its major selling points. The ghost, a young woman whose fiancé had been killed after a Christmas party in the house at the end of the eighteenth century, was said to walk through Boys Hall, calling out for him. The specifications on the £660,000 house included a history of the haunting as well as details of its seven bedrooms, indoor swimming pool, tennis courts and stables.

Boys Hall was not sold, although the ghostly marketing trick seemed to work at Chingle Hall, a moated manor house in Goosnargh, Lancashire. The owner, barrister John Bruce, had claimed that it, too, was 'the most haunted house in Britain'. As well as vouching for the ghostly presence of the English martyr John Wall, Mr Bruce had claimed that the house would be worth £5 million a year as a tourist attraction. In 1994 Mr Bruce managed to convince Professor Trevor Kirkham, an eye specialist at McGill University, Montreal, that the house was worth the asking price of £420,000. When Professor Kirkham discovered that Chingle Hall was in fact losing around £30,000 a year, he successfully sued for damages.

It was with difficulty, then, that Eddie and I set out to establish, if not exactly *the* most haunted house in Britain, then one that could truly boast multiple hauntings. Eddie had dealt with many cases involving several hauntings, but none matched my criteria: I was looking for a great old house with layer upon layer of history, and ghosts from every period. Quite by chance, I found exactly the right place: Littledean Hall, a Grade II listed house in Gloucestershire. I had been researching ghosts of the Civil War when I came across an intriguing account of a haunting at Littledean. Two Royalist officers had apparently been murdered in the dining room of the house and every year a phantom stain, like a pool of blood, had appeared on the exact spot where they fell.

I managed to contact the owner, Donald Macer-Wright, and arranged a visit. Mr Macer-Wright, who inherited the house from his father, had lived there since 1979. The house had been open to the public since 1982 and many of his visitors had reported apparitions there. He had tried to sell Littledean in 1991 for £500,000, but without success. A keen amateur archaeologist, Mr Macer-Wright said that the house, a converted Saxon church, had been built on a Romano-Celtic settlement, probably an iron works. It was still possible to see the original Saxon rooms underneath the main floor of the house and chart the extensions and changes to the house throughout the centuries. He was also an authority on the ghosts of Littledean.

On 20 June 1994 I set off from London for the West Country. As I drove into Gloucestershire, the green fields stretched way over the horizon and the sun shone fiercely. As you reach the Forest of Dean, you are taken back in time. A royal forest from time immemorial, it covers an area of ten square miles, including 34,000 acres of National Forest Parkland. The ancient oaks and beeches have witnessed the Roman occupation of Britain, the Danish wars and the Civil War. Today, it is one of the most beautiful areas of ancient forest in the country.

A small brown 'heritage site' sign marked the entrance to Littledean Hall, and as I turned up the drive I saw Eddie waiting in the car park. He had already introduced himself to Mr Macer-Wright, who was keen to start the tour of the house. It was 1 p.m.; I hoped that Eddie had had some lunch beforehand, or else we would get nothing done.

After five minutes Donald Macer-Wright strode through the courtyard to meet us. A tall, aristocratic figure of about forty, he was wearing scruffy working clothes and muddy wellingtons. 'Littledean', he said, 'is a house within a house. There are so many layers of history that you must first sit down and listen, so you can get an idea of its role through the ages.' He led us to the barn behind the courtyard,

271

which he had converted into a small museum, and plugged in a tape-recorder, which gave a potted history of the house. Eddie, meanwhile, wandered off to inspect the grounds.

Littledean Hall, the tape explained, had been continuously inhabited since the eleventh century and was the ancestral home of all the families of Deane and A'Deane of Gloucestershire, Berkshire, Oxfordshire and Dromore, Ireland. Before King Canute's victory in the Danish wars of the eleventh century, the Forest of Dean had been an ancient hunting ground. During the Roman occupation, Littledean was the site of a great temple to the goddess Sabrina, protector of the River Severn, which the house overlooks. William the Conqueror had given the manor at Littledean to the French baron William fitz Norman, son of Norman de la Mare, in 1080. He is recorded as being Lord of Dean during the Domesday survey of 1086. Norman's younger son, Ulric, took the surname Deane from the manor, which also gave the forest its name. Before Henry II's land reforms in 1154, the Deanes had single-handedly controlled the forest since the Norman Conquest, and were the most powerful family in the region. As a reward for helping Henry in the Scottish wars, the men of the Forest of Dean were given a grant to be free miners in the forest's iron mines.

Here I switched off the tape and went to look for Eddie. He was standing with Donald on a hillock behind the main driveway to the house and was holding a pair of curved ox horns. Behind him were the excavations of what looked like a Roman temple. His eyes were closed and his breathing had become rapid. He began to speak:

I can see garlanded oxen pulling a cart – it has four wheels and is made of rough wood. There are people in the wagon and there is a festive atmosphere. Two other oxen are hitched to the back of the cart and are being led along behind. The cart comes to a halt and the oxen at the rear are unhitched. They are being taken away for sacrifice, now wearing the garlands of the working animals. They are much smaller than the working beasts – I think they are much younger. I think that the period is Celtic – not long before the Romans arrived.

The two oxen are now led to a wooden pen, not much

bigger than each of them. A wooden bar is placed behind the animal and in front so that it cannot move. Ropes are passed under the belly to support it as its throat is cut. The blood is allowed to drop into a carved-out block of stone with a drain hole on the side which drops into another bowl. I cannot watch any more of this scene.

Donald had found the ox horns about ten years before and had wondered if they had been associated with ritual animal sacrifice at the temple site. He led us into his private garden, where he showed us a large stone block which he had unearthed a few years before. It was about sixteen inches long and carved out to form an elongated trough; it also had a drainage hole at one end. 'I never knew what it was, but it seems to fit Eddie's description,' said Donald. Eddie had wandered off and, when he returned, said that he sensed the presence of a woman who was very keen to communicate.

She is wearing a white toga decorated with gold embroidery. I think she was attached to the Roman temple here. She tells me she was a priestess. She would talk to the worshippers and answer their questions about the temple. She is showing me remembered scenes, conducting people into the temple – men, women, children. The temple was regarded as being a very magical place which created a feeling of wonder and awe in all who visited it.

Donald then began our tour of Littledean in the part of the house that could be traced back to the Saxon period. An archway marked a small flight of steps down to a lower level, which was the floor of the original house. It was just possible to stand up in the dark room with its dank earthen floor. Donald had tried to recreate a typical Saxon dwelling: a bench had been carved out of a huge block of stone by the wall near the entrance and a cauldron hung over a primitive hearth. At the far end of the room a wooden bed was set on a raised platform and covered with animal skins.

'Littledean seems to have evolved from a Saxon church,' said Donald, 'which was converted to a house at the time of the Norman Conquest. From 1066 onwards the house expanded into a manor until the early fourteenth century. After that it changed only according to social fashions. The house was built from stone taken from a nearby Roman site which was mined in an ancient quarry in the forest. The house is such a farrago. Here we are in the Saxon house; the front door of the main house is Norman; on the other side of the house are some Roman ruins; and there is a medieval well house in the grounds.'

Donald had grown up at Littledean Hall, surrounded by stories of ghosts; one of the first things he decided to do when he took over the house in 1979 was to get to the bottom of these stories. He had been watching Eddie with anticipation, but sadly nothing happened. Then Eddie suggested that we have a tea break as he had not had lunch and was feeling rather faint. As we sat down around a huge pine table in the kitchen, Donald fed us more history. He became so immersed in the story of Littledean that he did not notice Eddie becoming agitated. 'There's someone here,' he said loudly, silencing Donald at a stroke.

I feel that this room was a place of judgment. Someone was dragged from here kicking and screaming after judgment was passed; someone was condemned here. I think it was a witch; she was burnt at the stake near here. I think the haunting dates from the thirteenth or fourteenth century. I don't think she was a very pleasant character, but she was wrongly condemned. She appears outside sometimes.

She had very strong feelings of vengeance after she died. I can see her wearing very ragged clothes. The careless way she dressed and her reclusive personality made her an object of suspicion in the village. They dragged her in here on a cart after a witch hunt in the area. They brought her in here for questioning; it was a church investigation. She was so defiant and blasphemous that she condemned herself through her own mouth. She is still earthbound. It's going to be difficult to get her away.

This woman still follows the path she was taken on out of the hall to her death. She was taken out through the back of the kitchen and held there while they made the bonfire. They tried to extract a confession from her, but she refused.

'I often wondered whether this room was haunted,' said Donald. 'We once had a dog who would always howl late at night when he was in the kitchen. My mother became introverted, reclusive and depressed when she lived at Littledean – I wonder if she was sensing the witch?'

Donald told us that the kitchen incorporated part of the great hall of the former Manor of Dean. In the Middle Ages it had been forty-eight feet long, with a gallery and an entrance at the far end and a cross-entrance in the middle. As the hall of the largest manor house in the forest, it would have been used as a hall of justice, he said. A door led from the hall to a private chamber and below this was a chapel and an undercroft.

We then walked across the courtyard and around to the main entrance. The front view of Littledean was magnificent. A broad, gabled building of grey, lichen-covered stone looked out over acres of rolling green countryside; three rows of tiny diamond-leaded windows glinted in the afternoon sun and a snug, ivy-clad porch marked the entrance. An ancient cedar tree hugged the house, its long branches dipping towards a reed pond below the grassy banking.

Inside the hall, Donald told me that the ground floor was the main hub of psychic activity. Several visitors had witnessed the ghost of a black man in the hall and a dark stain resembling a pool of blood regularly appeared on the dining-room floor leading off the hall. 'We have some evidence for both stories,' Donald whispered as Eddie studied the family trees on the wood-panelled walls. 'Charles Pyrke, the son of Thomas Pyrke, who owned the house, is supposed to have been murdered by his black manservant in 1741 for raping the black man's sister.'

Eddie seemed to be picking something up in the hall, although he could not articulate the message for several minutes. Eventually, he managed to hold the contact:

I'm inclining my head to the left as though I have to; it seems to be a characteristic of whoever it is that is approaching me. It's a woman; she used to pace around this area quite a lot and she's trapped here. Now she wants to get away.
She says: 'He [Donald Macer-Wright] wants to hold on to

us. This makes it more difficult for us to leave.' I think this woman had some sort of deformity – her head twisted to one side and I feel her back was deformed, which made walking difficult. My impression is that she belonged to the seventeenth century and was brought up during the Civil War.

She says: 'They said I was accursed of God. Sometimes they regarded me as less than human. And it seems I am still afflicted.' I think she's been trapped by bitterness over how she's been treated. She was born here, and although she was not a servant, she seems to have been treated like one. 'Part of a large family,' she says. 'They didn't understand.' I think every time someone comes in she feels she has to hide. She says: 'They used to try to keep me out of the way when they had visitors.'

She seems to be in her late forties or early fifties; she's wearing a full-length skirt, a bodice and a tight-sleeved top garment, and a head-covering. Her hair is grey, but I think I'm seeing her towards the end of her life. When she was young she had long brown hair which she wore in ringlets. She wasn't very pretty, and she rarely went out of the house, so she was very pale.

She says: 'This house could be a cheerless place to live in.' They used to take her out occasionally in a coach, and when they arrived at their destination they would bustle her out. It was as if they were ashamed to let her be seen, which added to her misery. She died of a disease. She says: 'I just went into a decline and died. They used to think that because I was deformed I was stupid and they'd treat me like that. After a time I found it easier to act the part than show them I understood more than they realized.'

I feel her straightening up; it won't be long before she can get away. She says: 'You are kind, good Sir, for your patience and the help you bring.' There has to be a lot of forgiveness and understanding all round – by her of her family and by them of her. They realize how wrong they were, but she has got to forgive them too, or she will not make progress.

A woman is coming to her now; she's not a nun, but she

276

did lead a very religious life. They are going to make a stop on the journey, because she has to give the woman time to find it in her heart to forgive her family. Her companion will give her a lot of help; I think this is where we will have to leave her.

Something had struck a chord in Donald: 'I think you have just solved a mystery,' he said. 'There's a blocked-up window on the side of the house overlooking the pond; the roof also seems to have been altered and I've never understood why, as the house was re-roofed before the middle of the eighteenth century. The only way into that room is through a ladder and a trapdoor from the room below. I think it was probably an attic room that was used for solitary confinement and for punishment – perhaps the woman Eddie contacted was locked in there when guests arrived.'

Leading off the hall was a small, oak-panelled room with a large stone fireplace and a huge oak side table. This was the library of the Jacobean house. Sunlight streamed in through the leaded windows, casting dancing light spots on the polished wooden floor. On the small wall next to the fireplace was a print of a young black boy with a silver collar around his neck. The picture was a photograph of an eighteenth-century painting of Charles Pyrke's black slave boy, who grew up in the house. Eddie wandered over to join me by the picture and suddenly felt a sharp pain in his chest. He said:

I'm picking up a man. He was tall and always carried himself in a very upright manner. He was shot in the chest on this spot; I can feel him falling against the wall and sliding to the floor. He's lying in a heap on the floor.

The man says: 'It was the result of a quarrel, a dicing game.' They'd been playing in this room and someone sprang up and accused him of cheating. There was a lot of bad feeling between him and his partner, who simply pulled out a pistol and shot him. It's eighteenth-century – around 1740. I think he was about thirty-eight when he died.

He was a neighbour who came here for a gaming party. He owned land, enough to give him some social standing. The man who shot him was another landowner. There had been quite serious quarrels between them before then, but they had both been invited as guests that evening. When the argument started, the owner of the house realized that he should not have invited them to the house together. A lot of things followed on from the murder. One of the other men at the gaming party was a local magistrate; he couldn't judge the issue because he had been a witness to it. The trial had to be taken elsewhere and the main issue was whether the man who died had been cheating. This is what concerns him now.

'They impugned my honour,' the man says, 'that a man should die in such a way that he could not defend himself.' He tried to follow what happened after his death, and he seems to have some idea of what happened at the trial, but he was sure that everyone believed he was cheating. 'It was easier for them to assume that I was cheating,' he says, 'otherwise the man would have been charged with murder. But it was murder.'

He's pleased that I accept his innocence. The man who shot him was just looking for an excuse to kill him – there was such bad blood between them. I sense a peace with him which there wasn't before. His wife has come for him and they walked along as though they are dancing; they are going into the light now. He seems very happy. I shall let him go.

'There is a story about a pistol duel in the house in which a man was killed,' said Donald, 'and we think the Pyrke family was involved, although it was hushed up. The Pyrkes did the same thing over the death of Charles Pyrke, who disappeared in 1741 at the age of twenty-three.'

Nathaniel Pyrke, the grandfather of Charles Pyrke, was famous for burning King James I's chair in Gloucester and rampaging through Oxfordshire when William of Orange was crowned King of England in 1689. The Pyrkes had bought Littledean in 1644 from Charles Bridgeman, whose grandfather had in turn bought it from Richard Brayne in 1612. The last Deane to hold the house, Sir William de Deane, had been killed in 1319 in the Scottish wars, and had died without an heir. His cousins Richard and John received a legacy from the Earl of Hereford, and after 1327 Littledean was split between the heiresses. The manor passed to the Pomfrey family in the fifteenth century.

On the opposite side of the main hall was a light, airy room with two double windows and a polished wooden floor. This was formerly the main dining room, although it was dominated during our visit by a large billiard table. Above the fireplace was a picture of Sir Henry Lingen and his wife. Sir Henry was an ancestor of Thomas Pyrke and a prominent Royalist officer in the Civil War. Donald showed us the spot to the left of the fireplace near the door where the red stain occasionally appeared. Eddie seemed to be making contact:

> I am getting the strong impression of quarrelling going on. I think it's Royalist officers. One had insulted the other, who took this to be a matter of honour, and swords were drawn. They started fighting in here, in front of the fireplace, and one of them said: 'Let us continue this quarrel outside. We should not spill blood in this house.' So they went outside and resumed their fight, until their colleagues separated them, telling them not to be so foolish. No blood was spilt.
>
> The quarrel was the result of tension that had built up between them as they waited for the fighting to begin. They made up their differences just before they were both killed in action. A group of Roundheads stormed the house and there was a fight in the hall. The two men fought side by side in the main hall, but they were both brought down by pistol shots. They were content to die together.

Donald told us he was aware of a contemporary Roundhead account of the fighting at Littledean which was sent back to Parliament. In it, two Royalist officers were mentioned: Lieutenant-Colonel Congreve, Governor of Newnham, and Captain Wigmore, who was in charge of the garrison at Littledean. According to the dispatch, the house was surrounded by Roundheads: 'The Royalists had accepted quarter,' it said, 'and were ready to surrender when a soldier in the house fired a shot and killed a Roundhead.' According to Donald, this action had enraged the Roundheads so much that they set upon them and wiped out the garrison.

Littledean Hall was garrisoned by both the Roundheads and the Royalists during the Civil War. The first action in the Forest of Dean came in 1643, only a year after the start of the war, when Prince Maurice, brother of Prince Rupert and the nephew of King Charles I, attempted to capture Sir William Waller, who was returning from Wales with his Roundhead army. The Prince established a line of defence of 2,000 men from Newnham-on-Severn to Ross-on-Wye, making Littledean his headquarters. Waller narrowly escaped capture within a mile of Littledean.

Donald then led us to the staircase behind the hall and up to the first floor. He called the long thin landing 'the haunted corridor' as several visitors had seen shadowy figures there or felt unwell. In a low voice, he explained to me that the previous month two women had climbed the staircase and gone into a strange trance; their husbands had led them into the sitting room off the corridor, fearful that they were having a stroke. 'One of the women had said she was possessed by something,' said Donald; 'she could see her husband but she was unable to talk to him.'

Eddie wandered into the sitting room and two bedrooms – the Blue Room and the Rose Room – which both had strong psychic imprints from the Civil War, although he was sure that there were no trapped spirits there. Nor were there any on the haunted landing. We walked back downstairs, but on the last step, Eddie said:

I have an old man with me. I think he's in his seventies, or even older. He's stooping a bit. I think he still had his hair – it's grey, a little bit bushy – and some side whiskers. His wasn't a natural death. He was inclined to be a bit irascible and he still has this characteristic; he resents having people around him in the house. He's not aware that he's dead; he still thinks the house belongs to him. He had servants and treated them rather badly towards the end. I think he fell down the stairs; I see him in a heap at the bottom. He died so quickly.

I don't think it happened very long ago. I have to pick up

his period from the clothes he's wearing, but I can't see him at the moment – I'm just getting glimpses of his face. I get the feeling he's late Victorian or early Edwardian. He's not a very easy man to approach; he's got to realize that he's passed on, but he's finding it very hard to accept. He's very puzzled by the changes in fashion and all the people he sees that he doesn't know. But he's still reluctant to acknowledge that he's moved on; until he does this he cannot progress. 'Why should I be moved?' he asks, and I tell him that there's somewhere much better for him to go.

I think he's going to be taken away in a state of sleep; when he wakes up he'll see people he knows who have died, and this will help him accept it. I will leave him now.

Although Donald did not know exactly who the man was, he did say that the house had been let to private tenants between 1860 and 1890 and that one tenant had died there during the early twentieth century. Eddie's words seemed to corroborate Donald's story about the visitors' experiences: 'His wasn't a natural death . . . he fell down the stairs.' It occurred to me that the man might have been poisoned and become dizzy before he fell down the stairs to his death. The visitors had certainly felt dizzy at the top of the stairs.

Our final destination was the driveway outside the house, which marks the old Roman route to Monmouth and was used as the main road until 1816. At the time of our visit it was being excavated by archaeologists, who had revealed the paving stones of the old Roman road. As we walked towards the main road, I could see that Eddie was faltering. 'Perhaps we should call it a day now,' I said. 'It's four o'clock and you haven't had your lunch yet.' The relief on Eddie's face was immediate; I felt a little guilty because I always seemed to be pushing him, but I knew from experience that if I did not, our visits would be an endless round of tea breaks. A spring came into his step as we walked back to the house, but about halfway down the drive he suddenly stopped and closed his eyes.

There's a man here who knows I can help, but he's worried that I might go without contacting him. He's saying: 'I keep trying to impress myself on people in the hope that something can be done. I know I'm not supposed to be here. It's a terrible situation to find yourself in when you can't move away, you can't go on. I know it isn't right.'

He's very articulate and very much aware of his situation. He has been trying very hard to make people aware of him by manifesting here. 'But I don't seem to be able to make any headway.' He's frantic with concern because even the people who have seen him don't realize that he needs help to get away. 'They've got the wrong attitude,' he says. 'I'm a curiosity to them, but I don't want to be a curiosity. I want to be helped.'

I need him to calm down and explain why he's got stuck. I see a funeral cortège and carriage with the coffin in it being drawn by four horses. He's possibly late Victorian or even more recent. I can't see him, but the funeral looks to be that period. The carriage is ornate, with brass lamps on the front.

The thing that has trapped him is a very strong sense that he has left things unfinished. He took matters very seriously and worries about unfinished business. He shrugs his shoulders and says: 'But things never do get finished. You complete one stage and you create another problem and so it goes on.'

He had some interest in politics, but I'm not sure; he may also have had military connections – I can see him now in a red military tunic. He says: 'I did some important work in this house.' I don't think he owned it, but he spent a lot of time here. He's riding off on a black horse now, straight into the light – he's so pleased.

'There have been so many sightings of apparitions on the drive and by the courtyard that we have lost count of them,' said Donald over a welcome cup of tea in his sitting room. 'In the 1950s, my father saw a hunched figure in a long cloak dash across his path towards the house as he was coming up the drive. He thought it might have been an elderly woman who was staying at the house, so he got out of the car and went to look for her with a torch. He couldn't find anyone, and when he asked her the next day if it was her he'd seen, she said: "That was the ghost of Brayne."'

'John Brayne was a Roundhead captain during the Civil War who spied on the Royalists. He is said to have disguised himself as a gardener at Littledean to observe the King's men – we always thought the ghost was him, but it now seems unlikely from what Eddie has said. In April 1992 a friend of mine saw him disappearing into the wall of the house when he was reversing his car out of the courtyard. He was the first person to see the ghost in the daylight. A year later I saw the same thing.'

Donald was keen to show us the view from Littledean over the ox-bow lake in the mouth of the River Severn, but it was getting late and Eddie was ready to leave. I agreed to stay behind, so we waved Eddie off and walked up the hill past the Roman temple site. It was a beautiful clear summer's day and the view of the rolling Gloucestershire countryside was breathtaking. Field after iridescent green field stretched down to the river and every town and settlement for miles around could be clearly seen. I understood then why Littledean was of such strategic importance during the Civil War.

As we turned to walk back to the house I asked Donald whether he had many visitors to Littledean, but he did not answer. I was about to say something else when he interrupted. 'I have been trying to remember what another psychic told me when she came to Littledean last year,' he said. 'As she made her way around the side of the house, she got the impression of a huge fire, with a monk or priest standing by trying to stop something terrible from happening. It's strange how these things never make sense at the time, but it certainly matches Eddie's account.'

There was obviously much more to uncover at Littledean, but one thing was certain: it had more than satisfied my criteria for being the most haunted house in England.

Chapter 17

Tomorrow's Ghosts

The generations of men are like leaves on the trees. The
wind blows and one year's leaves are scattered on the
ground; but the trees burst into bud and put on fresh ones
when spring comes round.

Homer, *Iliad*

MS *Estonia*, September 1994

In the early hours of 28 September 1994, the Baltic ferry MS
Estonia sank in the freezing waters off the south-west coast of
Finland. More than 900 passengers drowned in the hour it took the
ship to sink; 130 people survived. Only 100 bodies were recovered.
It was Europe's worst ferry disaster since the Second World War.

Survivors told how the *Estonia* turned on its side after water had
gushed in through the vehicle loading ramp; fifteen minutes later
the ship began its slide to the bottom of the sea. Most of the
passengers were in their cabins, asleep; those who did make it out
of the ship spent terrible hours on life-rafts in the sub-zero Baltic
waters.

The day after the disaster, Eddie unexpectedly experienced the
emotions of passengers who went down with the Estonia. The
psychic impression soon faded, to be replaced with a direct

instruction: he was ordered by the spirit world to help those who had drowned. 'There was something very urgent about the instruction,' said Eddie. 'I was told that among the trapped souls were some whose families had already been taken to the spirit world; it was important that they were quickly reunited.'

Eddie called a meeting of his psychic development group to pray for the victims. At once, Eddie made contact with the spirit world; he sensed a bright light and realized that he had to take this light to the scene of the disaster.

We are being guided to leave the spirit realm and descend to the earth level. I can see a thread which we must follow on our downward journey this will help us maintain contact with the spirit world. [A few minutes later.] We have now descended to the sunken vessel. There is a deep gloom, and all I can see are shadowy figures moving around randomly. I sense their deep anxiety and bewilderment. These poor souls have struggled so hard against their dying that they have carried a feeling of despair into the next world. It is still with them and holding them back. Some are still searching for the families they lost when the ferry sank. But I cannot see any children among them; this does not surprise me as children are well protected at the psychic level.

These spirits now exist on the etheric level, so they feel none of the pressure from the water, which is part of the material world. They feel neither wet nor cold, nor do they have any problems breathing. This is causing them a lot of confusion. They ask: 'What has happened to us? Why can't we get away from here? It doesn't make any sense.'

Eddie then asked his colleagues to provide the psychic power to raise these souls from the earth level and out of their watery prison. He urged them to visualize a platform lying on the sea bed and to encourage the victims to gather on the platform. 'It was difficult to see exactly how many there were,' said Eddie, 'but I think around eighty came forward. Then we raised the platform through the water to the surface and gently guided them to the shore. When they saw land, they were very relieved;

some began to talk with their neighbours as they stepped off the platform.'

A number of men and women are coming forward. They are escorting the victims along the shore and up a wide ramp that extends towards the sea. I can't see where they are going . . . wait, now I can see them reclining on armchairs and sofas; it looks like the deck of a ship to me. The people who brought them here are encouraging them to rest and relax.

The ship is moving smoothly over the water and the sky in the distance is becoming brighter, as if the dawn is breaking. Now it is reaching its final destination and docking at the quayside. They are leaving the ship – I think there are about a hundred of them. Waiting on the quayside are the families who were separated from their loved ones. They are being reunited now, with love and tears of joy. A number of relatives who have been in the spirit world for some time are also coming forward to greet them. The job has been done. Now we must withdraw and leave them.

Eddie said a final prayer for them, but then heard a voice telling him to go back to the scene of the disaster as there were others who still needed help. 'I was back in the gloomy waters, but this time I was in contact with a man on or near the bridge of the ship. He was wearing a peaked cap and a heavy, dark overcoat. I felt sure that he was the ship's captain.

He is in deep distress. He feels responsible for the disaster and refuses to leave the ship because he cannot face the people who perished when the *Estonia* sank. I feel tremendous compassion for him.

Two men have now appeared by his side; both are wearing uniforms. I think one of them is the captain of the *Titanic*; I don't know who the other one is. They are trying to persuade the captain to leave with them. They have succeeded and now they are walking away from the sunken ferry, on to dry land and beautiful countryside. Now our work is complete. We can leave him.

286

On 2 October 1994, the *Mail on Sunday* ran a small article about Avo Piht, the captain of the *Estonia* who had survived the disaster and gone into hiding after discharging himself from a Helsinki hospital. The ferry owners had urged him to go to ground as he alone would have known what had happened during the final, fatal minutes of the voyage. His co-captain, Arvo Andersson, whom Eddie believed he contacted, went down with the ship. They took turns to skipper the *Estonia*, and on the night of the tragedy both were on the bridge of the ship because they were being assessed for a special pilot's licence. Captain Piht and the ferry operators could face criminal negligence charges if it is proved that they knew the seals on the bow doors were worn when they set sail.

The *Estonia* was not the first time Eddie had been drawn into a contemporary tragedy. In 1989 he was asked to contact a victim on the *Marchioness*, the pleasure cruiser that sank in the Thames; and in 1988 he made contact with victims of the Armenian earthquake. Each case gave him valuable experience in helping spirits trapped by disasters.

The *Marchioness*, August 1989

Eddie was drawn into the *Marchioness* case by chance. One evening in autumn 1989, after he had given a lecture at the College of Psychic Studies in London, he had been approached by a young woman who asked him for help. Andria Lennon thought she had been disturbed by a spirit who had subsequently attached itself to her. She had felt ill-at-ease for weeks and thought the change came about after a meeting with a friend of hers, Vicky Galbraith. Eddie had immediately sensed a psychic disturbance around Andria and asked her to visit him the following week at his home. As soon as he opened the front door to Andria, he picked up the spirit of a young woman who was desperate to talk to him:

I think she is about nineteen or twenty. She may have died in

the Pan Am jet that crashed over Lockerbie. No, wait . . . she's
telling me that she drowned . . . on the *Marchioness* in the
Thames.

She is still trying to shake off the shock of the event. She
says: 'I'm all right, but I feel a bit weighed down by the shock
of it all and the effect the disaster had on those around me.
Could you help me?'

I need to share her death experience with her if she is to be
released. She's showing me now . . . There was a sudden jolt,
then everything began to fly around the boat. The lights have
gone out. Now I'm just seeing deep, dark green. The boat has
turned over and the water is coming in fast. She's screaming
and everyone around her is panicking. It's no use. She shouts:
'It shouldn't happen to me! It shouldn't happen to me!'

Now I can see someone coming to her: an older woman,
matronly, who is very kind, yet firm. She says: 'Come along
dear, come with me. Come along. The worst is over.' They
leave together, and I see the light beckoning them. We can
let go of them now.

The *Marchioness* had sunk on the Thames on the night of
19 August 1989. The sixty-year-old pleasure cruiser had been hired
by a young London financier, Antonio de Vasconcellos, to celebrate
his twenty-sixth birthday. His friend, Jonathan Phang, a photographic
agent whose birthday fell in the same week as Antonio's, had
organized the party.

The company that controlled the *Marchioness* had said that the
safety limit for the boat was 120 people, but more than 150 had turned
up on the night. Shortly after midnight, a 1,750-ton dredger, the
Bowbelle, had crashed into the back of the boat, damaged her from
behind and forced her to swing directly in its path; within seconds, it
was struck again. The boat had sunk rapidly. Only eighty-seven
people survived; the river police recovered twenty-five bodies from
the Thames. At least thirty-eight were never found.

Andria and Vicky knew some of the victims of the *Marchioness*
disaster. They were particularly concerned about a young man
whom they knew only as Neville. He had regularly visited the
London gym where they were both members. They asked Eddie if

he could contact him for them. Eddie agreed, and on 7 October 1989 Andria drove Vicky to Eddie's house. After a cup of tea, Eddie sat down and began to search for Neville. Then Eddie sensed that there was a spirit presence and asked him to come forward. Neville, it seemed, was not earthbound like the previous victim of the *Marchioness* who had contacted Eddie. This man was in the spirit world and had come back to tell Vicky and Andria about some of his experiences in his new life.

He is inviting me to sit on the grass with him. I am trying to adjust my consciousness to his level. He says: 'Sure, I'm OK here. It's great. Everything is as it should be, if you know what I mean. I was a bit confused at first because of the speed with which everything happened – none of us was prepared. But it didn't take too long for any of us to settle down once we had accepted what had happened. That's what seemed important, accepting it. I can speak for everyone on that, although there are one or two who are still finding it a bit hard. But believe me, I wouldn't go back. Why go back to all that when you can just take it easy here?

'Oh, sure, I'd get bored if I was just sitting on the beach or lying on the grass, but it's not like that here. You can lie down on the grass and things happen all around you, if you let them. Imagine hearing little whispers – it took me a long time to figure out what they were; it's the grass talking to you, and it's the same with the trees and flowers. It's as though they are trying to communicate with you. I haven't figured out their language yet, but I expect I will in time. It's the same with colours; you look at something – the bark of a tree, perhaps – and it's as if you're looking inside it. Now you couldn't do that where you are – unless you're on mushrooms!

'I suppose you could say that it's about discovering things here. There are lots of people I can visit and who visit me. [Vicky says she would like to visit him.] People visiting from earth do so during their sleep; they can only do it safely if they have a lot of love, otherwise the path isn't clear and it can be dangerous. Well, I'll have to finish now. Love to you both.'

Eddie was familiar with the young man's description of the spirit world. 'His experience matches what I have heard from many other spirits who have just arrived in the next world,' he said. 'It is usually similar enough to their earth life to feel comfortable for them, but there are many things that enhance their new environment. They are so charmed that they never want to return to earth.'

Armenian earthquake, December 1988

> The destruction was almost total. Nine-storey apartment blocks had disintegrated. Dust hung like a fog over teams of rescue workers. Many dug with their bare hands to reach survivors whose faint cries could be heard from beneath the debris. Others, armed only with pickaxes, fought frantically to raise heavy steel girders. The ground itself had split and fractured, destroying roads and bridges.

This harrowing description of the Armenian earthquake in Simon Freeman's article in the *Sunday Times* of 22 December 1988 shocked hundreds of thousands of British readers. The previous Wednesday, the Armenian city of Leninakan (population 250,000) was reduced to rubble. It had been at the epicentre of the earthquake and most of its citizens were believed dead, entombed in their devastated homes. In the surrounding villages of Spitak, Kirovakan, Stepanavan and Akhuryan, shock waves had flattened hundreds of multi-storey buildings and killed thousands more people. The Soviet authorities admitted that around 700,000 people had been left homeless, although Western experts believed the true figure was closer to two million.

On 20 December Eddie had been watching the appalling scenes on television. It was late in the evening and he had turned off the set at the end of the news bulletin. But the desperate images were fixed in his mind as he sat down on the sofa. Suddenly he found that he was making contact with the disaster scene.

> I can see the debris of buildings – heaps of concrete and slabs of stone from walls and ceilings. I am standing on a tilting

290

slab of concrete, looking down on a small group of people –
twenty or so. They are close to panic, just waiting for another
shock wave. One man, calmer than the rest, is trying to
quieten them down and keep them all together. They are
victims of the earthquake; they don't realize that they have
been killed. They are earthbound at the moment – their fear
of the earthquake has trapped them.

I am trying to calm them down with my thoughts. I don't
know how I can get them away from this place. If a bright
light appears before them, they may think it is a flash from
another earthquake and they will panic and rush off in all
directions. No, I have to wait and hold them steady. I can see
now a small flock of sheep approaching them, but the victims
have not noticed them. One of the sheep has detached itself
from the flock and is now approaching the crowd. A woman
nudges the man next to her and points at the sheep; he
follows it slowly. Another sheep does the same with someone
else, until finally they are all gone. They are on their way to
heaven now.

After Eddie left the scene, he marvelled at the ingenuity of the
spirit world in escorting the Armenians to the next world. 'Sheep
were a familiar sight to these people and would have calmed them,'
he said. 'The spirit world always knows exactly the right way to lead
a trapped soul into the next world.'

Hiroshima commemoration, August 1987

On 6 August 1987 Eddie received the following communication
from a spirit source:

The dropping of the two bombs at Hiroshima and Nagasaki
marked the peak of scientific materialism on earth. It set in
train a reaction that is still growing, and seeded a slow change
of heart. Since then, people have been going through fear and
revulsion; only now are they emerging into hope. In times to
come, when the events of the first nuclear bombs are seen in

perspective, the sacrifice of so many lives will be understood.

The Japanese who died at Hiroshima have made progress in the spirit world. They gather to link with the groups commemorating the event on earth and provide feelings of great hope for the future. They want people on earth now to forget the sorrow and raise their eyes to see the light that the future holds.

On 6 August every year, the anniversary of the dropping of the first atomic bomb on Japan, anti-nuclear groups around the world meet to commemorate the attack in 1945. The bomb that landed on Hiroshima killed 100,000 citizens; the same number died in the following months from burns or radiation sickness. A second bomb, dropped on Nagasaki three days later, killed a further 7⁵,000 Japanese.

Eddie had seen at first hand the destruction the bombs had wreaked. In spring 1946 he was sent to Japan with the Royal Electrical and Mechanical Engineers as part of the Commonwealth Occupation Force. His destination was Hure, on the main island of Honshu. While he was there, he visited Hiroshima. 'We had seen photographs of the devastation there,' he said, 'but it was nothing compared with the experience of being there.

'We saw charred telegraph poles and thousands of tiny houses flattened by the force of the blast. A reinforced concrete building stood shakily in the centre of the town, its wooden doors and hand-rails burnt away.'

A few weeks later, Eddie met a Jesuit priest who had been running a Catholic mission in the hills above Hiroshima when the bomb struck. 'He described how the survivors had come streaming out of the town into the hills, many of them burnt by radiation or fire. The mission ran out of beds and soon the corridors were littered with bodies. He and his assistants did all they could to help the victims, but after a few days, his helpers fell ill with radiation sickness themselves and died. It was a hopeless situation.'

Eddie had often wondered if there was a logic behind such suffering. His communication on the anniversary of Hiroshima had helped him understand it a little, but he was still concerned. A few years later, in 1994, he received the following message from the spirit world, which gave a wider perspective.

History presents many sad examples of cruel massacres – in biblical times and later by the Romans and conquerors such as Ghenghis Khan – right up to the present tragedies in the Balkans and Rwanda. When the victims of these massacres have been in the spirit world for some time, they are able to forgive the people who caused their deaths. Through this act of forgiveness, they transmute the pain of their suffering into a love of humanity. They join together in this expression of love, and by doing so they raise humanity on earth one small – but very significant – step upwards, towards the spirit world.

While this is not the only way that humanity can advance spiritually, it is an important one. In the case of all these victims – Hiroshima, Rwanda and the Balkans – suffering on such a scale is never wasted, either for the individual or for humanity.

Tragedies will continue to happen, and some spirits will remain trapped at the earth level. Whether these belong to the bereaved families in Beirut or Belfast, or are the victims of racial conflict in the Balkans or Rwanda, we must accept that at some point this earthly suffering will translate itself into a new crop of modern-day ghosts.

In the years ahead, Eddie will doubtless be called again by the spirit world to assist in the release of these trapped souls. He is certain that, just as the Civil War and the World Wars left a terrible legacy of ghosts, so too will the conflicts, tragedies and natural disasters of the late twentieth century and the third millennium.

Epilogue

by Eddie Burks

'Whither goest thou?' said the Voice.
'I know not,' said I, 'but go I must.'
'Then follow me,' said the Voice.
'Do not tarry, for time is short and we have much to do.'
'Have I the strength to follow?' I asked, and the Voice said:
'The strength shall be given to you.'
'Where do we go?' I asked,
And the voice said: 'Be content to know that it is onwards and
upwards. Is that not enough?'

Anonymous

My contribution has been intensely personal; I have to carry responsibility for the psychic content and this I accept. I have spent many years recording my psychic experiences and in the process I have tried to reach a deeper understanding of the spirit world. I may have got somewhere in this, but I know better than to think that any conclusions I have reached are going to remain unchanged for long. They are not mistaken in essence, but at best they can only be an approximation of the truth. But better an approximation than a void of ignorance.

As with the scientific study of the material world, the more one learns about the spirit world, the more one realizes the immensity of what remains unknown. Like the explorer of an unknown continent, I find that the greater the area mapped out, the longer the boundary around it, and the greater the area still to be discovered.

While we are on earth our world seems to be the major or only reality. When we probe the world of the spirit, our perspective begins to change; we realize that in some remarkable way the visible universe depends on the world of the spirit. At the personal level our physical body reflects this dependence, for it ceases to function when it is separated from the etheric and soul bodies. The world of the spirit does not depend on the physical world: if the physical world were destroyed, the spirit world would continue to exist, just as our personal consciousness survives the death of the physical body.

It is this consciousness which provides continuity of existence. The world we see about us is interpreted by our consciousness: who is to say that my perception of the world is nearer the truth than somebody else's? For instance, the artist sees much that we miss – he perceives a different reality. One can argue that the world around us is subjective, that it is impossible to know its reality, or even whether it really exists outside our mental perception. Seventeenth- and eighteenth-century philosophers discussed this question at great length, but without reaching firm conclusions. In the end, one is thrown back on to common sense: accepting that there is something real 'out there', we still disagree with each other about its nature.

In the next life the soul perceives a heightened reality, but one which depends much more on the attunement of consciousness. As our consciousness becomes more refined, more spiritual, our perception brings us awareness of a reality which reflects that refinement. There is a saying that what is without is a reflection of what is within. It is true here on earth; in the next life it becomes the dominant truth. Consciousness is the arbiter of reality.

It is the mind that directs consciousness through the action of the will. An important aspect of our lives on earth is the opportunity we have to learn how to control the mental process. We also learn to control the imagination and the emotions; we have to struggle to find the proper function of the will – to use it constructively rather than for domination. The purpose of this learning is that in the next

296

life the mind comes into its own. An inability to control the mind can cause considerable difficulties; having a powerful imagination without the will to control it can be like trying to ride a wild stallion which is apt to rush off in any direction. This sounds allegorical, but it is very close to the actual experience in the spirit world.

The plight of the earthbound soul illustrates the situation which can arise when a strong negative emotion is carried into the next life: the power of the mind bound by this emotion can pin the soul down for a very long time and subdue the consciousness. As we progress in the world of the spirit, so the powers of the mind progressively unfold, enabling us, in the course of time, to explore not only previously hidden aspects of the physical universe, but also regions of the spirit world into which we have earned entry. And so we come to penetrate the mysteries of our existence stage by stage, each one offering confirmation of the love of the Creator as expressed in Creation. So far, we humans have not looked after the earthly part of that Creation very well; we have forgotten – or not yet learned – that we have a responsibility for all of it. But we have not even accepted responsibility for our fellow humans. We have a long way to go: there will have to be radical changes in our hearts and in our thinking.

So what am I reasonably sure of? First, that life goes on after death; all my experiences since 1970 have ineluctably persuaded me of this. The next life offers us endless opportunities to grow in love and spiritual understanding. The world we enter is more vivid than the physical world, but it is still recognizable, at least to begin with. We do not lose contact with the ones we love; in fact, we meet up again. Those we do not wish to see will not meet us, unless a reconciliation is necessary. This is all part of the great design; if we entered the next life and found ourselves in a totally different environment, there would be much confusion and no sense of continuity.

We take our personality, our memories, our fears, loves and prejudices with us into the next world. If, when we die, our fears, ambitions, feelings of bitterness or vengefulness are too strong, we can become earthbound and possibly manifest as ghosts. Fortunately, only a small number of people become attached to earth, although I believe that this proportion varies during different periods of history, and from place to place.

And what of God? We could refer to the philosophers and find ourselves as confused and uncertain as before. If I have made a case at all, it is simply that there is a great plan, one that is shot through with a transcendent love. Individual souls *do* matter – our purpose and destiny is to find our way back through our experience and accumulated knowledge to the Creator. But does God the Creator exist within his Creation, or is He the 'watcher on the hill' observing the mess we are making on earth? Spirits I have contacted have no such doubts. They say: 'We are aware of the presence of God in all things around us. We breathe in His spirit and he works His purpose through the myriad spirits who form the hierarchy of the spirit world.' And yet, it is the spark of God within each one of us – the part which is eternal and incorruptible – that will draw us back to our Source, no matter to what depths our soul may sink on its journey through life.

And so I remain an optimist, confident in the destiny of the human race, but aware of the painful metamorphosis that society must undergo before it emerges into the spiritual light of the coming age.

Select Bibliography

Abbott, Geoffrey, *Ghosts of the Tower of London* (Heinemann 1980)

Anon, *The Genuine History of the Life of Richard Turpin* (1734)

Ashley, Maurice, *Charles I and Oliver Cromwell; A Study in Contrasts and Comparisons* (Methuen 1987)
  The English Civil War (Alan Sutton 1990)

Bindoff, S.T., *Tudor England* (Pelican 1964)

Black, J.B., *The Reign of Elizabeth, 1558–1603* (OUP 1994)

Blyth, Henry, *Caro: The Fatal Passion* (Rupert Hart-Davis 1972)

Brooks, J.A., *Ghosts of London* (Jarrold 1982)

Brooks, John, *Ghosts of London* (Jarrold 1991)

Carlton, Charles, *Going to the Wars* (British Civil Wars, 1638–1651) (Routledge 1992)

Cavendish, Richard, *The Magical Arts: Western Occultism and Occulists* (Arkana 1984)

Colson, Percy, *White's: 1693–1950* (William Heinemann 1951)

Dale, John, *The Prince and the Paranormal* (W.H. Allen 1986)

Davies, Dewi, *Law and Disorder in Brecon*, 1750–1880

Day, Julius and Ash, Arty, *Immortal Turpin: The Authentic History of England's Most Notorious Highwayman* (Staples Press 1948)

Edwards, Father Francis, *The Marvellous Chance* (Rupert Hart-Davis 1968)
  Guy Fawkes: The Real Story of the Gunpowder Plot (Rupert Hart-Davis 1969)

299

Mary & Ridolfi: Design for Destruction (Royal Stuart Papers IX 1975)

Glasstone, Victor, *Victorian and Edwardian Theatres* (Thames and Hudson 1975)

Graham, Winston, *The Spanish Armada* (Collins 1987)

Hallam, Jack, *Ghosts Who's Who* (David & Charles 1972)

Harley Lewis, Roy, *Theatre Ghosts* (David & Charles 1988)

Hastings, Max, *Bomber Command* (Michael Joseph 1979)

Howard, Diana, *London Theatres and Music Halls* (Library Association 1970)

Jenkins, Elizabeth, *Princes in the Tower* (Hamish Hamilton 1978)

Jones, Christopher, *No. 10 Downing Street: The Story of a House* (BBC Publications 1985)

Kaplan, Philip and Collier, Richard, *The Few: The Battle of Britain, Summer 1940* (Blandford 1989)

Lander, J.R., *The Wars of the Roses* (Alan Sutton 1990)

Lazarus, Richard, *The Case Against Death* (Warner 1993)

Lejeune, Anthony and Lewis, Malcolm, *The Gentlemen's Clubs of London* (MacDonald and Jane's 1979)

Macadam, Alta, *Sicily* (A. & C. Black 1988)

MacQueen-Pope, W.J., *The Haymarket Theatre* (W.H. Allen 1948)

Ghosts and Greasepaint (Robert Hale 1951)

Mason, Peter D., *Wings over Linton* (Fenton Enterprises 1994)

McIver, Nick, *Great British Ghosts* (Longman 1982)

Middlebrook, Martin, *The Nuremberg Raid* (Allen Lane 1973)

Morton, H.V., *Ghosts of London* (Methuen 1939)

Morton, Andrew, *Diana: Her True Story* (Michael O'Mara Books, 1992)

Northcote Parkinson, C., *Gunpowder, Treason and Plot* (Weidenfeld & Nicolson 1976)

Poole, Keith B., *Britain's Haunted Heritage* (Robert Hale 1988)

Ridley, Jasper, *Lord Palmerston* (Constable & Co. 1970)

Rowell, George, *William Terriss and Richard Prince: Two Characters in an Adelphi Melodrama* (Society for Theatre Research 1987)

Rowse, A.L., *Eminent Elizabethans* (Macmillan 1983)

Somerset Fry, Plantagenet, *Castles of the British Isles* (David & Charles 1980)

Sweetman, John, *The Dambusters Raid* (Arms and Armour Press 1990)

Townsend, Peter, *Duel of Eagles* (Cassell 1970)

Turner, Dorothy, *Mary, Queen of Scots* (Wayland 1988)

Underwood, Peter, *A Gazeteer of British Ghosts* (Souvenir Press 1971)

Warren, C. Henry, *Great Men of Essex* (Bodley Head 1956)

Wedgwood, C.V., *The King's War, 1641–7* (Penguin Books 1983)

Williams, Neville, *Thomas Howard IV Duke of Norfolk: A Tudor Tragedy* (Barrie and Rockliff 1964)

The Cardinal and the Secretary (Weidenfeld & Nicolson 1975)

Williamson, Audrey, *The Mystery of the Princes* (Alan Sutton 1981)

Index